SCHOOL COUNSE
THEIR FAVORITE CLASSROOM GUIDANCE LESSONS:
A GUIDE TO CHOOSING, PLANNING, CONDUCTING, AND PROCESSING

ASGW

Edited by: Janice DeLucia-Waack, Ph.D.
Meghan Mercurio Sarah Korta
Katherine Maertin Faith Colvin
Eric Martin Lily Zawadski Carla Giambrone
University at Buffalo, SUNY

ASSOCIATION FOR SPECIALISTS IN GROUP WORK

Alexandria, VA

Others in the ASGW Group Activity Book Series (available at www.asgw.org)

Group Work Experts Share Their Favorite Activities: A Guide to Choosing, Planning, Conducting, and Processing Vol.1

School Counselors Share Their Favorite Group Activities: A Guide to Choosing, Planning, Conducting, and Processing Vol.1

Group Work Experts Share Their Favorite Multicultural Activities: A Guide to Choosing, Planning, Conducting, and Processing

Online Group Activities to Enhance Counselor Education

New in 2014:

Group Work Experts Share Their Favorite Activities: A Guide to Choosing, Planning, Conducting, and Processing Vol. 2

School Counselors Share Their Favorite Group Activities: A Guide to Choosing, Planning, Conducting, and Processing Vol. 2

DVDs also available from ASGW:

Group Work: Leading in the Here and Now (Carroll)

Developmental Aspects of Group Counseling (Stockton)

Leading Groups with Adolescents (DeLucia-Waack, Segrist, & Horne)

Group Counseling with Children: A Multicultural Approach (Bauman & Steen)

Group Counseling with Adolescents: A Multicultural Approach (Bauman & Steen)

Published by Association for Specialists in Group Work 5999 Stevenson Ave. Alexandria VA 22304 Copyright © 2014 by the Association for Specialists in Group Work ISBN 978-1-55620-344-2

TABLE OF CONTENTS

School Counselors Share Their Favorite Classroom Guidance Activities

ACADEMIC SKILL LESSONS

CAREER EXPLORATION AND PLANNING LESSONS

PERSONAL AND SOCIAL SKILLS LESSONS

Personal
Lesson

Social Skills
Contributors

(Cont.)
Page

Foreword
Janice DeLucia-Waack
University at Buffalo, SUNY

My students were the inspiration for this book. Every semester they scramble to put together classroom guidance activities for their internships. They borrow from their cooperating counselors some activities that are awesome and when we ask where they came from, they say "I made it up". So this book is a compilation of those tried and true activities that are being used in the field and have yet to be published. The lessons are wonderful. I did a training two days ago and used several of them. The students (and teachers) loved them! And most importantly, reported that they had learned about themselves and their relationships.

The response when we asked for classroom guidance lessons was overwhelming why this is our largest book so far in the *Association for Specialists in Group Work Activity Book Series*. The classroom guidance lessons are organized by the ASCA Areas: Academic, Career Exploration and Planning, and Personal/Social Skills. Within each section, they begin with the youngest students and end with lessons for high school students. Each classroom guidance lesson is very specific with what ASCA Standards met, materials, and a specific script. Processing questions are detailed to help ensure that students make meaning out of the lesson.

In addition, the opening chapters were written to provide an overview of how to create and utilize a series of classroom guidance lessons within a comprehensive school counseling program. National experts in the field such as Carolyn Stone, Carol Dahir, and Rebecca Schumacher address key issues as you plan and integrate these classroom guidance lessons.

I hope you enjoy this book and use the classroom guidance lessons as much as I do!!!

Chapter One
The Big Picture: Comprehensive School Counseling, Core Curriculum, and Program Mapping
Carol Dahir
New York Institute of Technology

The Comprehensive School Counseling Program

In the traditional Gestalt sense, the whole is greater than the sum of its parts. One cannot have a comprehensive school counseling program without a school counseling curriculum; and for some, the concept of program and curriculum is one and the same. A comprehensive program is designed for every student so that school counselors, embracing the law of parsimony (Myrick, 2003), have shifted their focus from a *Some Students' Agenda* to an *Every Student Agenda* that assures the acquisition of skills and knowledge, and equity in educational opportunity (Walsh, Barrett, & DePaul, 2007).

As a result of the development of the **American School Counselor Association** *(ASCA) National Standards* (Campbell & Dahir, 1997), ASCA joined the ranks of the academic disciplines by providing a content framework to clearly define the role of school counseling programs in the American educational system. The standards are statements of what students should know and be able to do as a result of participating in a school counseling program and follow the three domains of counseling programs: *Academic, Career, and Personal/Social Development*. These domains offer school counselors, administrators, teachers, and counselor educators a common language that also is readily understood by colleagues who are involved in the implementation of standards across other disciplines.

Student competencies, which help to identify student knowledge and skills, follow each of the standards. Competencies guide the development of the program content for student growth and achievement in the *Academic, Career,* and *Personal-Social* domains are an integral part of individual planning, school counseling curriculum, responsive services, and system support (Gysbers & Henderson, 2012). Competencies may be organized developmentally by school level and thus inform the sequence of strategies and activities, reflecting local school system issues, priorities and concerns.

Why Build a School Counseling Core Curriculum?

In this heightened frenzy of implementing and evaluating the common core standards, where do school counselors fit in? Is it our work to support our teachers, who for the umpteenth time since *America 2000* (1990) are delivering curriculum based on new academic standards? Or is it our goal to redefine the old "guidance curriculum" and align it with the *ASCA National Standards* and the common core? ASCA, too, has shifted in its thinking and has replaced the term "guidance curriculum" with "school counseling core curriculum" with the belief that using the same vocabulary as administrators and teachers will lead to shared goals and a purposeful understanding of the role school counselor. Curriculum is purposeful and based on the needs of the students in our school and in this age of accountability, school counselors now include student learner objectives and measurable outcomes in every lesson.

But why curriculum when I was not trained as a classroom teacher? Yes, but as educator and a counselor you have an ethical and moral responsibility to "provide students with a comprehensive school counseling program that parallels the *ASCA National Model* with emphasis on working jointly with all students to develop personal/social, academic and career goals (ASCA, 2010. A.3.a)". What better way to ensure that every student benefits from the work of the school counselor and the school counseling program? A successful school counseling core curriculum identifies what your students need to know and be able to do in these three important areas of *Academic, Career,* and *Personal-Social Development.* These skills are integrated into the core academic mission of the school in a planned, sequential and developmentally appropriate way.

The involvement of school faculty and administration is essential for effective and successful curriculum implementation. In most circumstances, the curriculum is intended to serve the largest number of students possible and this is accomplished through advisory programs, large group meetings, and of course, classroom presentations. The curriculum is planned, ongoing, and systematic with units of instruction and incorporates the school improvement plan, the *ASCA National Standards* and competencies, school data, and input from teachers, administrators, school staff, parents, and community stakeholders. The curriculum gives attention to particular issues or areas of concern in the school building or district such as reducing bullying behaviors, goal setting, career awareness, conflict resolution, or organizational skills. In this book, the following classroom guidance lessons address those topics respectively: *There's Power in Being a Bystander: Use it or Lose it!, Ready..Set.. Goals, Interdependence Day, Conflict Resolution,* and *Strategies for Success.*

Designing and Delivering Classroom Guidance Lessons

Lessons are delivered through the following methods. *Classroom Instruction:* School counselors provide instruction, in collaboration with classroom teachers, staff, and/or other stakeholders; about topics such as motivation, getting along with others, goal setting, decision making, career and college planning, respecting self and others, peer pressure, conflict resolutions, etc. Existing curricula such as *Second Step, Steps to Respect, Respect for All, Bully Busters, Student Success Skills,* and *Positive Behavior Intervention Supports,* as well as the school counseling core curriculum may also be used as part of classroom instruction.

Interdisciplinary Curriculum Development: School counselors work in conjunction with staff to develop lessons which connect content areas and the school counseling core curriculum. Examples may include but are not limited to organizational and study skills, test taking strategies, decision making, character education, peer problem solving, and community service, etc. Specifically, *Teaching Students to Ask for Help, Introduction of School Counselors and Middle School Needs Survey, Homeroom Quilt, A Chain is Only as Strong as its Weakest Link,* and *Puzzling Communication* lessons all focus on creating a positive classroom environment.

Group Activities: School counselors provide instruction and guidance to students in a small group setting in and outside of the classroom pertaining to the domains of academic, college and career readiness, and personal-social development. This has a different purpose than group counseling. In some schools that have a teacher advisory model, school counselors collaborate with classroom teachers and staff to design and develop specific activities as a component of the core curriculum.

Classroom lessons and curriculum activities are an integral part of the total comprehensive counseling program and important to every student's affective development. Although school counselors have to carefully organize their schedules to deliver the school counseling core curriculum, it provides ample opportunity to involve every student in this important component of the school counseling program.

Developmental Scope and Sequence

A scope and sequence can outline the Pre-K through grade 12 monthly curriculum topics in a developmental and comprehensive manner for all students. The curriculum unit plan outlines all the lessons included in that unit; and the specific lesson plan outlines the students learning objectives, structure, and general information contained in that specific lesson. The PreK-12 scope and sequence establishes the priorities for each grade level based on the district strategic priorities and school data which are delineated by the pre-K, elementary, middle, or high school levels.

Program Mapping

Mapping serves as a planning tool to identify the standards, competencies, and the subsequent services and activities for each grade level. Gaps in academic, career, and personal-social development can be easily identified through the mapping process. Mapping benefits the entire school community by providing a comprehensive timeline for service delivery and can be used to either develop or accompany a Pre-K through 12 scope and sequence. Mapping provides an identification and recording of all of the components of the delivery system, including school counseling core curriculum. Most importantly, program mapping helps us to plan a balanced approach to providing academic, career, and personal-social development activities to every student we are responsible for.

As the pressures on schools to raise the bar of academic performance persist, school counselors can collaborate with classroom teachers and administrators to use their skills to identify and rectify barriers that inhibit closing the achievement and opportunity gaps. Comprehensive school counseling programs and the school counseling core curriculum provide school counselors with an opportunity to assume a pro-active role in identifying and responding to complex academic, social and personal issues in a preventive and interventive manner.

References

U.S. Department of Education. (1990). *America 2000: An education strategy.* Washington, DC: Author.

American School Counselor Association. (2010). *Ethical standards for school counselors.* Retrieved from www.schoolcounselor.org

Campbell, C., & Dahir, C. (1997). *Sharing the vision: The national standards for school counseling programs.* Alexandria, VA: American School Counselor Association.

Gysbers, N. C., & Henderson, P. (2012). *Developing and managing your school guidance program* (5th ed.). Alexandria, VA: American Counseling Association.

Myrick, R. D. (2003). *Developmental guidance and counseling: A practical handbook.* (5th Ed.) Minneapolis, MN: Educational Media Corporation.

Walsh, M. E., Barrett, J. G., & DePaul, J. (2007). Day-to-day activities of school counselors: Alignment with new direction in the field and the ASCA national model. *Professional School Counseling, 10,* 370-378.

Chapter Two
Creating a Theoretical and Pragmatic Framework for Classroom Guidance Based on RtI, SEDL, and DASA Standards

Janice DeLucia-Waack
University at Buffalo, SUNY

While the new directives, standards, and even abbreviations can be overwhelming for school counselors, much of this information can be very exciting and useful for school counselors. It has sometimes been hard to integrate the role of the school counselor into the classroom even difficult to ask teachers for time to intervene with students individually, in small groups, and particularly in classes. Yet, most of the new developments and guidelines in education are highlighting the role of the school counselor, particularly the importance of classroom guidance in teaching essential skills and information to all students. This chapter will make suggestions on how to integrate the role of school counselor and classroom guidance into the essential mission of the school.

Some Positive Reframes on Old Terms

All Staff are Working Toward Student Academic Success

Sometimes "counselor" is accentuated in the role of school counselor, which may underemphasize the other unique skills and knowledge they possess. It is important to vocalize when working with teachers, parents, students, and administrators that the school counselor's first priority, along with all school staff, is to promote academic success. Communication from teachers about what academic skills they incorporate into their classes (organization, study, test taking) is helpful so that when students come to you, you already have a sense of what skills they have been taught so you can reinforce and build upon their skills, rather than re-teaching or suggesting different strategies. It is also a good opportunity for school counselors to provide classroom guidance on those topics as a way to get into the classroom and interact with students preventatively.

Expertise in Career Exploration and Planning is Unique to School Counselors

It is important to publicize the comprehensive training and unique expertise school counselors have in career development/exploration, and post-graduation planning. Specifically, college readiness and preparation are key parts of this expertise. Introducing yourself and outlining your background as a resource for all constituents is critical as you speak to students, parents, and teachers. The beginning of the year is always a good time to introduce (or reintroduce) yourself, your role, and all the ways you can be helpful to all in the school. The classroom guidance activity *Introduction of School Counselors and Middle School Needs Survey* by Rabey et al. is a good example of how to introduce yourself as a school counselor and assess needs of middle school students.

The **American School Counselor Association** *Student Standards* (ASCA, 2004) strongly advocate for interventions, including classroom guidance, in three areas: *Academic, Career Exploration and Planning, and Personal/Social Skills.* In addition, Response to Intervention (RtI; http://www.nasponline.org/resources/handouts/rtiprimer.pdf) guidelines outlines three levels of intervention; the first being classroom interventions aimed at all students, typically academic skill focused. The new *Educating the Whole Child, Engaging the Whole School: Guidelines and Resources for Social and Emotional Development (SEDL;* http://www.p12.nysed.gov/sss/ sedl/) and *The Dignity for All Students Act (DASA;* http://www.p12.nysed.gov/dignityact/) emphasize the importance of teaching personal and social skills K to 12. Taken together, there is strong support for classroom guidance in the three areas for all students. Teaching academic skills includes time management, organization skills, note-taking, and test-taking skills. Terneus's lesson *Decisions, Decisions* is designed for elementary students while *Getting*

Ready for Middle School by Logan and *Ready..Set..Goals!* by Sam Steen and Joy Rose are for middle school students, and *Time Quadrants* by Parsons is for middle and high school students.

Career exploration and planning varies by level, but is essential. For middle school, it may be more general: work values and skills and how they impact students' learning and work skills. Beeching's *Now for Later* asks middle school students to contemplate their future as a way to begin to think about careers. In a very innovative way, Brooks and Luke use a popular game to begin the discussion about careers, *The Power of YuGiOh: Using Your Powers to Explore Careers.* In high school, the focus is much more on what students will do after high school – college, job, apprenticeship, trade school, or military. *NCAA Expectations* by Cavalluzzo outlines expectations for college athletes while Alger and Luke's *Resume Writing for High School Students* guides students this this process Career exploration is mandated at the elementary level in some states (e.g., New York) so activities at this level would focus basic elements of jobs and careers. Lessons such as *Amazing Grace: Her Dream Comes True* by Cleveland, Austin and Thomas and *Create A Career Caricature* by Ross-Menelli and Luke use books and characters to begin career exploration.

In addition, the personal/social area has generated more dialogue pertaining to the SEL and DASA standards and in a preventative way, how to provide knowledge of basic social skills that all students need: communication skills, coping skills, and emotion management skills. Lessons like *Fur-sonalities: Animals and Friendship Skills* by Conner and Ziomek-Daigle for elementary, *Managing the Uncontrollable* by Jennifer L. Marshall for middle, and *Conflict Resolution by Tamika Collins* for high school students all address key issues in this area.

The classroom guidance lessons in this book are organized by topic and then school level (grade level within) so it is easy to find developmentally appropriate lessons for all ages and topics.

Collaboration and Coordination are Key to Successful Interventions

Collaboration. School counselors are not alone in the school in terms of providing information and success strategies for academic skills, career exploration and planning, and personal/social skills. All school personnel are focused on ensuring academic success. Thus, some content called for by the new standards may already be delivered by other staff. Communication is key. School counselors are part of a Pupil Personnel Services (PPS) team with the school psychologists who are focused on *Response to Intervention* around academic skills, learning difficulties, and emotional difficulties. Also on the PPS team, school social workers may focus on family and community collaboration and addition to social and emotional issues.

In addition, other teachers or staff will overlap in content areas and skill development. This overlap offers potential to reinforce and extend skills and join faculty in their classrooms to co-teach certain topics and themes. The library media specialists are experts in researching topics, so they can be very helpful with information about careers as well as current information and books about personal/social issues (for use in bibliotherapy). Home and careers teachers spend a significant amount of time on career lessons, so coordination with them is critical. Either co-teaching some lessons or having access to the lesson plans provides important information to discuss with students. Information gathering can be based on the lessons students have already completed as they plan for the next grade/level. In addition, the health and physical education teachers now have a curricular mandate that includes decision-making, problem-solving, and some mental health concepts. Thus, it is essential for school counselors to know what their colleagues are teaching to build upon those concepts, and co-teach and collaborate with student planning and evaluation.

Coordination. School counselors should be thinking integration and coordination. Every new requirement or regulation that is added, such as SEDL and DASA, does not necessarily require augmenting your school counseling program. Much of what is called for may already be happening in your school. It is helpful for the PPS staff to map out, almost like a curriculum map for teachers, what classroom guidance is already provided. Additional Tier 1 classroom guidance (and Tier 2 and 3) interventions can then be designed to be systematic, build upon previous lessons, and meet multiple objectives. For example, if teachers are already teaching organization and planning skills using an agendamate in the classroom, school counselors can reinforce those skills, rather than teach them.

Reframe Your Goals and Topics Positively

Reframe everything positively. Instead of focusing on bullying prevention, emphasize creating responsible, respectful citizens. This is a more realistic goal than stopping bullying in your school. In reality, bullying happens about 32% of the time; thus, 68% of the time, students are respectful. Using a Brief Solution Focused Therapy model, the focus is on the exceptions - situations when students are respectful and caring and ways to increase those behaviors. Programs such as PBIS focus on those positive behaviors. This also applies to the teaching of anger management skills. What students want to admit they need anger management skills? But defined as managing emotions and learning coping skills, students are much more willing to come to a group that focuses on learning those skills as opposed to being labeled as angry.

Response to Intervention (RtI) as a Call for Classroom Guidance

The RtI pyramid suggests three levels of intervention. Tier One is for all students - what skills do all students need? This is classroom guidance. Key information and skills are provided for all students by school counselors in academic, career development and planning, and personal/social skills. Tier 2 includes more intensive interventions for students who need additional help learning the above skills or at -risk; typically psychoeducational groups again tailored to those three areas. Tier 3 involves intensive one on one interventions for a small group of students that require additional services.

Let me share some examples. Tier 1 classroom guidance for academic skills is important for students who are transitioning. For these students, several classroom guidance lessons early in the year on test-taking strategies, how to plan and organize time for projects and papers, and how to plan and study for tests might be helpful. In addition, students in these transitional grades who are already at risk may also be part of a Tier 2 intervention - a small group for school success skills beginning the first week of school to help them acclimate. Additionally, after 10 weeks, students failing two or more subjects may move into a Tier 2 intervention.

If you use an RtI model for career planning in 8th grade, a significant amount of time is spent on career exploration in home and careers class, usually taking an interest inventory on the computer, scoring it, and then discussing general interpretations in class. Students might do a project on a particular career area that they are interested in and research salaries, degrees needed, and possible colleges. In English class, students might research a career by reading a biography of someone with that career, interviewing someone with that career, and seeking out resources about that career. The library media specialist could be involved with both of these classes. In addition using that information, the school counselor can begin to talk about high school, a four-year plan, and post-graduation planning. Tier 1 classroom guidance lessons on how to schedule for 9th grade may be useful. Tier 2 career planning for 8th graders would involve meeting in small groups based on career interest areas with the school counselor to discuss possible careers and plans for high school. Tier 3 would include individual meetings with students and their parents to finalize a student plan for high school.

Conclusions

It is almost natural to get anxious every time a new standard materializes as school counselors wonder "What else will I need to do?" However, it is useful to look at the new SEDL and DASA standards that provide substantial justification for classroom guidance and small group interventions focused on affective, cognitive, and social development. The RtI model provides a framework, including a common language, to explain to all school staff how school counseling interventions fit within the goals and mission of the school.

It is my hope as you look at the activities in this book, you will recognize the many effective interventions that you already have in place and compliment yourself!!! Then you may be able to think creatively about what else you can do to help students. The Editors' goal is provide you with activities that you may be able to adapt to improve and expand your classroom guidance curriculum.

References

American School Counselor Association (2004). *ASCA student standards.* Alexandria, VA: Author.

Chapter Three
Collaboration with Administration and Teachers: Developing Value and Support for Classroom Guidance

Rebecca A. Schumacher
University of North Florida
Jacksonville, FL

Laura Ache
Englewood High School
Jacksonville, FL

Throughout the illustrious history of school counseling, the profession has responded to societal demands. As the 20th century ended, a tidal wave of educational reform influenced the educational landscape, most notably the *Nation at Risk Report* (National Commission on Excellence in Education, 1983), and the *No Child Left Behind Act* (NCLB, 2001). Standards based education and accountability became ubiquitous in education. Once again, the profession responded to societal demands and launched the process of transforming school counseling practices from a reactive, service delivery approach for some students to standards based, data driven comprehensive programs for every student (ASCA, 1997, 2003). Today, the *American School Counseling National Model* (ASCA, 2012) guides the work of counseling where evidence-based practices, accountability, and results are no longer anticipated or expected - but demanded! Aligned with the mission of schools, The *ASCA National Model* is designed to support every student in academic achievement, career/postsecondary planning, and personal/social development.

Delivering a data driven comprehensive school counseling program has reduced school counselor time spent in isolation with a few students and increased time working with all students (ASCA, 2012; Education Trust, 2009; Martin, 2002). Additionally, a programmatic approach has required counselors to increase involvement with administration and teachers. Although collaboration has been a traditional way of work for school counselors, a programmatic approach has significantly increased the importance of collaboration. A collaborative relationship with teachers and administrators "strengthens the impact of the school counseling program by collectively focusing on common goals" (Dahir & Stone, 2012, p. 390). Therefore, collaboration has become essential for counselors to be able to support and impact all students.

Classroom guidance is but one key strategy of the core curriculum of the *ASCA Model* (ASCA, 2012). Yet being able to enter a classroom and deliver lessons is not necessarily a function that school counselors automatically can do or even assume can be done. A school counselor needs permission to work in classrooms. It becomes imperative that counselors purposely build capacity and form working relationships with the key stakeholders – both administrators and teachers - in order to acquire permission and build the support necessary to deliver classroom guidance.

This chapter will first briefly review the definition and recent findings about collaboration. Second, data and types of data will be described, followed by a discussion for how the use of data cultivates collaboration. And last, we share a story - an example, of how collaboration with administrators and teachers resulted in developing value and support for classroom guidance programs in one high school. So, let us now turn to key points about collaboration and the collaborative relationship.

Collaboration

Collaboration is a style of interactions and relationships (Friend & Cook, 2012). The Oxford Dictionary defined "collaboration" as "the action of working with someone to produce or create something" (The Oxford Dictionary, 2013, para. 1). Thus, for school counselors to effectively deliver programs that impact students and support school success, working with others is key (Dahir & Stone, 2012). Forming these connections raises questions about the characteristics or factors found in such relationships.

Fortunately, the literature affords insights into administrator, teacher, and counselor relationships (College Board Advocacy, 2009; Dahir & Stone; 2012; Gibbons, Diambra, & Buchanan, 2010; Perusse, Goodnough, & Bouknight, 2007; Shoffner & Morris, 2010; Zalaquett & Chatters, 2012). One of the more significant and recent studies was a joint research project conducted by The College Board, the National Office for School Counselor Advocacy (NOSCA), America School Counselor Association (ASCA), and the National Association of Secondary

School Principals (NASSP). This report, *Finding a Way* (2009) described essential factors for collaboration between principal and counselors. Combining interviews and survey results from over 2,300 principals and counselors, the study found the following characteristics comprising effective principal-counselor relationships.

   1. Open communication that provides multiple opportunities for input to decision making;

   2. Opportunities to share ideas on teaching, learning and school wide educational initiatives;

   3. Sharing information about needs within the school and the community;

   4. School counselor participation on school leadership teams;

   5. Joint responsibility in the development of goals and metrics that indicate success;

   6. Mutual trust between the principal and school;

   7. A shared vision of what is meant by student success;

   8. Mutual respect between the principal and school counselors;

   9. Shared decision making on initiatives that impact student success;

   10. A collective commitment to equity and opportunity may be integral to a school counselor's role and function. (College Board, 2009, p.8)

   While this project was conducted with principals, it is logical to also apply these findings to relationships with classroom teachers. Shared beliefs, mutual trust and respect, as well as open communication seem to capture the primary themes from the study's findings. Collaborative relationships are further strengthened when school counselors demonstrate their value and worth to the greater good of the school's mission. Yet how can school counselors create this worth and value to help with the already heavy burdens that administrators and teachers confront?

The Impact of Data

   In the age of accountability, data has become one of the most essential and powerful factors for school counseling (Dahir & Stone, 2012; Dimmit, Carey, & Hatch, 2007). School counselors' use of data demonstrates the impact of a school counselor's work on students, conveys the value for school counseling, and informs counselors where programmatic changes may be needed (ASCA, 2012). Types of data used in counseling programs are process, perception, and results data (ASCA), which are briefly reviewed next.

Process Data

ASCA (2012) defines process data as "the method of evaluation using figures to show the activities, rather than the results from the activities, such as numbers of students served, groups and classroom visits" (p. 142). For example, process data related to classroom guidance lessons might be 123 students in five 4th grade classrooms received three classroom guidance lessons in the first two months of the school year. Certainly interesting data, but process data offers no insight into students' success, impact on student achievement, nor the worth or value for school counseling.

Perception Data

Perception data (ASCA, 2012) "measure what students and others observed or perceived, knowledge gained, attitudes and beliefs held, or competencies attained (p. 142). Completing surveys, pre and a post tests, demonstrations for learned skill/knowledge, role-plays, or project presentations are methods that assess student outcomes. Pre and post tests are typically used for classroom guidance. For example, prior to the classroom lesson, 33% of the students knew three or more resources for scholarship and financial support; after the lesson, 91% of the students knew three or more resources. Providing these results to administrators and with a plan on how to improve lessons and better serve students show administrators and teachers that school counselors are aware of their pitfalls and have already brainstormed ways to improve. Value and worth for what counselors can contribute to student success are beginning to emerge.

As most administrators are concerned with what goes on in classroom, most of their time and attention is focused on helping teachers improve. School counselors want to ensure that their classroom guidance lessons are not burdening classroom teachers with more work, but supporting teachers, which will immediately provide value and worth, or creditability, to classroom guidance curricula.

Outcome Data: Results

Results data is by far the most powerful and telling data type. Outcomes - "how students are measurably different as a result of the school counseling program" (ASCA, 2012, p. 142), provide evidence for how the school counseling program made a difference for students' school success. Examples of results data include improved grades, attendance, or behavior; data collected over time. For example, after delivering classroom lessons about study skills, tracking homework completion rates and grades at the end of the marking period, conclusion of the semester, and the end of the year all convey results data. Reporting results continues to strengthen the worth and value for school counseling and the work of counselors, and conveys a powerful message to administrators and teachers for how school counselors contribute to student success.

Administrators are constantly measuring, reviewing, and assessing school data. School data is a priority of an administrator's position in the school and ultimately affects the bottom line of what can and cannot take place in a building. For example, providing school counseling curricula that could negatively affect student scores on a state-mandated exam runs the risk of no support for classroom guidance. Conversely, classroom guidance curricula that align and reinforce what teachers are doing in the classrooms and show results, reinforce and support what administrators are working to accomplish. Alignment of classroom lessons with standards and supporting the standards of classroom instruction further strengthens the use of guidance lessons.

Ultimately the use of data shows a worth and value for what school counselors do, how school counseling can support the work of administrators and teachers, and the impact school counseling programs can have on student success and student achievement. And with teachers under great pressures to provide bell-to-bell instruction in their content areas, data can prove to be the catalyst that allows school counselors to enter into the classroom and deliver guidance lessons, support the work of classroom teachers, and boost knowledge and skills toward students' success and achievement. In sum, data is a powerful path that can lead to demonstrating worth and value of guidance lessons, and ultimately shape a collaborative and collective spirit between counselor and teacher, and counselor and administrator.

Recognizing that data can facilitate collaboration with administration and teachers, next we discuss how the cycle of data use for classroom guidance is applied. Before determining what strategy should be used, one must first consider the purpose or what is the "need" for classroom guidance.

Defining the Need

As anyone would not just begin a task without prior thought and planning, the same can be said for planning classroom guidance. "Needs" data is one of the most influential pieces of information school counselors can use when building collaborative relationships with administration and teachers. Administrators' goals are to support teachers and instruction and the school counselor can build most of their relationships with administration and faculty by showing how their classroom guidance lessons will support the teachers in helping students learn.

There are a number of methods to determining student needs. Reviewing school data for grades, behaviors, and attendance is one method to identify student needs. A needs-assessment survey is also a useful tool administered to teachers asking common student issues that prevent their students from achieving to their potential. Student surveys surrounding personal/social issues, career domains, and academic needs, in conjunction with teacher input also informs the type of lesson the school counselor may provide. Test scores, grades, placements, behavioral data, and attendance are also common ways to uncover "needs". Common themes such as peer relationships, organization, and time management may emerge. School counselors can then use this data to inform administrators about the issues and ask for support in setting up classroom guidance with teachers in high-risk areas where it might be difficult to gain any class time.

When using needs assessments, we recommend that assessments be done quarterly at faculty meetings where little use of time is needed, and the assessments can be personalized to those teachers paired with the school counselor's caseload; whether that be by grade level or alphabet. Table 1.1. summarizes ways in which one method, or a combined mix of methods can determine students' needs. Once students' need(s) are determined, the inclination may be to address all needs, but it is advisable to focus on one particular need. The reason for selecting one is to be able to measure what you are trying to accomplish. This is critical and worth emphasizing - *select one need* -enables measurement of what happened as a result of the strategy or strategies employed to address the need. You may have multiple goals to address this need with multiple strategies to accomplish the goal(s). However, it will be difficult to impossible to determine what impacted your students if a number of needs are addressed simultaneously. How will you know what worked or did not work? Remember that what you do with your students is constantly cultivating value to your work, and ultimately increasing a collaborative relationship with administration and teachers. There are multiple strategies that school counselors may use, such as development of specific programs (e.g., tutoring, mentoring, peer helping), or small groups. However, for the purpose of this chapter, classroom guidance is the focus.

Table 3.1 *Sample Pre-Planning Question to Determine Students' Needs*

Methods	Evidence Sources
Review Existing Data	Data offers rich evidence. Examples: test scores, attendance, discipline referrals, graduation rates, enrollment in AP courses.
Conduct Observations	Classroom observations frequently provide insights into curriculum content and potential for integrating counseling standards with subject content.
Have Conversations	Talking with teachers, administration, and students inform about perceptions and beliefs.
Administer Surveys	Needs surveys provide feedback from large numbers, whether administered to students, faculty, and/or parents/guardians.

The process for delivering classroom guidance is a circular one; one constantly being re-evaluated and refined to build collaborative relationships with teachers and administrators. Here are suggested steps for each phase of classroom guidance:

a) Identify needs of the students. Methods can vary in how the needs are determined as described earlier in the chapter (see Table 3.1.);

b) Select the most prevalent need. It is advisable to review the needs with teachers and administrators (again building relationships) to identify which one need will be addressed;

c) Determine the curriculum that will most effectively address the need;

d) Establish the goal(s) that address the need;

e) If using a pre/post, administer the pre-test and deliver the classroom guidance;

f) Constantly monitor the classroom guidance and revise the lessons as needed;

g) Once the classroom guidance is completed, collect post data to calculate perception data, and share outcomes from the pre/post tests with teachers and administrators;

h) Collate process data and begin to monitor results data;

i) Continually communicate results data with teachers and administrators, and

j) Determine "next steps" based on student needs for further classroom guidance.

To capture this process, the below figure portrays the cycle of classroom guidance delivery.

Figure 1.1 Cycle of Classroom Guidance

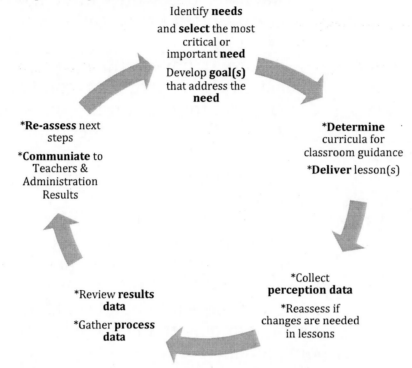

The Story

Next is one example of collaborative efforts of administration, teachers, and school counselors at a Title I High School in the Southeast area of the United States, and their cycle of classroom guidance. At this high school, each school counselor had approximately a 500 student caseload divided by grade level. To determine the needs of their students, the department conducted a needs assessment survey with the faculty at the end of the first quarter. The needs assessment measured student needs, as seen by the teachers, in four separate categories: *Academic, Career, Personal/Social, and Community*. Each category had a listing of 12to15 different needs and teachers were asked to select the top two or three needs of their students in each category. The top selections by domain were as follows:

Academic Development:
1. Organization and test taking,
2. Classroom speakers,
3. Classroom guidance lessons on study skills.

Career Development:
1. Getting financial aid information for post secondary educational options and exploring job opportunities after high school,
2. Applying knowledge of personal abilities, skills, interests, and values to future goals,
3. Exploring career choices and making career decisions.

Personal and Social Development:
1. Conflict resolution,
2. Student problem solving,
3. At-risk identification and implementation of interventions to enhance success.

Community Involvement:
1. Job shadowing, work based learning, part time jobs,
2. Developing a sense of community pride,
3. Understanding and helping the community recognize and respecting cultural and ethnic diversity.

Next, these results were presented and discussed during one of the regularly held counselor-administrator meetings. It was obvious that there were gaps in students' knowledge about postsecondary information and career readiness, which meant that the school's mission of providing all students equitable access to knowledge and skills for post-secondary readiness was not being fulfilled. To address this need, administration approved four counselors to provide a combined total of more than 200 individual classroom visits.

The 9th grade received the initial cycle for classroom guidance. The data clearly indicated that for 9th graders a goal needed to address developing a better understanding for how postsecondary education impacts one's adult lifestyle. Using information from the needs-assessment, 9th graders received classroom guidance lessons designed to educate them about potential earnings based on education level. In a short pre-survey, students were asked to identify their post-secondary goals and explain the correlation between education and income. As part of the curriculum, US Labor Department data was used in interactive lessons where students worked in small groups and were asked to choose their "dream life" scenario, and complete their personal budget, based off of their own numbers and experiences. Next, students were then assigned envelopes containing data about their group's education level as well as what they could expect to earn in one-month's time. As real life budget numbers were revealed, students had to recalculate their budgets, showing either positive or deficit income at the end of the month.

Prior to the lesson, most students acknowledged desire to obtain some sort of post-secondary education, but could not clearly and specifically define their goals. After the lesson, students gave specific answers to the question "What is your educational goal?" including specific mention of associates, bachelors, masters, or terminal degrees. Students were also able to articulate one thing they learned about education and salary, revealing a clear correlation between higher education and expected income, with answers ranging from understanding how quickly money can be spent, the importance of life planning, and that potential earnings cannot be left to luck. From the pre and post measures, these 9th grade students had clearly grasped that higher income is not by chance and higher education improves potential earning power.

Armed with this perception data, the 9th grade school counselor met with administration about using these types of lessons school-wide to impact the student's awareness of post-secondary options. Looping the results of the 9th grade lessons to the school's mission of providing all students equitable access to knowledge and skills for post-secondary readiness, this lesson was replicated and used by the 10th grade counselor. Results data will be tracked once these 9th grade students enter 12th grade and finalize their postsecondary planning.

Data results in this situation supported the worth and value for how school counseling programs can benefit students. Jointly and collaboratively, administration, teachers, and the counselors in intentional conversations determined how better to address the mission of the school, ultimately how to impact all students in the school. By demonstrating results, the school counselor conveyed worth and value for how to contribute to student success and developed support of administration and teachers for not only classroom guidance but small group counseling. Data was the critical factor in developing collaboration.

Conclusions

Overall, comprehensive school counseling programs are goal oriented and based on the needs of the school and students. Once needs are identified and prioritized, and goals defined, school counselors then begin the phase of determining what strategies will address the specific needs to accomplish these goals. Classroom guidance is but one strategy that a school counselor may use to tip the balance to accomplish the goal(s) established from needs identified by data. Classroom guidance is not a standalone entity nor an isolated event, but rather one strategy to deliver a data driven comprehensive program. Other strategies may include such student focused strategies such as small groups, individual work, tutoring program, peer program, bully-proofing program, or system-focused strategies such as a review of school practices, parent programs, grading policies, or attendance policies. The beauty of classroom guidance as a Tier I intervention is the comprehensiveness of reaching all students.

Data is also a crucial element in building the school counselor, teacher, administrator relationships. It can be the catalyst and the justification for the work of school counselors, and ultimately affirm or erode the administration's trust in not just classroom guidance, but all work of school counselors. Demonstrating results and impact on students is the ultimate outcome and purpose of the work of school counselors. Doing so continues the process of worth and value for what school counselors can contribute to student success and continues to cultivate the collaboration of school counselor, teacher, and administrator.

References

American School Counselor Association. (1997). *Executive summary: The national standards for school counseling programs.* Alexandria, VA: Author.

American School Counselor Association. (2003). *The ASCA national model: A framework for school counseling programs.* Alexandria, VA: Author.

American School Counselor Association. (2012). *The ASCA national model: A framework for school counseling programs* (3rd Ed.). Alexandria, VA: Author.

College Board Advocacy. (2009, May). *Finding a way: Practical examples of how an effective principal-counselor relationship can lead to success for all students.* General format, Retrieved from http://professionals.collegeboard.com/profdownload/findinga-way.pdf.

Dahir, C. A., & Stone, C.B. (2012). *The transformed school counselor* (2nd Ed.). Belmont, CA: Brooks/Cole/Cengage Publisher.

Dimmitt, C., Cary, J.C., & Hatch, T. (2007). *Evidence-based school counseling: Making a difference with data-driven practices.* Thousand Oaks, CA: Corwin Press.

Education Trust, National Center for Transforming School Counseling (2009). *The new vision for school counselors: Scope of the work.* Retrieved from www.edtrust.org/sites/edtrust.org/files/Scope%20of%20the%20Work_1.pdf

Friend, M., & Cook, L. (2012). *Interactions: Collaboration skills for school professionals,* (7th Ed.). Pearson Publishing.

Gibbons, M. M., Diambra, J. F., & Buchanan, D. K. (2010). School counselor perceptions of and attitudes about collaboration. *Journal of School Counseling, 8,* 1-28. http://jsc.montana.edu/articles/v8n34.pdf

Gysbers, N.C. (2010). *Remembering the past, shaping the future: A history of school counseling.* Alexandria, VA: American School Counseling Association.

Martin, P.J. (2002). Transforming school counseling: A national perspective. *Theory Into Practice, 41,* 148-154.

National Commission on Excellence in Education. (1983). *A nation at risk.* Washington, DC: U.S. Government Printing Office.

No Child Left Behind Act of 2001, Publ. L.No. 107-110. (2001).

Oxford Dictionary (2013) Retrieved from http://oxforddictionaries.com/us/definition/american_english/collaboration

Perusse, R., Goodnough, G. E., & Bouknight, T. (2007). Counselor education and educational administration: An exploratory survey of collaboration. *Journal of School Counseling, 5 (24),* http://jsc.montana.edu/articles/v5n24.pdf

Shoffner, M., & Morris, C. W.(2010). Preparing pre-service English teachers and school counselor interns for future collaboration. *Teaching Education, 21,* 185-197. doi: 10.1080/10476210903183894

Zalaquett, C.P., & Chatters, S. J. (2012). Middle school principals' perceptions of middle school counselors' roles and functions. *Secondary Education, 40*(2), 89-103.

Chapter Four
Leadership Principles for Classroom Guidance Lessons as a Task Group

Amy W. Upton   John C. Dagley
University of South Alabama

The history of teaching and learning in small groups is longstanding. For decades, and perhaps even centuries, children and adolescents have learned in small groups. Of course, the first small group was the family-of-origin for most young children, with other sub-group learning opportunities coming along when students started attending schools. In the pioneer days of America, school-based learning took place in a small "one-room" schoolhouse wherein young students ranging in age from 7 to 15 or so were taught by a single teacher in a series of small-group exercises organized loosely around ages and levels of learning. Dependent upon local resources, learning focused on the basics – namely, reading, writing (spelling), arithmetic, and history. The teaching process typically consisted of lectures, recitations, repetitive skill-building activities, and more than anything else, small-group interactions in the form of cross-age tutoring. Thus, a long history exists of "groups" and classroom guidance as organizational tools for facilitating learning.

In recent decades, the focus of task groups in schools has largely been on "the-group-as-a-whole" Often, the focus has been on sports teams, or on groups charged with a specific task, i.e., homecoming activities, disaster relief fund drives, peer helping programs, debate teams and others. Each of these efforts may still be on the school agenda, but today's task groups would be undoubtedly more educational and social-emotional in emphasis. The purpose of this chapter is to help school counselors provide effective leadership in classroom guidance using a task group perspective to impact student achievement and development as 21st century learners.

ASCA National Model and Task Groups

Today's school counselor uses a wide variety of approaches and techniques to deliver a school counseling program built at the local level, as inspired by the national model outlined by the **American School Counselor Association** (ASCA, 2012). That model outlines a school counseling program comprised of curriculum-based efforts, individual planning, needs-based responsive services, and system-support initiatives. This guiding model has been purposefully structured to help students achieve academic, career and personal/social goals required for effective living. Small and large groups comprise a significant part of the delivery system. Of the four types of groups described in the professional literature (Task, Psychoeducational, Counseling, and Therapy; ASGW, 2000), Task groups stand out as an approach that most easily fits into the structure of schools, primarily because Task groups can be led inside classrooms. While the primary focus of the group goal is on the performance of the "team" or "task force," individual student growth is also important. It is this complication that makes classroom guidance and task groups challenging objectives for school counselors as the focus is always split between the individual and the group.

School counselors are charged with the responsibility for serving schools in a myriad of ways, foremost of which is the implementation of a comprehensive school counseling program. The *ASCA Model* (2012) recommends school counselors spend up to 80% of their time in direct and indirect student services. Both large group classroom guidance and small groups are part of a comprehensive program, and are considered direct student services. Classroom guidance, serving as the large group delivery platform of the school counseling curriculum, provides all students direct contact through the curriculum. Academic learning objectives continue to grow, almost exponentially; additionally, so do more personal and group/team-oriented personal behavioral objectives. The focus has intensified and sharpened on each student's need to become more future-focused and strategic, more resilient, more understanding, more teamwork-oriented, more accepting of others who seem different, more resourceful, more motivated, and more responsible. The *ASCA Model* emphasizes each of these learning objectives, and collectively presents the professional school counselor with a considerable curriculum to deliver (along with a number of other responsibilities).

Traditionally, school counselors through all levels (Pre-K to12) have led classroom guidance lessons focused on specific aspects of the guidance curriculum such as the academic, personal/social and career development student competencies (ASCA, 2004). Task groups, especially classroom guidance lessons, have been about both "process" and "outcome," with classroom guidance being highly valued as a process "and also" an outcome goal in headlined challenges, like bullying prevention, conflict resolution, violence prevention, multicultural and international living, (Conyne & Harpine, 2010; Orpinas & Horne, 2006). Both individual and group goals can be achieved. If public education calls for students to embrace 21st century skills such as collaboration, global awareness, and problem solving, and the world of work is demanding more teamwork and project-based achievement of tasks, then school counselors can serve individuals and society through implementing classroom guidance as Task groups.

Unique Leadership Challenges

A significant challenge confronting leaders of classroom guidance lessons from a task group perspective is the fact that a *class is not a group* in the usual sense. Classes exist as a unit before and after classroom guidance, so the group dynamics are a bit different than what is experienced in a small group counseling experience. Therefore, when school counselors lead Task groups they experience that leadership parameters within an existing classroom are often unique and a bit unlike other groups they lead. Group dynamics still occur, and group leadership skills are still required, but "groups within a group" offer different challenges. "Cohesion," for example, often considered the "sine qua non" of small groups, has already been established by the time an outsider (school counselor) arrives. The limited time allocated for classroom guidance reduces the likelihood of re-creating whole-class cohesion, so counselors must focus on helping members of smaller units within the class to come together to achieve the targeted goals of the task group. In that sense, cohesion rests with the task, not the group, per se.

Additional challenging variables that often confront school counselors include significant time limits, a general lack of confidentiality, an open-membership, a larger than usual number of group participants (sometimes up to 30 or more), a quasi-acceptance of an outsider (not the regular teacher), and an agenda that is sometimes more or less structured, and possibly more personal than their regular classroom. Each of these variables is important. Plus, above all, in today's academic environment where test performance is a constant focus of the entire school, anything not directly related to academic performance is viewed with high skepticism, even though all parents and educators want children to build critically important life skills beyond academics.

Leadership Principles

School counselors lead classroom guidance group sessions from a base of planned objectives, both process and outcome. Leadership responsibility is an important part of the role of school counselors, and nowhere more so than in groups. Inhibitive or potentially harmful behavior of a student or students within a group can be more easily contained and shaped when a leader has been timely, not necessarily prescient, in their observations and re-directions. This can be accomplished by the school counselor moving around the classroom; observing, listening and assessing interaction as the group and sub-groups work. Hence, structure becomes imperative. School counselors need to be master observers and quick deciders as to when and how to intervene to facilitate positive task group interaction, and as to when to stop and re-direct harmful interactions. Positive support can be more impactful than re-directing.

School Task groups need to be tied to curriculum-based goals. It is imperative that the school counselor prepare the lesson plan within stated objectives in their school's comprehensive school counseling plan, and align it with local, state and nationals standards for students. Group interaction should also be in line with regular school behavioral guidelines. It is always in the participants' best interests for the classroom guidance structural and behavioral guidelines to be readily apparent. Students need to know what to expect from the lesson and from the leader, and to be aware of skills, attitudes and knowledge they should be gaining from the lessons (DeLucia-Waack & Nitza, 2009). By discussing the expectations of the classroom guidance group and by providing clear and concise instructions at the onset of the group lesson, school counselors provide students with the needed structure and direction to begin a group. In addition to clear structured directions, school counselors may also choose to describe typical roles, both positive and negative, that tend to occur in specific task force groups. For example, a leader may introduce part of an activity by saying something like "sometimes it's easier to allow one or two individuals to accept all the responsibility for contributing thoughts and ideas, relative to our task, but we need comments and assistance from each, so let's help each other contribute." With that introduction, leaders set expectations with positive encouragement, rather than intervening after-the-fact if and when "monopolizers" emerge.

Leadership Strategies

Focus on Goals of Lesson

As in all groups, Task group leaders spend time early in the classroom guidance lesson focusing on the purposes and goals. In this book Land and Ziomek-Daigle share an excellent example of clear goals in the *Balloon Tower Challenge*. The first goal of this lesson is that the students "define cooperation and teamwork, and identify individual roles within a group or team." This goal of setting a defined perspective of cooperation provides a solid foundation for the group to begin the activity, and creates an agreement (a group norm) so that they may move forward together.

Focus on Experiential Learning

In addition, Land and Ziomek-Daigle's *Balloon Tower* also is an exceptional example of a lesson that directly relates its goals to desired outcomes by providing students an opportunity to experience "learning group participation skills" first-hand. A similar connection between goals and the classroom guidance lesson is present in *Getting Help: The Art of Asking Questions*, a middle-school lesson by Falco, Williams and Conner. In this, the simple task of teaching students how to ask questions is turned into an interpersonal exchange where participants learn how to master one of the most useful skills in any learning environment – how to ask for help in a way that it can be given.

Focus on Balance of Process and Content

A skill of special merit is for the leader to maintain a twin focus during classroom guidance on both process and outcome. Sometimes the process can become so engaging that outcome goals may be neglected. In such a case, process may trump outcomes unless the leader stays vigilant. Such may be the challenge in the *Homeroom Quilt* lesson by Behm et al. In this lesson, it would be important to discuss at length the process (and the outcome) of creating a group quilt to its purpose.

The unique challenge in most Task groups is to keep the "process" alive and well. Often the task takes over and process goals get lost, unless the leader anticipates such a situation and plans for it. One way that a school counselor can provide leadership is to allow time for processing questions at the conclusion of the activity. Time must be allowed for the students to return to the purpose of the group and reflect on their individual and collective efforts to achieve the group goal.

Each lesson in this book provides processing questions to be used at key points in the activity to facilitate meaning attribution. Kilgore, Freels, and Fineran's lesson, *Puzzling Communication*, includes processing questions after each round that can lead the groups into the next round with a better understanding of their communication strengths and weaknesses impacting completion of the task so that they can improve their communication skills going forward. Additionally, Lukehart and Guth's lesson *Diversity Rocks* included questions about themes of their groups, and about similarities and differences of group members in an effort to facilitate group discussion midway through their lesson. In these examples, waiting until the activity is completed to introduce processing questions may reduce the lesson's meaning; do it earlier.

Assessment of Learning

An important leadership task in classroom guidance is to measure outcomes. It is more common, and also somewhat useful, to collect formative (process) data during the group, but it is even more important to assess outcomes. To what degree did the group achieve its objectives? Processing questions are included at the end of lessons to assess how well students have achieved the identified goals. In Kitchens and Evans' lesson *Friendship Trail Mix*, the processing questions "How is our classroom like our trail mix?," and "How is our classroom different than our trail mix?," assess whether the group successfully met goal #2: "Recognizing the diversity in our classroom through comparing similarities and differences among classmates, and learning we can all be friends." Sometimes the nature of the group makes outcome assessment a challenge, but in schools, it's increasingly important.

Lesson Design

The selection or design of the lesson is also important. Bibliocounseling can be used quite creatively in Task groups throughout the age range of schools, particularly because writings/readings can be impactful as experienced by readers, in similar yet very different ways. It is that range of experience that provides the content for "processing" personal reactions. The use of the *Amazing Grace* book by Cleveland, Austin and Thomas is an excellent example of using writing and readers' responses to provide a "book club" sort of processing interaction of gender roles/restrictions.

Several other classroom guidance lessons in this book possess exceptional potential for inspiring interaction. In several ways, Eisenman provides an excellent example of an almost continuous focus of "sharing the experience" in *The Group Cohesion Web*, wherein students build an interconnected web of yarn. Similarly, the *Create a School* lesson by Paone provides a scenario inviting small groups to consider setting up targeted rules (e.g., dress code) for things they experience daily. The leadership challenge would be to maintain an appropriate modicum of decorum in a free and open exchange on such a stimulating topic. As this lesson calls for multiple groups to be developed within this activity, setting the size of each group at a manageable level (Paone recommends groups of six) is a key first step in managing the groups. Additionally, the school counselor could direct each group to choose one member of their group who serves to keep the group on task, and the discussion in line with the goal.

Summary

Leadership principles for conducting classroom guidance from a Task group perspective begins with shaping goals to meet the curriculum endorsed by the local school system, and end with assessment of outcomes directly related to those learning objectives. Between pre-planning and the post-group assessment, School counselors use their expertise to lead students formed into Task groups to achieve desired objectives of both the "groups" and the "individuals." Focused on 21st century learning goals, students in sub-groups within a classroom are guided through a well-planned and smoothly facilitated set of exercises in such a way that they are able to experience both individual and collective growth.

References

Association for Specialists in Group Work (2000). *Association for Specialists in Group Work professional standards for the training of group workers* (Rev.). Retrieved from www.asgw.org pdf/training_standards.pdf

American School Counselor Association. (2012). *The ASCA National Model: A framework for school counseling programs (3rd Ed.).* Alexandria, VA: Author.

American School Counselor Association. (2004). *ASCA National standards for students.* Alexandria, VA: Author.

Conyne, R., & Harpine, E. (2010). Prevention groups: The shape of things to come. *Group Dynamics: Theory, Research, and Practice, 14*, 193-198. doi: 10.1037/a0020446

DeLucia-Waack, J.L., & Nitza, A. (2010) Leading task groups in schools. In B. Erford (Ed.), *Group work in the schools* (pp.171-186). Upper Saddle, NJ: Pearson

Orpinas, P., & Horne, A. (2006). *Bullying prevention: Creating a positive school climate and developing social competence.* Washington, DC: American Psychological Association.

Chapter Five
Data and Accountability: Evaluation of Classroom Guidance Activities

Christine Suniti Bhat
Ohio University

Caroline J. Lopez
Chapman University

The **American School Counselor Association** (ASCA) emphasizes the need for school counselors to carry out both formative and summative evaluations in a comprehensive school counseling program. Accountability is a core element of the ASCA *National Model* (2012), allowing school counselors to "demonstrate the effectiveness of the school counseling program in measureable terms" (p. xiv). Evaluative data are utilized to answer the vital question: "How are students different as a result of the school counseling program?" (ASCA, p. 99). If school counselors are to justify the use of valuable instruction time for classroom guidance lessons, they must be prepared to demonstrate efficacy by clearly showing what students have learned or how they have grown as a result of the guidance efforts. This chapter will provide a brief overview of the concept of accountability, discuss the types of data school counselors can collect, and suggest ways data can be utilized.

Accountability is one of the four quadrants in the framework of the *ASCA Comprehensive School Counseling Model* – the remaining quadrants are *Foundation, Delivery,* and *Management* (ASCA, 2012). Using data, school counselors can demonstrate how programming including classroom guidance can improve student outcomes in terms of attendance, achievement, attitudes, or behaviors. Data related to guidance elements of a comprehensive school counseling program provide information on how much of an impact programming is having on student outcomes, as well as how programming may need to be strengthened. Three types of data provide concrete and powerful evidence to the school community and key stakeholders regarding the positive impact of the work of school counselors.

Three Types of Data:
Process, Perception, and Outcome

Three types of data are useful for school counselors to include in program activity results reports: process, perception, and outcome data. Each type of data answers a different question. Process data answers the question: "What did you do, and for whom?" (ASCA, 2012, p. 51). Perception data answers the question: "What do people think they know, believe, or can do?" (ASCA, p. 51). Outcome data answer the question: So what?" by demonstrating the impact of a program or activity (ASCA, p. 52). ASCA provides a format to document such data with the "Small Group Results Report" that is available for download upon purchase of the 3rd edition of the *ASCA National Model*.

School counselors can easily provide Process data by documenting the guidance lesson, the number of lessons offered, and the number of students served. For example, Jennifer Park's *A Village of 100* is a two-lesson activity that teaches about social justice and inequities. If this guidance activity was delivered to 6th grade students, process data in the form of attendance may be recorded as follows: lesson 1: 105 students present; session 2: 96 students present.

Perception data may be quantitative or qualitative, and requires students or participants to self-report on knowledge gained or attitudes changed as a result of the guidance lesson. Utilizing quantitative research tools such as surveys and a pre-post research design, school counselors can gather data before and after classroom guidance. Surveys typically use a Likert scale, with a range of responses (for example a Likert scale of 1 to 5 (1=Strongly Disagree, 5= Strongly Agree). For example, José M. Álvarez's lesson *Show Me the Money: Career Choice, Financial Aid, and Information Systems* encourages students to think critically about their career choices and teaches students about financial aid. The pre-survey presented at the end of this activity can help the counselor assess (a) knowledge, with questions such as: *I know what FAFSA is and how to apply for it*, and (b) attitudes, such as, *"I feel excited about visiting colleges/universities.* A post-lesson survey administration could assess gains made by students, while a post-post survey administration could assess longitudinal gains or changes after a period of time (e.g., 3 months).

Pre-surveys can be used to improve instructional methods and thereby, improve learning outcomes. An example of this can be seen in Figure 1 which reports the results of a sexual harassment guidance lesson for middle school students. Pre-survey data indicated that 95% of students believed it was important to report instances of sexual harassment; however, only 26% indicated that they could identify sexual harassment behaviors. Using this data the school counselor recognized that students already knew it was important to report and therefore, designated more time in the lesson toward explaining what qualified as sexual harassment behavior. Adjusting the classroom guidance lesson based on this data resulted in significant gains on post-survey data. After the lesson, 66% of students were able to identify sexual harassment behaviors.

Figure1: Sexual Harassment Lesson

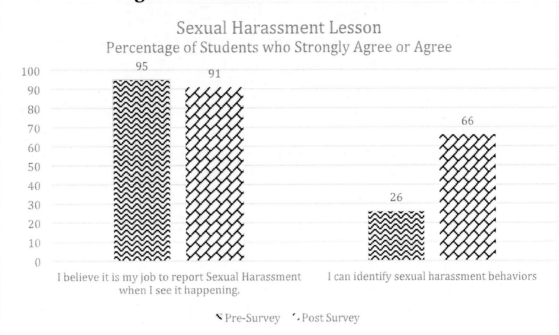

Quantitative data can be easily displayed using tables, charts, or graphs. As noted in Figure 1, a bar graph can graphically display gains that are made between pre and post survey administrations. Perception data can also be collected by qualitative means such as sentence-completion items. For example, in Lopez and Bhat's lesson *There's Power is Being a Bystander*, one of the goals (understanding the role of the bystander in intervening) can be assessed by the following: "I can take action as a bystander by _____"), or by conducting focus groups with participants before and after the activity.

Outcome data demonstrate the impact that changes in student knowledge, attitudes and behaviors have on achievement and behavior. For example analyses of discipline referrals related to cyberbullying in the months before, during, and after students have participated in a cyberbullying prevention program can demonstrate changes in behaviors.

School Counselors Share Their Favorite Classroom Guidance Activities

Guidance lessons focused on motivation and retention can track attendance data or graduation rates (achievement outcome data) to demonstrate the impact of programming on student outcomes. If a school counselor at a middle school delivered a guidance curriculum on assertiveness versus aggressiveness, the goal is to demonstrate that aggressive behaviors have lessened in the weeks after the program. Although it may not be possible to infer causality, it is useful to be able to demonstrate a link between the guidance programming and a reduction in aggressive outbursts.

Data to Highlight the Impact of School Counseling on Student Outcomes

As discussed in the previous section, different types of data provide information to guide the work of school counselors. If pre and post data show no improvement on some items, the school counselor can work to improve guidance activities related to that particular area in the guidance curriculum. Data may also be disaggregated so that outcomes may be studied by biological sex, race or ethnicity, grade level, or socio-economic status. Analyses with disaggregated data permit the school counselor to target interventions with specific populations in the school based on need as demonstrated by data.

Data can be shared with all constituents in a school including the administration and school board, teachers, parents, and students. In some states such as California with the *Support Personnel Accountability Report Card* (SPARC, http://www.sparconline.net/) and Ohio, with the *Ohio School Counselor Accountability Report* (OSCAR, http://www.ohioschoolcounselor.org/Default.aspx?pageId=1712885), school counselors prepare accountability reports and publicize them on the school website or in other ways. This serves the dual function of (a) educating constituents about the impact of the work of school counselors and (b) providing information useful in advocacy efforts to support the work of school counselors.

Data Analysis Tools

Some school counselors shy away from engaging in data-driven accountability, thereby losing valuable opportunities to demonstrate in concrete terms that guidance activities positively impact students. School counselors do not need specialized statistical software to engage in data analysis. Tools such as *EZAnalyze*, a Microsoft Excel Add-On (http://www.ezanalyze.com/features.htm), make data analysis and creating graphs easy. With *EZAnalyze*, school counselors can do the basic descriptive statistics including mean, median, standard deviation, and range. It also provides options for disaggregating data and creating graphs. Another strategy school counselors could consider is to partner with universities in their area to complete evaluation studies of school counseling programs. Statistical procedures such as t-tests could be conducted to assess if pre and post-test differences are significant. Further rigor could be added to accountability studies with the use of psychometrically sound instruments with robust reliability and validity. For example, Hammond and Roseman in *Anxious Adolescents* utilize the *Holmes-Rahe Social Readjustment Ratings Scale* to measure growth and progress of students in handling stress.

Resources to Support Accountability Efforts

The *Center for Excellence in School Counseling and Leadership* (CESCaL, http://www.cescal.org/resourceFinder.cfm) assists school counselors as they design, develop, implement and evaluate evidence-based school counseling activities. The website add website contains a resource board where graduate students and practicing school counselors can create and share classroom guidance lesson plans, PowerPoint lessons, pre and post-tests, and results reports. The site also provides ready-made templates for developing school-wide guidance curriculum action plans, classroom guidance action plans and results reports. Accountability resources are also provided by state departments of education.

Conclusions

Over the past two decades the focus on accountability has increased. With the Educational reform movement, high stakes testing, and federal and state legislation, school counselors are routinely called upon to demonstrate how students are different as a result of the services they provide. Measuring the effectiveness of classroom guidance lessons is imperative in order to determine if learning objectives have been met and to serve as a guide to enhance current guidance curriculum.

References

American School Counselor Association (2012). *The ASCA National Model: A framework for school counseling programs* (3rd Ed.). Alexandria, VA: Author.

Chapter Six
Ethical and Legal Considerations in Classroom Guidance

Carolyn Stone
University of North Florida

The legal and ethical complexities of working with minors in schools require school counselors to remain vigilant about the rights and responsibilities of students and their parents/guardians, as well as the implications of those rights on their work (ACA, 2005; ASCA, 2010; Imber & Van Geel, 2009). These ethical complications are acutely present in small group and individual counseling but also in delivering classroom guidance lessons (Thompson & Henderson, 2010; Vernon, 2004). The legal and ethical complexities surrounding classroom guidance lessons are primarily the result of school counselors delivering personal/social emotional services in a setting designed for academic instruction (Baker & Gerler, 2007; Galassi & Akos, 2004; Gibson & Mitchell, 2007; Moyer, Sullivan, & Growcock, 2012; Sink, 2005). A major consideration discussed throughout this chapter is the fact that there is no guarantee of confidentiality in classroom guidance and therefore, school counselors must be careful to avoid putting students in situations where highly sensitive and personal material may be discussed such as groups for incest survivors. An example would be helpful and if any activities from book – cautions would be great to add.

This chapter will revisit and highlight some of the basic principles of ethical issues for classroom guidance work; i.e., confidentiality, informed consent, best practices, appropriate topics, skill level, parents/guardians' rights, multiculturalism, and obligations to administrators and teachers. Special emphasis is on the competing interests and obligations that extend beyond the students to parents/guardians, administrators and teachers and minors developmental levels which require that the school counselor be able to adequately attend to the number and nuances of considerations before entering the classroom to provide a lesson.

Informed Consent and Safety in Classroom Guidance

Classroom guidance requires that the school counselor provide a minimum level of informed consent, maybe not as often or as involved as is needed for small groups and individual counseling where disclosure of sensitive information is a given, but at least a minimum level of informed consent is needed along with parameters and instructions for engagement. The parameters and instruction for engagement would include reminding and/or providing ground rules that promote respectful behavior especially when classmates are sharing information. It is also important for the school counselor to explain to students if they have personal information that would be better shared privately that they can see you individually. Remind or teach students how to get an appointment to see you.

Confidentiality, which is addressed in Standard A.2 of the ASCA *Ethical Standards*, means that the professional school counselor provides informed consent, i.e., disclosing the terms to provide the counselee the purposes, goals, techniques and rules of procedure under which he or she may receive counseling. How does this look for classroom guidance?

For example, a school counselor was delivering a classroom guidance lesson when a student shared highly sensitive information. Students were being asked to share past experiences with feelings such as when they felt afraid, happy, or excited and when asked to tell about a time they felt sad, a student brand new to the school offered, "My dad just killed my mom and then killed himself." In this very real case, the counselor asked the student if he would like to share his story; he then graphically described his parents' murder/suicide.

While in the classroom setting, the emotional safety of all students is primary (ASCA, 2010, D.1.). School counselors cannot possibly predict what students are going to say in classroom guidance lessons but a good rule of thumb is to prepare for the worst and have a plan as to how you will address situations where students share inappropriate information about their families. A good skill to develop is thinking through implications of lessons and possible responses with an eye on the possible twists and turns of students' responses. Also, being prepared to skillfully intervene without dismissing a student or making him or her feel devalued is an important tool to be able to use.

In this real situation, if only the counselor had honored the student with a sincere acknowledgement that his parents death is indeed a situation that would make him feel sad, and move on to the next person, perhaps the fallout could have been avoided. To do more than sincerely acknowledge and move on opens up the possibility of more trauma for the child who lost his parents and the other children hearing details. This student is not developmentally able to understand the implications of sharing his story in front of his classmates. He does not understand that this can bring sympathy but also possible taunting and bullying. By allowing him to tell such personal sensitive information in a classroom setting the student was put in a positive of even further harm. Clearing the calendar and quietly and figuratively scooping him up immediately after the classroom session and bringing him in to your office for unconditional positive regard would be an important next step. Helping him find those people with whom he can safely share his story and connecting him with resources would be ongoing support for this student.

Newspaper Article following the Incident: School Forming Death Talk Protocol

A panel of school officials wants to avoid a repeat of a recent incident in which a student graphically described his parents' murder-suicide to his sixth-grade classmates. The Mesick Middle School principal and three school counselors are setting a protocol to follow whenever discussing the deaths of a student's immediate family members. Meanwhile, counselor Linda B., who school officials said asked the boy if he wanted to share his story with classmates, was suspended for two days during an investigation, Superintendent Ron Ford said. The board then took "appropriate remedial action," he said, though he would not be more specific. The counselor since has returned to work. The panel's efforts were spurred by a student's talk in Carole R.'s sixth-grade class on Oct. 6 regarding his parents' deaths downstate in September. The boy moved to Mesick to live with relatives and enrolled in classes here. Both R. and B. declined to be interviewed, Principal Deann Jenkins said. Several parents, including Jay Clough, whose 11-year-old daughter was in the class, told the school board and administrators of the incident. "My first impression was that it should've been brought to the parents' attention before they talked about it in the classroom," Clough said. "So now, instead of one kid that needs counseling, you've got a whole classroom of kids that need counseling" (Carr, 2003).

When highly sensitive, graphic details are revealed by a student before a school counselor can intervene, it is necessary to think through and address any negative repercussions. Given the age and developmental levels of the students, an appropriate response might be to notify parents about what transpired and give suggestions on how to talk to their child about what they heard in the class, especially since the student revealed in this very real case, the details of a murder/suicide. The teacher and counselor might need to collaborate to talk to the class as a group or help groom the classroom to accept and support the new student.

Confidentiality and Classroom Guidance Lessons

The developmental levels of children mean confidentiality cannot be guaranteed and sensitive information about the private world of students and their families is often discussed by children openly without warning and before the school counselor can intervene to protect (Corey, 2011; Greenberg, 2003; Venkatesh, 2006). The reality of working with minors in small groups or classroom guidance groups requires school counselors to come from the posture that confidentiality will be breached. Filtering working with students through the lens that whatever is said in the classroom will be tweeted, posted on Facebook, or discussed at the lockers down the hall within seconds or minutes helps counselors take the necessary precautions to watch what they allow one student to talk about in front of other students. Some minors frequently change friends and loyalties, and with this fluid behavior, there is the danger of a student wanting attention, seeking revenge or just acting thoughtlessly in revealing another student's personal pain. Regardless if the topic is as innocuous as school success skills or as serious as children in divorce situations, it is imperative to remember confidentiality will be breached. Before allowing students to discuss issues that explore family troubles or personal issues, school counselors must ask themselves if the potential emotional cost to students and their families is worth the gains that could result from having allowing the student to share in a setting where confidentiality will be breached.

Information Learned in Classroom Guidance

When delivering classroom guidance lessons, school counselors often observe or identify students who need additional services. A student innocently shares that her dad walks around the house nude, sending off alarm bells for the school counselor. Mary Hughes the elementary school counselor in this very real court case, *Hughes v. Stanley County School District* (1999), told the student to talk to her mother. Hughes was fired for not reporting alleged child abuse. M.B., a third-grade girl, told Hughes, that her father, G.B., walked around the house naked after a shower. In another conversation, M.B. told Hughes that G.B. "touched her in the area of her breast during a playful wrestling match," and in a third conversation, Hughes learned that M.B. walked in on her father while he was masturbating. M.B., however, had a history of fabricating and exaggerating facts, so Hughes was unsure how seriously to take the allegations. Accordingly, she spoke with the high school counselor to get a second opinion, and both felt that Hughes should speak with the girl's parents. So, going against school policy to report suspicion of abuse, Hughes contacted the parents in an attempt to validate or dismiss the allegations. The parents told her that the allegations were essentially true and G.B. had taken steps to avoid reoccurrence in the future. While Hughes did check up on the situation with M.B. daily, she never reported the allegations to the authorities. The failure to report came to light when the police questioned Hughes in connection with a complaint that G.B. had sexually assaulted a neighbor girl. G.B. pled guilty to the sexual assault charge with the child, and Hughes was fired for failure to report the previous allegations (Swinton, 2005).

Clear Imminent Danger or Serious and Foreseeable Harm

The use of serious and foreseeable as the indicator school counselors will use to determine if a breach of confidentiality is necessary is a shift from the previous idea of "clear and imminent" danger. Clear imminent danger is insufficient to cover situations in which the school counselor may know of a danger that is not directly in front of them, but could not be classified as "clear and imminent". Therefore, the term "serious and foreseeable" was adopted in the 2010 ethical codes to provide a larger blanket of protection for students and counselors.

During a drug awareness lesson, a seven year old reveals he sneaks his mother's cigarettes and smokes them when she is away. Webster defines imminent as about to happen, looming. Clear imminent danger has always been a concept that was defined by most school counselors as broader than looming, as they are acutely aware that their obligation extends beyond their minor students to their parents/guardians who have retained the right to be the guiding voice in their children's lives. Is clear imminent danger a 7-year-old smokes cigarettes; or when a 17-year-old smokes cigarettes?   If you substitute the concept of clear imminent danger for serious and foreseeable harm, does this help you make the decision as to whether or not you notify the 7-year-old's parents/guardians or the 17-year-old's parents/guardians?

Serious and foreseeable harm also describes a concept used in negligence (tort) law to limit the liability of a party to those acts which carry a risk of foreseeable harm, meaning that a reasonable person would be able to predict or expect the ultimately harmful result of their actions. The legal and ethical complications of any human service profession are daunting but on any given day a school counselor puts into play the "reasonable person" approach and navigates such charged, delicate subjects as abortion, harassment and suicide. School counselors exercise professional judgment when a reasonable person would know that a student has reached the limits of being able to negotiate a situation in isolation from parental involvement.

Serious and foreseeable harm is more appropriate in the case of a student that is in a downward spiral into a dangerous zone. No, we cannot say with conclusiveness that a 7-year-old smoking cigarettes is clear imminent danger and that this student is going to succumb to the temptation to use other drugs. However, is it evident that this 7 year old child is involved in serious and foreseeable harm and the counselor will want to involve his parents, however, because of the difference in developmental and chronological levels it is unlikely that most school counselors would notify parents regarding the 17-year old who is smoking.

Teachers Protecting Classroom Instruction Time

School counselors sometimes have difficulty being allowed into certain teachers' classrooms for guidance lessons. School counselors try to determine the teacher's motives. Often it is because the teacher is trying to protect classroom instruction time. School counselors usually know better than anyone those teachers who are operating high on the personal social consciousness continuum and will easily discern between a teacher who is afraid you may discover something negative about them such as their classroom management approach and those teachers who legitimately worry about giving up even a minute of instruction time. The politically astute counselor will figure out how to frame his or her classroom guidance lessons to connect them to the academic success equation. It is a reasonable and legitimate response for a teacher to be protective of classroom instruction time. Teaching is a very demanding job and teacher's evaluations are more and more dependent on student success on high stakes tests. It is also the skilled school counselor who will negotiate the political landmines to assuage the fears of those teachers who worry the school counselor might discover something negative about them or their classroom. It may be tempting to write off the teacher who will not let you into his or her classroom, but politically and for students' sake it is better to figure out how to keep the lines of communication open and to address whatever concerns the teacher has so that you can deliver classroom instruction. Providing information to the teacher in general terms about how the lesson will advantage his or her students and involving the teacher in determining or approving at least a portion of the content will go a long way in forming an ally for your program.

Classroom Guidance as a Tier 1 Response to Intervention (RtI)

You have been receiving referrals from teachers who continually say that they have two or three students who are not completing work. You decide to use classroom guidance as one of the initial tools to try and address the problem as the messages that will be delivered can benefit all students. You are using the RtI Tier 1 approach, a multi-level instructional framework aimed at improving outcomes for all students. RtI is preventative, and provides immediate support to students who are at academic risk. RtI typically has different levels of intensity. Tier 1 is for at-risk students who have been identified through a screening process as needing research-based instruction, sometimes as part of a class wide intervention such as classroom guidance. A certain amount of time (generally not more than six or eight weeks) is allotted to see if the child responds to the intervention. Tier 2 is more intense such as an individualized behavior management program or small group counseling and this is for students who do not respond to the first level of group-oriented interventions. Tier 3 is typically even more individualized such as one-on-one counseling. If the child does not respond to instruction in this level, then he or she is likely to be referred for a full and individual evaluation under IDEA (National Dissemination Center for Children with Disabilities, 2012).

When Parent/Guardians Oppose Classroom Guidance Topics/Curriculum

Parents/guardians sometimes question the curriculum school counselors are using in the classroom or ask that their child not be included in classroom guidance lessons for fear they will be exposed to material they object to or that they will lose their place as the guiding voice in their children's lives. Parents/guardians send their children to school for academic instruction and when the school counselor enters the equation this is viewed by small minority of parents/guardians as moving too far away from classroom instruction into the personal, social and/or emotional domain. Usually this happens around lessons involving acceptance of the diversity of others such as lesbian and gay students and their families, sex education, or any curriculum that parents/guardians view as infringing on their religious beliefs.

As advocates, school counselors educate themselves about the prevailing community standards, and they learn to predict and skillfully negotiate the political landscape. It is easy for school counselors to feel so strongly about the work of advocacy that their responses might be undemocratic, however these responses lead to mistrust, distrust, and stalemates that do nothing but maintain the status quo, with students getting lost in the process (Savage & Harley, 2009). It helps to review materials with administrators to ensure their support and to anticipate possible concerns – and be prepared to address them – should they arise.

Although schools are allowed to make exceptions for parents/guardians who do not want their children exposed to discussions of certain topics, schools are not legally obligated to do so. In 2006, two families in Lexington, Massachusetts, objected to their elementary school children's curriculum which used a book depicting single-parent families, a family with two dads and one with two moms and the book "King and King", a story that depicts a wedding scene between two princes. When the school refused to provide prior notice and allow them to exempt their children from "instruction recognizing differences in sexual orientation," the two sets of parents sued the school district (*Parker v. Hurley*, 2007). Dismissed by the district court and the U.S. Court of Appeals, District Court Judge Wolf, wrote, "Parents do have a fundamental right to raise their children. The Parkers and Wirthlins may send their children to a private school … . They may also educate their children at home… . However, the Parkers and Wirthlins have chosen to send their children to the Lexington public schools with its current curriculum. The Constitution does not permit them to prescribe what those children will be taught" (*Parker v. Hurley*, 2007). That dismissal was unanimously upheld in the U.S. Court of Appeals (*Parker v. Hurley*, 2008).

In 2005, the Alliance Defense Fund represented a group of students and parents that sued Boyd County High School in Kentucky, saying they should be able to "opt out" of a court-ordered anti-harassment training that violated their religious rights. The training was implemented in response to an earlier ACLU case; the judge in that case found that anti-gay harassment in the school constituted a widespread problem and ordered staff and student diversity training to focus on issues of sexual orientation and gender harassment. U.S. District Judge David L. Bunning wrote that students and staff have no religious right to opt out of such training, since the training did not force students to change their religious views (ACLU, 2009c; Koschoreck & Tooms, 2009; *Morrison v. Board of Education of Boyd County*, 2006).

Maintaining positive relationships with parents/guardians is important as this enhances the counselor's ability to provide services to students (Huss, Bryant, & Mulet, 2008). Parents/guardians are generally protected by statute and the courts to be the guiding voice in their children's lives and school counselors want to build, not erode, credibility and maintain a strong working relationship with parents/guardians. This mission is forwarded when school counselors respect parents' right to ask questions about curriculum, yet, just as math teachers can teach math and science teachers can teach science school counselors as part of the educational process can deliver their school counseling which includes classroom guidance. The school counselor can hopefully avoid having parents try and opt out of curriculum by advocating for common ground. Failing to find a compromise it is really up to the school counselor in collaboration with the administration to determine if a parent should be allowed to opt their child out of certain classroom guidance lessons or if it is imperative to the overall well-being of all students in the school that each child participates in the lesson(s). It becomes a more difficult decision to refuse a parent's request when it involves value-laden issues; therefore, involving the administration is a critical step.

Some topics require advance parental notification and this is a chance for the school counselor to connect the lessons to academic success. Notification does not necessarily mean written parental permission. It may simply mean that the counselor is giving notice of what will be taught and if anyone has concerns then they can contact the counselor to request more information or to opt out. This would be applicable to controversial topics such as teaching sex education lessons of which school counselors are sometimes involved.

According to ASCA's *Ethical Standards for School Counselors* (ASCA, 2010), "Professional school counselors respect the rights and responsibilities of parents/guardians for their children and endeavor to establish, as appropriate, a collaborative relationship with parents/guardians to facilitate students' maximum development" (B.1.a). "It is therefore imperative for professional school counselors to develop a good working relationship with parents/guardians to promote the importance of privacy, confidentiality and privileged communication and to ensure that these principles will be managed in a manner that ensures students receive the counseling services they need" (Huss et al., 2008, p. 362). Parental notification is enough for classroom guidance lessons as a written parental permission is not realistic. While, legally, a school counselor can provide classroom guidance and other services without parental consent (Hansen, 2012), it is an ethically sound practice to post in the newsletter or announce in some way the school counselors intention to provide classroom guidance lessons.

Classroom Guidance as a Vehicle to Identify High Needs Students

School counselors are trained observers and oftentimes through their skills of observation hone in on students in need when delivering classroom guidance lessons. It is not uncommon for the school counselor to question a teacher about a student they observed that they think might be in trouble. For example, in this real case, a school counselor observed a child who had signs of Tourette's syndrome but his parents were unaware of the syndrome, wrote it off as "just his tics" and no educator had ever asked them to discuss these "tics" with their son's pediatrician. Given the highly sensitive nature of talking to parents about their son's possible problem it may be an unpleasant task, yet, the consequences and fallout in not involving the parents/guardians poses a greater risk to the student. The school counselor need not and probably should not try and label any disorder such as "your child may have Tourette's syndrome" or "I believe your child may be anorexic." It is far better to discuss the symptoms you are observing and why you are concerned and encourage parents to talk with medical professionals than to try to diagnose medical concerns yourself. Bardick, Bernes, McCulloch, Witko, Spriddle and Roest (2004) stressed making "honest, objective statements defining the behaviors of concern followed by insistence on obtaining the opinion of a trained professional" (p. 170) in situations such as notifying parents/guardians of their child's potential medical concerns. For example in the case of a suspected eating disorder, telling students that you care about them but believe they are not fine and need help is the brave thing to do. Even if the parents/guardians are also in denial, you have forced them to discuss the situation, and perhaps have planted some seeds so they will at least consider the possibility their child is not well.

Skill Level in Classroom Guidance

School counselors must practice within their competence level. Sometimes teachers or administrators will request the use of topics or material that the counselor has not been trained to deliver. *Chapter Nine* discusses resources that are specifically designed for classroom guidance lessons.

Topics for classroom guidance in schools require careful consideration, as schools are not the place for certain topics and/or the school counselor may need additional training to deliver certain topics. For example, in a real case, a school counselor was asked to help the class deal with the terminal illness and very imminent death of a student in their class. The school counselor sought the help of her local Hospice Organization who agreed to come in and provide classroom guidance on several occasions prior to and after the death of the student. The school counselor knew she could seek advice and materials and conduct the lessons herself but the skill level and training of the Hospice staff was in her judgment far superior as they lived this work every day of their professional lives. Ethically she felt it was only right to reach out for more expertise where she lacked it while still staying involved and connected and being part of the delivery of the Hospice work while they were in the classroom.

Smead (1995) indicated that "group work is more suited for children whose psychological needs are equally balanced" (p. 49). School counselors cannot be expected to adequately address every issue that is presented to them and it would be especially difficult for the school counselor to address the very rare, therapeutic issue that may need as wide an audience as a classroom setting. It is not that school counselors are less talented or less competent than their colleagues in agency or community settings, it is that certain topics need an expert who has done intensive work on the subject and who specializes or at the very least stays abreast of all the research as to best practices in this area (ASCA, 2009a).

The example of the Hospice counselor coming into the classroom also brings up the issue of parents/guardians' rights to decide if they want their child to participate or if they would rather handle the situation at home. Again, getting permission is not required but in some situations it is best practice to at least notify the parents about the upcoming classroom lesson/discussion and give them a chance to opt their child out of the lesson/discussion.

Multicultural Considerations and Classroom Guidance Lessons

Classroom guidance lessons always have at the heart a multicultural awareness and sensitivity embedded throughout the messages and activities. However, oftentimes multiculturalism is the primary focus of a lesson. For example, in a hypothetical case a school counselor had a new arrival to her school "Lilith" who was the only person in memory to wear the hijab, a headdress some Muslim women wear for modesty reasons. Often, Lilith's classmates were just curious and meant no harm when they asked her borderline rude questions. However, some student did mean harm when they pulled at her hijab or made negative comments. You have talked to Lilith who is a mature, level headed student and she has asked for your help as she feels isolated and misunderstood. You have decided to deliver a series of classroom guidance lessons to her grade level on diversity and acceptance of differences and with Lilith's permission you will also discuss the hijab significance and raise awareness and facilitate support for people who dress differently in honor of their religion. You will discuss other groups also such as the dress of the Hasidic Jewish people so that there is a broader brush stroke and not too focused on Lilith.

The **Association for Specialists in Group Work** (ASGW, 2012) encourages finding ways to connect students to others that can help connect them to the larger group. Additionally, Lilith needs an ally. ASGW guidelines states, "Determine if group membership needs to be expanded or altered to allow for a greater level of connection and support for group members who are isolated in the group due to one or more dimensions of multicultural identity or experience. This collective strength helps "validate and reframe members' experiences to foster their resilience" (Chen, Budianto & Wong, 2010, p. 256). "Group Workers ensure that a framework exists for members to feel supported for their diversity in the group members" (ASGW, p.1). In this case the group is the entire school and the school counselor decided to form a Guidance Team to help connect Lilith to others who are also being isolated because of their differences. The Guidance Team was given a high profile and participated in special projects which raised their standing and helped to celebrate their differences.

Conclusions

The ASCA *Ethical Standards for School Counselors* (2010) dictate that school counselors owe students loyalty and a trusting relationship. Students are school counselor's primary clients, yet, because school counselors are part of an educational community their loyalty and obligation extends to parents/guardians, teachers, administrators, the school district and the community. The ASCA *Ethical Standards* direct counselors to respect parents/guardians' rights and responsibilities for their children and advise a counselor to make "reasonable efforts to honor the wishes of parents and guardians concerning information that he/she may share regarding the counselee" (p. 2). ASCA (Standard D. 1) includes references to counselors' responsibilities to other school professionals such as faculty, staff and administrators, specifying that the school counselor "informs appropriate officials of conditions that may be potentially disruptive or damaging to the school's mission, personnel and property while honoring the confidentiality between the counselee and counselor" (p. 3). School counselors respect students' confidences and balance minors' rights with parents/guardians' rights. Knowing when to invoke confidentiality at the exclusion of a parent's right to know is a daily struggle. School counselors may find that by communicating the purpose and goals of their classroom guidance lessons, they strengthen partnerships with parents. It is unrealistic for members of the school and larger community to expect that school counselors should have all the skills, knowledge, and time required for adequate knowledge of all topics. The astute school counselor uses the rule of parsimony and delivers classroom guidance lessons as a Tier I intervention and to reach as many students as possible. Classroom guidance is a critical tool and must be used with caution to predict how lessons may lead to the disclosure of sensitive personal information in the open classroom setting; indeed a bit of crystal ball gazing on the part of the school counselor is required to provide all student with a safe environment.

References

American Civil Liberties Union. (2009c, July 20). *Morrison v. Boyd Co. Board of Education: Case profile.* Retrieved from http://www.aclu.org/lgbt-rights_hiv-aids/morrison-v-boyd-co-board-education-case-profile

American School Counselor Association. (2005). *The ASCA National Model: A framework for school counseling programs.* Alexandria, VA: Author.

American School Counselor Association. (2009). *The professional school counselor and student mental health.* Alexandria, VA: Author.

American School Counselor Association. (2010). *Ethical standards for School counselors.* Alexandria, VA: Author.

Association for Specialists in Group Work. (2012). *Multicultural and social justice competence principles for group workers.* Retrieved from http://www.asgw.org/pdf/ASGW_MC_SJ_Priniciples_Final_ASGW.pdf

Baker, S. B., & Gerler, E. R. (2007). *School counseling for the twenty-first century* (5th Ed.). Upper Saddle River, NJ: Merrill Prentice Hall.

Carr, T. (2003, October 24). School forming death talk protocol. Traverse City (Mich.) *Record-Eagle*, pp. 1-2.

Chen, E. C., Budianto, L., & Wong, K. (2010). Professional school counselors as social justice advocates for undocumented immigrant students in group work. *Journal for Specialists in Group Work, 35,* 255-261.

Corey, G. (2011). *Theory and practice of group counseling* (7th Ed.). Pacific Grove, CA: Brooks/Cole.

Galassi, J., & Akos, P. (2004). Developmental advocacy: Twenty-first century school counseling. *Journal of Counseling and Development, 82,* 146.

Gibson, R. L., & Mitchell, M. H. (2007). *Introduction to counseling and Guidance* (7th Ed.). Upper Saddle River, NJ: Merrill Prentice Hall.

Greenberg, K. R. (2003). *Group counseling in K-12 schools: A handbook for school counselors.* Boston: Allyn & Bacon.

Hansen, S. (2012). *Confidentiality guidelines.* Retrieved April 6, 2012, from http://www.school-counseling-zone.com/confidentiality.html.

Hughes v. Stanley County School Board, 594 N.W.2d 346 (S.D. 1999)

Huss, S., Bryant, A., & Mulet, S. (2008). Managing the quagmire of counseling in a school: bringing the parents onboard. *Professional School Counseling, 11,* 362-367.

Imber, M., & Van Geel, T. (2009) *Education law.* (4th Ed.). Mahway, NJ: Erlbaum.

Koschoreck, J.W. & Tooms, A.K. (2009). *Sexuality matters: Paradigms and policies for educational leaders.* Lanham, MD: Rowman & Littlefield.

Morrison v. Board of Education, 2006 U.S. Dist. LEXIS 6373 (E.D. Ky. Feb. 17, 2006).

Moyer, M.S., Sullivan, J.R., & Growcock, D. (2012). When is it ethical to inform administrators about student risk-taking behaviors? Perceptions of school counselors. *Professional School Counseling, 15*, 98-109.

National Dissemination Center for Children with Disabilities. (2012, August). Response to Intervention (RTI). Retrieved from http://nichcy.org/schools-administrators/RtI

Parker v. Hurley, 474 F. Supp. 2d 261; 2007 U.S. Dist. LEXIS 12751

Parker v. Hurley, 514 F.3d 87; 2008 U.S. App. LEXIS 2070

Savage, T. A., & Harley, D. A. (2009). A place at the blackboard: Including lesbian, gay, bisexual, transgender, intersex, & queer/questioning issues in the education process. *Multicultural Education, 16*(4), 2-9.

Sink, C. A. (Ed.). (2005). *Contemporary school counseling: Theory, research, and practice.* Boston: Lahaska Press, Houghton Mifflin.

Smead, R. (1995). *Skills and techniques for group work with children and adolescents.* Champaign, IL: Research Press.

Swinton, D.C. (2005). Criminal liability, failure to report child abuse, and school personnel: An examination of history, policy and case law. *Education Law & Policy Forum, 1*, 1-28. Retrieved from http://www.educationlawconsoRtIum.org/forum/2005/papers/swinton.pdf

Thompson, C. L., & Henderson, D. (2010). *Counseling children* (8th Ed.). Pacific Grove, CA: Brooks/Cole.

Venkatesh, S. (2006). *Group counseling.* Retrieved from http://changingminds.org/articles/articles/group_counseling.html

Vernon, A. (2004). *Counseling children & adolescents* (3rd Ed.). Denver, CO: Love Publisher.

Chapter Seven
Selecting and Adapting Developmentally Appropriate Classroom Guidance Activities
Kelly Wolfe-Stiltner
Haverhill Elementary School
Fort Wayne, IN

School counselors must be intentional and purposeful when selecting lessons to utilize in the classroom. Classroom teachers are teaching in a high stakes environment and school counselors must maximize class time to implement guidance activities. The purpose of this chapter is to provide guidance for selecting and adapting guidance lessons to meet the needs of your students.

Step One: Define the Purpose

When implementing lessons in the classroom the school counselor starts by defining the purpose of the lesson. The school counselor needs to consider what they want students know, believe, or be able to do as a result of this lesson. The lesson must incorporate state and/or local school counseling student standards, and the **American School Counselor Association** *National Standards for Students* (ASCA, 2004). Examples of ASCA Standards are identified in each activity in this book such as *A:A3.2 Demonstrate the ability to work independently, as well as the ability to work cooperatively with other students; C:B1.2 Identify personal skills, interests, and abilities and relate them to current career choice; and PS:A1.2 Identify values, attitudes and beliefs.*

Step Two: Build the Lesson

With specific goals for the lesson, the school counselor can now begin to build the lesson. When selecting activities, the developmental level of the specific students must be considered. The activity selected must match the comprehension and vocabulary level of the students at that level. Students in younger grades will need lessons that are more concrete in their design, with lesson moving to more abstract as students get older. The school counselor also has to be cognizant of the attention span of students. Students who are younger will require lessons that vary activities more frequently than students who are older. With younger students activities can last 20 to 30 minutes while varying the activity every 5 to7 minutes, while older students can sustain attention for activities that last 40 to 50 minutes with activities that vary every 10 to 12 minutes. The Kitchens and Evans *Friendship Trail Mix* lesson varies activities and discussion topics every 5 to 10 minutes to keep K to Grade 2 students engaged in the lesson. A *Candy Full Career* moves middle school students through different topics every 5 to 10 minutes. The *Happy is As Happy Does* lesson varies from student listening, independent work time, and sharing time to keep students involved throughout the lesson.

Step Three: Finding Resources

There are many books and resources on the Internet that are available to research ideas for lessons. *Chapter Nine* by Lopez and Bhat addresses how to find resources. When reviewing materials from any source it is important to consider if the lesson can be adapted to the purpose, standards, developmental level, and needs of their students. Often times with a little creativity or a few small changes, lessons can be adapted to meet our needs. Jennifer Marshall's lesson *Managing the Uncontrollable* activity is geared toward middle school students but could easily be adapted for high school or elementary school students.

Step Four: Creating a Format for the Lesson

Once the school counselor has identified the lesson material, it is beneficial to have a lesson plan or activity plan outline to document the lesson. *Chapter Eight* by Tosado addresses how to create an effective lesson plan. Important components of this outline will be objectives, standards, time frame, procedure, evaluation, and materials needed for the lesson. Each activity in this book has clearly identified goals, ASCA standards met, materials needed, specific directions, processing questions to clarify learning, and adaptations and cautions.

A helpful format for a classroom guidance lesson is: **Introduction, Main Content** or **Concept** to be taught, **Summary,** and **Processing**. When introducing the lesson, consider how you can utilize an emotional hook to engage your students. One way I do this at the beginning of a career lesson is give each student a card with a career on it and tell them I have alleviated a lot of stress and hard work that goes into determining a future career by choosing one for them. The students will often react in a variety of ways: disappointment, confusion, or anger. We then discuss if that is the best way to make a career choice and then lead into how our lesson is going to help them determine what to consider when choosing a career.

In Kindergarten, our yearly theme is caring so we are packing an *I CARE* package throughout the year. I always start the lesson with adding an item to the *I CARE* package that relates to the lesson theme. A few of the items we have added are ice cubes for calming down, an ear for active listening, and caution tape for our safety lesson. The students are always excited to see what will be in the package each lesson. In this book, the Conner and Ziomek-Daigle lesson *Fur-sonalities: Animals and Friendship Skills* grabs the students attention by letting them know they are going to talk about how their personalities are related to the personalities of animals.

The main part of the lesson teaches the skills or important information you want students to learn. The Landis lesson *Holland Dating Game* in a creative way introduces the six Holland career interest codes. The *Behavior Lemonade* lesson by Beeching and Fineran makes lemonade to help students understand how their behavior affects their lives.

In an era of 21st century skills, classroom guidance lessons need to prepare students to be productive citizens of a global economy. It will be important to find ways to incorporate activities in guidance lessons that will require collaboration, use of technology tools, problem solving, critical thinking, and creativity. The Christy Land and Jolie Zoimek-Diagle lesson *Understanding How We Work in a Group: The Balloon Tower* challenge offers students the opportunity to practice collaboration, problem solving and critical thinking. In addition, developmentally appropriate language and materials are essential. Depending on the age, efforts to sustain attention must be addressed. The *Balloon Tower* lesson keeps students engaged by actively involving them in the lesson.

Finally, you will need to wrap-up the lesson and assess for understanding. An easy way to assess for understanding is to provide a quick exit question or exit slip for students to respond to related to the lesson goals. The *Balloon Challenge* lesson asks students to write a ticket about how they contributed cooperatively to the group to get out the door. The product generated in the lesson is another easy way to assess for understanding. In the *Resume Writing for High School Students* activity, the school counselor reviews resumes to assess for student skil l building.

Step Five: Evaluation of Process and Outcome

After a classroom guidance lesson, it is crucial to assess effectiveness in meeting your planned goals. A review of evaluation data will help to determine if the objectives and standards were met.

In addition, consider time constraints and how they were handled. Review the structure of the lesson and materials used for possible future changes. Consider student reactions to the lesson such as amount of participation and engagement in the lesson to determine if changes are necessary. Teacher feedback about the lesson itself and student comments are helpful. *Chapters Three* and *Five* in this book detail how to use data to evaluate classroom guidance effectiveness in more detail.

Conclusions

Selecting and adapting guidance lessons is a crucial component of a comprehensive school counseling program. The school counseling curriculum will not be successful unless lessons are built on a solid foundation of clear goals and competencies for students. The school counselor must consider many components when selecting and adapting lessons and thoughtfully reflect on the lesson once completed.

References

American School Counselor Association (2004). *ASCA national standards for students.* Alexandria, VA: Author.

Chapter Eight
Guidelines for Writing a Lesson Plan for Classroom Guidance Activities
By Luis Antonio Tosado II
University at Buffalo, SUNY

While pre-service teachers as part of their training learn to write and implement lesson plans and curriculum, professional school counselors have limited experience with either. Thus, it is important for professional school counselors to have a framework to guide them when developing classroom guidance activities. Drawing from both the teacher education and school counseling literature, this chapter will suggest recommendations on key components of effective classroom guidance lesson plans.

What is a Lesson Plan?

A classroom guidance lesson plan is a detailed description of the professional school counselor's intended course of instruction for one class period. The specific details of each lesson plan are determined by the desired outcome for students. When designing lesson plans, items to be considered include: differential needs of the students and school; difficulty of the subject matter; developmental appropriateness of the topic; local, state, and national mandates; materials needed; and methods of evaluation.

Why Should Professional School Counselors use Lesson Plans?

Lesson plans serve as a tool to assist professional school counselors in organizing and delivering specific elements of a developmental counseling curriculum. Furthermore, they help school counselors stay focused and task oriented so that the desired objectives and outcomes are attained. Detailed lesson plans also make it easier to share lesson plans with other counselors and to document student contact.

Basic Components of a Classroom Guidance Lesson Plan

Classroom guidance lesson plans should include: demographic information about the students, learning objectives and the **American School Counselor Association's** (ASCA) *Student Standards* to be met, materials, procedures, and plans for evaluation and follow up (ASCA, 2012). The ASCA *National Model for School Counselors* includes a lesson plan template. Borrowing from the teacher education literature, other lesson plan components; such as the anticipatory set, guided practice, closure, and independent practice; will also be discussed in this chapter.

Demographic Data

This section of the lesson plan includes information such as the title of the lesson, the name of the school counselor presenting the lesson, the date the lesson was or will be delivered, the grade level or age group for which the lesson is appropriate, and the length of time required to complete the lesson.

ASCA Standards

The ASCA *Student Standards* (2004) are divided into three domains; *Academic, Career,* and *Personal/Social* with distinct standards, competencies, and indicators. Incorporating the ASCA *Student Standards* into classroom guidance lesson plans allows all stake holders (students, administrators, teachers, parents, and community partners and members) to connect the role of the school counselor with student outcomes. The ASCA *Student Standards* specifies attitudes, knowledge and skills that students should be able to demonstrate as a result of participating in a comprehensive developmental counseling program.

School counselors should also develop awareness, knowledge and skills in implementation of the *Common Core Standards* (National Governors Association Center for Best Practices & Council of Chief State School Officers, 2010, http://www.corestandards.org). Understanding of and integration of *Common Core Standards* into classroom guidance lessons will allow school counselors to assist in meeting desired school and grade level outcomes. Below is an example of a *Common Core* 8th Grade Statistics and Probability standard:

> CCSS.Math.Content.8.SP.A.1 Construct and interpret scatter plots for bivariate measurement data to investigate patterns of association between two quantities. Describe patterns such as clustering, outliers, positive or negative association, linear association, and nonlinear association.

A professional school counselor with knowledge of the *Common Core* might integrate the standard above with a guidance lesson by having students interpret scatter plots using actual data from their feeder high school to investigate college enrollment patterns of their previous students based on PSAT and GPA.

Learning Objectives

Learning objectives, also known as behavioral objectives, specify what students will be able to do as a result of participating in the guidance lesson. Professional School Counselors should develop objectives that are *SMART; Specific, Measurable, Attainable/Achievable, Relevant,* and *Time bound* (Haynes, 2010). For example, following the 40-minute classroom guidance lesson (time-bound – how many minutes), students will explain (attainable-achievable) the difference between bullies, victims, and bystanders (specific, measurable, relevant) in promoting a safe school environment.

Materials

In addition to identifying materials needed before a classroom guidance lesson, school counselors should consider the preparation of materials before the actual classroom guidance activity (e.g., pre-cutting materials and pre-sorting supplies such as markers, rocks, shells, beads, buttons, etc. into plastic bags or pencil boxes for younger students). School counselors can also provide materials to the classroom teacher before the guidance lesson and have students complete portions of the assignments before the guidance lesson. Proper preparation of materials and a well-developed plan for distribution and collection should make the lesson flow smother and classroom transitions easier.

Procedures

The procedures are detailed directions for delivering the classroom guidance lesson. Well-developed and clearly written procedures serve as step-by-step directions for use by the school counselor or other school counselors who may also implement similar lessons. Cavalluzzo's lesson *NCAA Awareness and Prospective Student-Athlete Steps* has detailed procedures, including step-by-step directions and a minute-by-minute breakdown of activities including a PowerPoint for reference. Kilgore, Freels, and Fineran's lesson *Puzzling Communication* includes brief scripted statements to be used when delivering the lesson.

Anticipatory Set

Before beginning the actual lesson, it is helpful to use an attention grabber to get students excited about the lesson. Known as the anticipatory set, this brief activity might include a multimedia presentation (e.g., video footage, audio recording, simulation, etc.), handouts, reading a story or passage, a role-play, showing a photograph, or questions written on the board. Land and Ziomek-Daigle's activity *Understanding How We Work in a Group: The Balloon Tower Challenge* uses an anticipatory set of a humorous video clip of unsuccessful teamwork to introduce a lesson on teamwork and cooperation. An anticipatory set should be short to introduce but not take up too much instructional time.

Direct Teach

This part of the lesson involves the school counselor teaching the specific content related to the objectives. Here the counselor introduces new vocabulary, skills, and concepts through lecture, discussion, multimedia, and modeling among other methods. In a career development lesson (using a PowerPoint), the school counselor might introduce and define the six Holland Codes (Realistic, Investigative, Artistic, Social, Enterprising and Conventional). In a variation of this intro Landis's *Holland Dating Game and Body of Interests,* the counselor creates "Singles Ads" based on the Holland codes to help students identify specific personality characteristics, interests, and hobbies associated with each code to make them more real for the students.

Guided Practice

This entails students completing an exercise or activity that demonstrates their understanding of their new knowledge and skills. The professional school counselor walks students through the process step-by-step to measure student's level of mastery. It is helpful to have both the classroom teacher and the school counselor circulate for classroom management and to assist students. Without the circulation and checks for understanding an exercise becomes independent practice; as the counselor and teacher are unable to observe the student, evaluate their level of mastery, or provide them with immediate feedback. In the activity Colavito, Moore, and Rose; *Discovering our External Assets;* school counselors are provided with a good example of a questionnaire (*Discovering External Assets* Questionnaire) which might be used during guided practice to check for understanding.

Independent Practice

If time permits, students may participate in an independent activity or exercise to reinforce learning. Independent practice may be performed in or outside of the classroom guidance lesson. In *Getting Ready for Middle School Lessons 1and 2* by Logan, counselors can use the first four questions in the handout *How to Succeed* as independent practice in the classroom. Further independent practice might include having students complete the homework question on the handout and the *Getting Ready for Middle School Summer Calendar.*

Closure

Last, the professional school counselor brings closure to the classroom guidance lesson by summarizing the objectives covered and processing activities. The counselor may ask students to show or share what they learned during the class period. Thomas and Austin's lesson *Family Work Values: Tools from the Past, Lessons I, II, and III* provides clear examples of what information the counselor should summarize, what to ask students to share, and sample discussion questions.

Plan for Evaluation

Evaluation is essential to determine if the desired outcomes were attained. The evaluation answers the fundamental question: "How are students different as a result of the school counseling program?" The *plan for evaluation* should include process data (number of students participating), perception data (surveys and assessments to be used), outcome data (academic, attendance, and behavior) and a plan for follow up if the data suggests that a re-teach lesson is necessary (ASCA, 2012).

Conclusions

While there are sample classroom guidance lesson formats, school counselors are free to develop lesson plans incorporating their individual preferences. While professional school counselors are not teachers it is important for them to be familiar with common pedagogical practices, lesson plan components and how to write lesson plans.

References

American School Counselor Association (2004). *ASCA student standards.* Alexandria, VA: Author.

American School Counselor Association (2012). The *ASCA national model: A framework for school counseling programs* (3rd Ed.). Alexandria, VA: Author.

Haynes, A. (2010). *The complete guide to lesson planning and preparation.* London, GBR: Continuum International Publishing.

Chapter Nine
You Don't Have to Reinvent the Wheel: Resources that are Readily Available and How to Search for Them

Caroline J. Lopez
Chapman University

Christine Suniti Bhat
Ohio University

The **American School Counselor Association** (ASCA, 2012) *National Model* recommends that school counselors spend 80% of their time in the delivery of direct and indirect services to students, with the remaining 20% of school counselors' time focused on the foundation, management and accountability components. The School Counseling core curriculum is a component of direct student services comprised of "instruction" and "group activities" that promote the academic, career, and personal/social development of students (ASCA, p. 84). With increasing caseloads and professional responsibilities, it behooves school counselors to utilize classroom guidance curriculum and other resources that have already been developed and/or are evidence-based and readily available. This chapter will provide strategies for finding and utilizing readily available guidance curriculum lessons and resources.

Evidence Based Classroom Guidance Curriculum

Due to legislation such as *No Child Left Behind* (NCLB) and the recent national initiative of *Common Core Standards,* there has been greater emphasis on using evidence-based curriculum to support the effectiveness of school counseling interventions (Goodnough, Perusse, & Erford, 2012). *Student Success Skills* is a program to assist K to 12 students develop skill sets including cognitive and meta-cognitive skills, social skills, and self-management skills. There are three distinct programs: *Ready to Learn* for students in grades and 1; *Ready for Success* for students in grades 2 and 3; and *Student Success Skills* for students in grades 4 to 12. Math, reading and social skills of students who have received the curricula improved (Brigman & Campbell, 2003; Webb,

Brigman, & Campbell, 2005). The *Kelly Bear Program* (www.kellybear.com) contains three different curricular themes: *Violence Prevention, Drug Awareness and Prevention Program,* and *Character and Resiliency Education Skills.* Curriculum lessons are geared for grades pre-K to grade 3. *Second Step: Violence Prevention Curriculum and Steps to Respect* (www.cfchildren.org) is another evidence based curriculum focused on teaching social and emotional skills for grades pre-K to 8. Topics such as empathy, impulse control, problem-solving and anger management are included. The *Ronald H. Fredrickson Center for School Counseling Outcome Research and Evaluation* (CSCORE: http://www.umass.edu/schoolcounseling/about-us.php) is another resource for research-based programs, such as *Project Achieve* and the *Missouri Center for Career Education.*

Web Resources

Increasingly, school counselors are utilizing forums and blogs on the web to share resources including curriculum lesson plans and resources. Blogs are personal webpages where an individual records his or her opinions, post videos, pictures and links to other sites. These posting are often in chronological order and centered on a theme or topic. One advantage to searching blogs is that it is often updated on a regular basis so you can easily stay abreast of current trends, topics, issues and resources. Examples of helpful blogs include, *School Counselor Blog* which contains a section called "School Counselor Spotlight" where school counselors are featured for their innovative ideas, creative lessons and helpful resources (Schultz, 2013). In the past, this blog has hosted a discussion via Twitter titled "Creating and Implementing Lesson Plans" where school counselors were able to connect and share resources (Schultz, 2013, November 6). The blog *Scrapbook of a School Counselor* has a section dedicated to sharing K-5 and middle school classroom guidance lessons on various topics including, friendship, kindness and cyber bullying (Panariso, 2013).

The website *Pinterest* is another useful source for collecting information on classroom guidance lessons and materials. Pinterest, www.pinterest.com, is an online pin board that allows users to create and manage multiple pin boards of photos, videos, and links to websites. One can also subscribe to the pin boards of other users. A "school counseling lessons" key word search on Pinterest provides access to numerous pins related to classroom guidance activities, such as *iKnow Test-Taking Lessons* and *Counseling Hearts: Swimmy-Beginning* of the school year activity. Online message boards are another helpful resource. Karen

McGibbon's lesson *Happy is as Happy Does* utilizes a worksheet obtained from a message board dedicated to teachers.

Collaboration with Organizations

School counselors can collaborate with businesses, universities and community organizations via formalized partnerships or through resource sharing to enhance the guidance curriculum. Unique resources offered by such collaborations include professional development training, guest speakers, field trips and evaluation tools.

National Organizations

Junior Achievement (JA) provides training, materials and support necessary to conduct financial literacy curriculum in schools. The organization helps connect schools with local business people and community leaders who can visit the classroom and share their workforce experience. Junior Achievement curriculum (www.juniorachievement.org) focuses on one of three areas: financial literacy, work readiness or entrepreneurship and is available for all grade levels. Depending on a school's location, fieldtrips can be arranged for a capstone experience at JA's Finance Park which allows 7th to 12th grade students to practice personal finance in a real-life setting of stores, shops, and financial institutions. Examples of curriculum include *JA More than Money (2013)* which teaches students in grades 3-5 about earning, spending, sharing, and saving money. It also identifies businesses that students can start or jobs they can perform to earn money.

Kids 2 College (www.kid-2collge.org) is a national program through the Salle Mae Fund which brings early college awareness and a college-going culture to schools through a six-session classroom guidance curriculum for middle school students and includes pre/post surveys. The Sallie Mae Fund provides the guidance curriculum lessons and training free of charge to schools. *Break the Cycle* (www.breakthecycle.com) is a national nonprofit organization dedicated to ending dating abuse and promoting healthy relationships. They provide curriculum and training to schools for both the middle school and high school level.

Statewide Organizations

As a result of state legislation geared toward creating safe schools and college and career readiness, state departments of education are now recognizing the need to support school counselors in the development of classroom guidance curriculum. The **West Virginia Department of Education** provides a wealth of resources for school counselors including

K to 12 guidance curriculum materials and lesson plans that connect directly to the ASCA National Standards (http://wvde.state.wv.us/counselors/guidance-curriculum.html). *I Have a Plan Iowa* provides a variety of guidance lessons on career development and academic achievement (www.ihaveaplaniowa.org) such as *The Roads to Success* curriculum (grades 7 to12) to assist students develop educational plans for the future and make informed decisions about college and career. *Virginia Career View* provides career guidance lessons for students in grades K to 8 in the state of Virginia, www.vaview.org ; resources include online career exploration games and printable activity sheets. The **Indiana Department of Education** (2013) provides research based prevention and intervention resources including a school wide prevention program, *Success for All* and targeted interventions such as *Reducing Anger in Adolescents.*

Local Organizations

School counselors can partner with local non-profit organizations and universities to deliver curriculum to students. One such example of a school-university partnership is in California. *Students Talk About Race* (STAR) (Multicultural Center, 2013) is a project of the Multicultural Center at California State University, Long Beach (CSULB). STAR trains CSULB college students as well as teachers, counselors and other college students in the Los Angeles area to become facilitators in cross-cultural communication. The eight week STAR curriculum is designed to create "a compassionate and candid forum, addressing difficult issues of diversity with vulnerability and humor" (Multicultural Center).

Professional school counseling organization websites are great sources for classroom guidance activities. The website for the New York State School Counseling Association contains a "Counselor Support" section that contains resources for a comprehensive school counseling model, including classroom guidance lessons.

Bibliotherapy Resources

Bibliotherapy is an excellent method of providing younger students with information on relevant topics. An excellent starting point for finding books on topics such as bullying, friendship, grief and loss can be found on the blog *Books That Heal Kids* (www.booksthathealkids.blogspot.com),which provides a summary and review of therapeutic books for children. A keyword search "School Counseling Books" on the Pinterest website provides user with pin boards of bibliotherapy books. Lastly, a useful tool for school counselors is the app *Book Crawler* which can be downloaded on iOS devices. This tool allows users to scan the barcode of books and creates a catalog inventory of books read, books owned, and books to plan on reading. The book cataloging program allows the user to tag, filter, sort, categorize and flag their book collection. Users are able to mark books that they have loaned out and can categorize their collection by themes (grief, loss, bullying) for quick reference. School counselors may also choose to catalog books containing guidance curriculum lessons and categorize them by *Academic, Personal/Social* and *Career Domains.*

Integrating Technology into Classroom Guidance

As a result of rapid technological advances, school counselors are now encountering classrooms filled with tech-savvy students. Increasingly, this tech generation of students gathers information from the world around them through various forms of technology including websites, online software, apps, and online videos. In order to make classroom guidance lessons more relevant and timely to students, school counselors should begin to incorporate these various forms of technology into lessons. Video clips can be incorporated into lessons and obtained through sites such as YouTube, www.youtube.com. For example Lopez and Bhat's lesson *There's Power in Being a Bystander* utilizes a media clip obtained from YouTube that highlights the pain experienced by a real victim of cyberbullying. YouTube contains videos such as *Music for Classroom Management- The Tattling Song.* School counselors can subscribe to video channels on YouTube including the **Sesame Street Channel** which contains a section called *Everyday Challenges.* This section includes videos such as the *Bye-Bye for Now Song, Twiddlebugs Take Turns* and the *Elmo Doesn't Give Up Song.* Additional channels available for subscription include **Randomactsofkindness** which contains lessons on kindness and **SoulPancakes** which contains videos on life topics including stepping out of your comfort zone and the science of happiness. The website *Film Clips for Character Education,* www.filmclipsonline.com, offers film clips from popular Hollywood movies for purchase. The movies have been pre-screened for age-appropriateness and DVD menus have the option of Spanish audio or subtitles for English Language Learners. Lesson plans and strategies for connecting lessons to state standards are included in the study manual. Video clips touch on issues such as bullying, peer pressure, responsibility, sportsmanship and leadership. Film clips are taken from popular movies such as *Babe, Remember the Titans* and *Liar, Liar.* Sandra Logan's lesson *Getting Ready for Middle School* utilizes videos from TeacherTube.

One technological tool that can be used to increase active participation during classroom guidance lessons is the *i>Clicker* (www.iClicker.com) which enables presenters and participants to interact through question-and-answer polling, and records results to improve learning outcomes. School counselors are able to easily and immediately get feedback on questions posed during a presentation and receive the results in real-time. Using the *i-Clicker* remote control to answer a question allows students to respond to sensitive topics such as bullying with the assurance of anonymity.

School counselors are now using software such as *Naviance* (www.naviance.com) as an online tool to use during classroom lessons on college and career readiness. This software assists students to develop individual academic plans within the setting of a classroom guidance lesson. Students are able to take personality tests, explore career interests, determine courses needed to reach goals, develop individual academic plans, search for scholarships and track admission applications. These activities can be completed in conjunction with the College and Career Readiness Curriculum (grades 6 to12) offered through *Naviance*, which includes lesson units such as *Middle School Academic Planning, Learning Style Inventory, Skills Needed for Postsecondary Success,* and *Informed Decisions on Career Paths.*

Conclusions

School counselors may benefit from using technological resources that help save the time required to find, develop and evaluate lesson plans. With the numerous resources that are readily available to school counselors it is important to develop a system for categorizing the various resources necessary for a lesson plan including PowerPoint's, handouts, videos, surveys. LiveBinder, www.livebinder.com, is an online organization tool that allows you to create binders or categories where you can save or bookmark websites, personal documents, videos and photos. An entire school wide curriculum can essentially be organized into this online binder. Resources can be categorized by grade level, ASCA domain and guidance lesson theme units and the content of an entire binder can be shared with others.

School counselors do not need to re-invent the wheel as they plan and deliver guidance curriculum. As the profession of school counseling matures, more and more guidance curriculum resources are available to school counselors. Rather than developing such resources, the time of school counselors might be better utilized in delivering guidance curriculum and evaluating the effectiveness of such programs to enhance knowledge and skills of students in the academic, career, and personal/social domains.

References

American School Counseling Association. (2012). *The ASCA national model: A framework for school counseling programs* (3rd Ed.). Alexandria, VA: Author.

Brigman, G., & Campbell, C. (2003). Helping students' academic achievement and school success behavior. *The Professional School Counselor, 7,* 91-98.

Goodnough, G.E., Perusse, R., & Erford, B.T. (2011). Developmental classroom guidance. In B. Erford. (Ed.), Professional school counseling (pp. 154-177). Saddleback, NJ: Pearson Education.

Indiana Department of Education. (updated 2013). *Best practice/research-based* prevention and intervention resources for school counselors. Retrieved from http://www.doe.in.gov/student-services/student-assistance/best-practiceresearch-based-prevention-and-intervention

Multicultural Center (2013). *Students talk about race.* Retrieved December 17, 2013 from http: //www.csulb.edu/divisions /aa/grad_undergrad /mcc/events/star/

Panariso, T. (2013) *Classroom guidance.* Retrieved from http://schoolcounselorscrapbook.blogspot.com/p/classroom-guidance_16.html

Schultz, D. (2013, November 6). November #SCCHAT: *Creating and implementing lesson plans* [Web log post].School Counselor Blog Retrieved from http://www.schcounselor.com/

Schultz, D. (2013). *School counselor spotlight.* Retrieved from thttp://www.schcounselor.com/p/school-counselor-spotlight.html

Webb, L.D., Brigman, G.A., & Campbell, C. (2005). Linking professional school counselors and student success: A replication of the student success skills approach targeting the academic and social competence of students. *Professional School Counseling, 8,* 407-413. doi: 10.1037/t05345-000

Chapter Ten
Using Questions to Make Sure Students Learn What You Wanted Them to Learn From the Classroom Guidance Lesson

Christine Suniti Bhat
Ohio University

School counseling core curriculum consists of an instructional program delivered by school counselors or other educators to students in school (ASCA, 2013). This curriculum is most efficiently delivered in large groups, and is referred to as guidance curriculum. These types of curriculum have an educational focus as well as a personal and interpersonal growth and development focus. The school counseling curriculum offerings have specific learning objectives but they are not purely instructional. They have an application component to facilitate and encourage students to apply what they are learning though the curriculum to their individual situations. Processing questions provide group activity leaders with an avenue to engage students in application of learning. Here-and-now interaction facilitates the application of concepts learned in class.

The types of processing questions selected are guided by the purpose of the classroom guidance lesson. For example, with guidance curriculum focused on preventing binge drinking and delivered to all 6th graders, the main objective is prevention. A similar curriculum delivered to all juniors may have both prevention and an intervention focus as there may be students who have not begun using alcohol and others who have done so. When guidance curriculum is offered to a smaller group of students who have been abusing alcohol, the focus is to intervene with these students. In all of these examples, learning new knowledge is important but learning new skills and behaviors is key to lasting change. Processing questions provide students with opportunities for intrapersonal learning through reflection and interpersonal learning through discussion with fellow students. Such questions also assist students with processing whole group dynamics and progress so that they learn about interpersonal effectiveness in group situations.

In the **Association for Specialists in Group Work** (ASGW) *Best Practice Guidelines* (Thomas & Bender, 2007), section C is devoted to Processing:

> Group Workers process the workings of the group with themselves, group members, supervisors or other colleagues, as appropriate. This may include assessing progress on group and member goals, leader behaviors and techniques, group dynamics and interventions; developing understanding and acceptance of meaning. Processing may occur both within sessions and before and after each session, at time of termination, and later follow up, as appropriate (p. 117).

Processing helps members make sense of what has taken place in the group (guidance lesson) and helps members apply or generalize what they have learned to their lives outside of the group setting (DeLucia-Waack, 2006; Stockton, Morran, & Nitza, 2000). Processing has been described as the most important phase when utilizing group activities (Jacobs, Harvill, & Masson, 2009). Types of processing questions might differ based on the goals of the guidance curriculum, the number of class meetings that are devoted to a single topic, and the level of comfort students have with each other. This latter factor is often related to the time of year – at the beginning of the year when students in a class do not know each other well their interactions are similar to the beginning stages of a group. As the year progresses, student interactions are more likely to be similar to the middle and ending stages of groups. Through appropriate processing questions students can internalize changes in thoughts and externalize changes in behaviors and skills.

School counselors leading classroom guidance lessons must allocate sufficient time to process activities adequately and must give thought to questions to pose in order to maximize learning and application of concepts to real-life situations. At the end of each lesson in this volume, processing questions are provided. School counselors are encouraged to utilize these questions or to adapt them to the students that they serve. It is not necessary to use every processing question provided after the activity. Leaders must judiciously choose processing questions that are most appropriate based on the goals of classroom guidance activity and the needs of students. For school counselors who wish to develop their own processing questions, examples of different types of processing questions utilizing two dimensions, the stage of development of the guidance group and the type of interaction are presented. Since guidance curriculum is often delivered to whole classes, the stage of development may be linked to the time of year. In the beginning of the year, students are getting to know each other and may be tentative and afraid to take risks. This is likely to change as the year progresses and students get to know each other better.

References

American School Counselor Association (ASCA, 2012). *The ASCA National Model: A Framework for School Counseling Programs* (3rd Ed.). Alexandria, VA: Author.

DeLucia-Waack, J. L. (2006). *Leading psychoeducational groups for children and adolescents.* Thousand Oaks, CA: Sage Publications.

Jacobs, E. E., Masson, R. L., & Harvill, R. L. (2009). *Group counseling: Strategies and skills.* Belmont, CA: Thomson/Brooks/Cole.

Stockton, R., Morran, D. K., & Nitza, A. G. (2000). Processing group events: A conceptual map for leaders. *Journal for Specialists in Group Work,* 25, 343-355. doi: 10.1080/01933920008411678.

Thomas, V. R., & Pender, D. A. (2008). Association for Specialists in Group Work: Best Practice Guidelines 2007 Revisions. *Journal for Specialists In Group Work, 33*(2), 111-117. doi:10.1080/01933920801971184. Retrieved from http://www.asgw.org/pdf/Best_Practices.pdf

Wilson, F. R., Rapin, L. S., & Haley-Banez, L. (2000). Association for Specialists in Group Work. Professional Standards for the training of group workers. Retrieved from http://www.asgw.org/pdf/training_standards.pdf

**Examples of Processing Questions Suitable for the Stage of Development
and the Type of Interaction**

	Stage of Development Beginning	Stage of Development Middle	Stage of Development Ending
Type of Interaction: Intrapersonal	Were you surprised by your reactions to the video? What emotions did you experience as you shared your fears? What concerns did you have as we began this lesson or activity?	What frustrates you about your ability to be assertive? How honest are you being with yourself? What thoughts do you have about your ability to refuse alcohol when a peer offers it to you?	What was the biggest take-away idea for you? What are your plans to sustain some of the gains you made in group? Use three words to describe yourself as you finish this curriculum. How are these different from the words you described yourself with in our first group?
Type of Interaction: Interpersonal	Who did you think you were most similar with? Tell that person why. When did you feel most connected with someone in the group? Who was that and why do you think you felt connected? What was the most surprising thing that you learned about group members as they introduced themselves?	Share with someone in the class why it is hard for you to ask for help. Share with each other one strategy that you use to help control and redirect your anger. Share your thoughts both negative and positive after giving someone in the group a genuine compliment.	How can you help your friend in this class to maintain the gains you have both made here? Who will you ask for help when you find it hard to resist drinking alcohol at a party? What would you say to each member of this group regarding how they have affected you?
Type of Interaction: Whole Group	What one word would you use to describe the climate in our first session? Did you notice any shifts in energy during the lesson? What do you notice about how this group is interacting?	What do you notice above how the class behaves when there is conflict? Do you observe that there are sub-groups within this class? How does this sub-grouping affect our interaction? Why do you think we are stuck?	How is this class different now as compared to when we first began? How will this experience affect the way you interact with each other in the classroom in future? What words can you use to describe this group as we finish up?

Chapter Eleven
Integrating Classroom Guidance Lessons Through Collaborative Classroom Instruction

Luis Antonio Tosado II
University at Buffalo, SUNY

Ileana Gonzalez
Johns Hopkins University

The classroom is a dynamic environment affected by student diversity and varying pedagogical practices of classroom teachers. The **American School Counselor Association** recommends that school counselors spend 80% of their time in direct and indirect student services (ASCA, 2012). The percentage of time this delivery occurs in the classroom varies by grade level (e.g., elementary 35 to 45%, middle 25 to 35%, and high school 15 to 25%). A skilled school counselor not only integrates the school counseling core curriculum in the classroom, but also models effective teaching and classroom management techniques. For the professional school counselor, successful integration of classroom guidance activities involves collaboration with teachers and other professional staff members to deliver the developmental school counseling core curriculum. Therefore, in this chapter the focus will be on integration of classroom guidance activities through a model of Collaborative Classroom Instruction with suggestions of practical tools.

Collaborative Classroom Instruction
How to Begin the Collaborative Process

In order to begin the collaborative process, it is imperative that teachers understand and believe in the mission of the comprehensive counseling program. This buy-in process takes considerable time and effort. Counselors need to be aware of what is happening daily in the classroom including when and how teachers deliver curriculum to students; conversely while teachers need to be aware how implementation of a comprehensive school counseling program will help close the school wide educational gaps. Once this mutual understanding of roles is established, counselors and teachers can work in conjunction in order to deliver guidance lessons.

Professional school counselors implementing collaborative classroom instruction should also be familiar with ASCA *Student Standards* and *Common Core Standards* (National Governors Association Center for Best Practices & Council of Chief State School Officers, 2010, http://www.corestandards.org). Just as teachers link curriculum to national, state and local standards in their subject areas, so too must school counselors. The curriculum is aligned with the counselor's vision, mission and goals and fosters knowledge, attitudes and skills in the content areas of academic achievement, career development and personal/social growth (ASCA, 2012). For example, if counselors are delivering a lesson relating to calculating college costs, this topic can easily be applied to curriculum delivered in a mathematics class. To collaborate, counselors need to be aware of curriculum being taught, and level and implications of the rigor for college and career readiness in the future.

Common Collaborative Classroom Interventions

In the teacher education literature, collaborative teaching models are often used to develop specialized instruction for students receiving Special Education services (Cook & Friend, 1995). In addition, teachers from different content areas may also partner together to teach collaboratively such as English and Social Studies so that students read books written during the time period they are studying. Ideally, school counselors also plan lessons with teachers as a model of collaborative classroom instruction to ensure all students receive a common school counseling core curriculum. Several collaborative teaching models (Cook & Friend) have been adapted to facilitate integration between school counselors and classroom teachers.

Lead Teacher. In this model, the school counselor takes the lead in teaching the subject matter while the classroom teacher observes or assists by managing classroom behavior or assisting individual students. The teacher does not provide direct instruction to the students. This model might be used when presenting an introductory lesson to incoming middle (6th grade) and high school (9th grade) students on topics such as the role of the school counselor, credits, transcripts, suicide, counseling services, or other topics that might be more appropriate for school counselors.

School Counselors Share Their Favorite Classroom Guidance Activities

Stations or Centers. In this model, the counselor and teacher are responsible for different aspects of the lesson while students rotate station-to-station receiving instruction from the counselor, teacher, or another professional. This might be useful when the two professionals have different areas of expertise. An English teacher may sit at a station discussing grammar and proofreading college essays while the counselor works with students at another station on components of the college essay. The Steen and Rose lesson *Ready..Set..Goals!* may be modified by placing the counselor at one station to teach and supervise the writing of long-term goals while the teacher is at a second station teaching and supervising the writing of short-term goals.

Team Teaching. Also known as co-teaching or tag teaming, this refers to scripted or impromptu instruction planned and delivered by both the counselor and teacher at the same time. For example; the counselor might explain the steps in the traditional *Stop, Think, Make a Good Choice* activity while the teacher role-plays the process for the class.

Parallel Teaching. The counselor and teacher split the class into two smaller groups of students, each taking one group, and deliver the same lesson to their respective group. In this model, the students remain with one adult throughout the duration of the lesson. This is helpful in lowering adult-student ratio or when important to maximize the number of students sharing and discussing.

Alternative Teaching. In this approach, the counselor and teacher split students with one teaching the main lesson to a large group and the other teaching a similar lesson to a smaller group of students with needed differentiation. For example in the lesson by Logan *Getting Ready for Middle School, Lesson I and II,* the teacher might deliver the lesson to students transitioning to the local middle school while the school counselor works with a smaller group of students whose parents are migrant workers and military members and will not be returning to the district (the smaller group will focus more on the transition to a new school district).

Differentiated Instruction. Differentiation is defined as the process of "adapting educational activity to suit the diverse needs and characteristics of the learners" (Haynes, 2010, p. 139). Collaboration with the classroom teachers is instrumental as the teacher is the most knowledgeable source of the learning styles and academic performance level of students in their classroom. The teacher and counselor can work collaboratively to modify and adapt the lesson to meet the needs of all students and ensure lessons are developmentally appropriate. For example in the Cleveland, Thomas, and Austin lesson *Chicken Man: Making the Best of all Jobs,* a teacher with English Language Learners (ELLs) in the classroom may differentiate by informing the counselor that a bilingual student may need to sit next to the ELLs to read and/or interpret the story for the students.

Professional school counselors may wish to differentiate activities by outcome, task, support, or a combination of the three, depending on student needs. When differentiating by outcome might mean one student writes a paragraph while another draws a picture. When differentiating by task, school counselors may ask one student to express a feeling while another may state differences between a happy and sad feeling. A school counselor differentiating by support may allow one student to work independently while accommodating another with the use of a bilingual dictionary. In Gomez's *Family Drawings and Career Guidance Lesson 1*, the outcome can be adapted for high school students by assigning students to write an essay and genogram based on family education and career or audio record a family interview and based on responses, write the essay. Students needing special accommodations can work in groups to complete this task.

Constructing Culturally Relevant Lessons

Professional School Counselors must ensure that they adhere to culturally appropriate practices when preparing and presenting lessons. Culturally responsive teaching is defined as "using the cultural characteristics, experiences, and perspectives of ethnically diverse students as conduits for teaching them more effectively" (Gay, 2002, p. 106). Just as lessons are differentiated for students at varying educational levels, differentiation may also occur for students from different cultural backgrounds. Learners must be able to see themselves represented in the curriculum. While not having a title that specifically addresses diversity, Thomas and Austin's lesson *Family Work Values: Tools from the Past, Lessons 1, 2, and 3 is* an example of a lesson that demonstrates cultural responsiveness by allowing all students to take pride in work and achievement by becoming aware of their own family's values and achievements; and then processing how they will implement those values in their own lives. Counselors interested in lessons that specifically address culture might want to review *Connecting Students to the Civil Rights Movement Through Music* (Wilson and Ziomek-Daigle), and

Don't Say Ain't: Addressing Linguistic and Cultural Differences Between Home and School Culture by Goodman-Scott.

Culturally competent school counselors use their awareness, knowledge, and skills of the *Multicultural Counseling Competencies* (Sue, Arredondo, & Mcdavis, 1992) and the *Multicultural and Social Justice Competence Principles for Group Workers* (Singh, Merchant, Skudrzyk, & Ingene, 2012) when integrating classroom guidance lessons through collaborative classroom instruction. Understanding these competencies and principles provides a starting point to recognize and challenge oppressive practices (e.g., racism, classism, ableism, sexism, etc.) that would otherwise alienate, marginalize, and deny equity and access to a school counseling core curriculum that promotes college and career readiness for all students.

Conclusions

Collaborative Classroom Instruction involves professional school counselors working with classroom teachers to plan and deliver core curriculum or classroom guidance activities. As school counselors and teachers work together through collaborative classroom, instruction school wide gaps will narrow and desired outcomes will be achieved.

References

American School Counselor Association (2012). *The ASCA national model: A framework for school counseling programs* (3rd Ed.). Alexandria, VA: Author.

Cook, L. & Friend, M. (1995). Co-teaching: Guidelines for creating effective practices. *Focus on Exceptional Children, 28*, 1-16.

Gay, G. (2002). Preparing for culturally responsive teaching *Journal of Teacher Education,* 53, 106-116. DOI: 10.1177/0022487102053002003

Haynes, A. (2010). *The complete guide to lesson planning and preparation.* London, GBR: Continuum International Publishing.

Singh, A., Merchant, N., Skudrzyk, B., & Ingene, D. (2012). *Association for specialists in group work: Multicultural and social justice competence principals for group workers.* Retrieved from Association for Specialists in Group Work website: http://www.asgw.org/pdf/ASGW_MC_SJ_Priniciples_Final_ASGW.pdf

Sue, D. W., Arredondo, P., & McDavis, R. J. (1992). Multicultural counseling competencies and standards: A call to the profession. *Journal of Counseling & Development, 70*, 477-486.

ACADEMIC SKILL BUILDING CLASSROOM GUIDANCE LESSONS

School Counselors Share Their Favorite Classroom Guidance Activities

Class Friendship Chain

Submitted by Jennifer H. Greene and Sandra M. Logan

School Level: Elementary.

Target Population: Ideal for Grade 2, appropriate for Grades 1 to 3.

Goals:
1. Understand appropriate vs. inappropriate behaviors in a friend.
2. Students can identify at least one friend.
3. Help students to feel connected to classmates.
4. Create a visual reminder for classroom teacher to refer to.

ASCA Standards:
A:A3.2 Demonstrate the ability to work independently, as well as the ability to work cooperatively with other students
PS:A1.6 Distinguish between appropriate and inappropriate behavior
PS:A2.6 Use effective communications skills
PS:A2.8 Learn how to make and keep friends.

Estimated Time: 30 to 40 minutes.

Materials: White board and markers, Handouts (Ingrid, White, Haiston, & Swift, 1996) pencils, markers or crayons, student scissors, stapler.

Lesson

1. The School Counselor introduces this activity by saying "Today we're going to be talking about friendship and what makes a good friend." Then ask students to silently think of a good friend. Then ask them to think of things that a good friend does and things that a good friend says. Ask a few students to share an example.
Emphasize examples that can be generalized to multiple situations. If examples are too specific, give the generalization to the students by saying something such as "It sounds like you're saying that good friends share with others?" Write these examples on the board for use later. (8 to 10 minutes)

2. Pass out the handout. Explain to students that they will be creating a class friendship chain using their responses that were previously brainstormed. Ask them in this order to:
    a. Write their answers first
    b. Color the sentence strips second, and
    c. Cut out the strips last.
Circulate among the students as they are working to answer any questions and let them know that they will have an opportunity to share them with the class if they choose. Make sure to check in with each student to assess his or her understanding of friendship skills. (7 to 10 minutes)

3. When the first student volunteer finishes cutting out his or her strips, have him or her come up to the front and ask if he or she would share one of the friendship skills from his or her strips. While the student shares their example, you can attach their three sentences strips into a chain with a stapler. This is the beginning of the class chain. If a student decides not to share, ask if you can share one of his or her examples with the class. (2 to 3 minutes)

4. Continue until all students' strips are a part of the classroom friendship chain. (8 to 10 minutes)

5. Use these questions to Process the activity:
   ✓ How many of you can think of someone who is a good friend?
   ✓ Does that good friend do the things we named?
   ✓ When have you done or said the things that are a part of our friendship chain?
   ✓ What happens when you do or say those things?
   ✓ How many of you are a part of the friendship chain of this class (that should be everyone because they all put their names on their strips)?
   ✓ What is one new friendship skill you would like to try this week?

6. To end the activity, summarize the students' responses about what makes a good friend and remind the class that each of them is a part of the class friendship chain that will be hanging in their classroom as a reminder of these qualities. (5 to 7 minutes)

Cautions: It is sometimes helpful to write some of the students' ideas on the board at the beginning, but if only a few are written sometimes, students restrict themselves to those few. There may be some students who have a difficult time identifying a friend. Counselor should walk around the classroom to gauge if any students need assistance.

Adaptations: Some students may be able to draw their ideas on the strips rather than write. If time is a concern, the counselor may distribute small pieces of paper & have students draw directly on them.

References

Class Friendship Chain. Adapted from Ingran, J., White, L, Haiston, D. N. & Swift H. (1996). *Cobb County Elementary Guidance Handbook.* Cobb County School System. Unpublished document.

About the Counselors:

Jennifer Greene is a Doctoral Student at University of Central Florida. Previously, Jennifer was a School Counselor at an international school in Georgia that offered the International Baccalaureate Primary Years Programme to refugee, immigrant, and American born students. jengreene@knights.ucf.edu

Sandra Logan is a Doctoral Fellow at University of Florida in Gainesville. Previously, she was an Elementary and Middle School Counselor in Southern California. Also, she has served as President of the Orange County chapter of the **California Association of School Counselors**. Logan.here2help@gmail.com

Directions: Write something that a good friend does or says on each strip. Include your name on at least one strip.

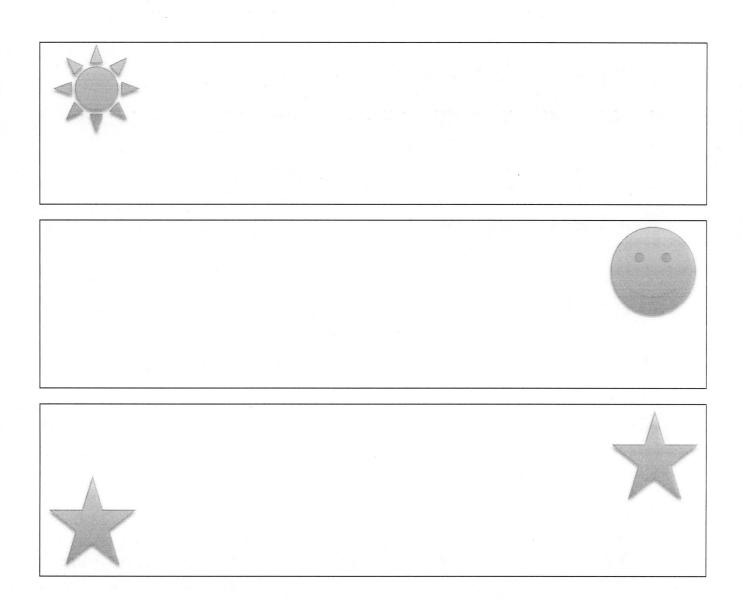

Adapted from Ingran, J., White, L, Haiston, D. N. & Swift H. (1996). *Cobb County Elementary Guidance Handbook.* Cobb County School System.

Decisions, Decisions
Submitted by Sandra Terneus

School Level: Elementary.

Target Population: Grades 3 to 5.

Goals: Students will:
1. Practice making decisions.
2. Have knowledge of decision-making styles.
3. Identify factors which influence their decision.

ASCA Standards:
C:A1 Develop career awareness
C:A1.5 Learn to make decisions.

Estimated Time: 20 to 30 minutes.

Materials: Deck of cards, whiteboard, marker.

Introduction: Counselor begins by saying: People make decisions every day. What are some decisions that you have made already? Did you decide what you were going to wear to school today? What else have you decided today? There are three basic styles of making decisions.

- The first style is called **Intuitive**. It means that a person makes a decision because it just feels right in their gut. Have any of you made a decision because it just feels right?
- The second style is called **Dependent**. It means that a person depends on others to help him or her make a decision such as parents, teachers, and other people of authority. Have you ever asked anyone for help in deciding what to do?
- The third style is called **Rational**. It means that a person examines data, scores or information to help him or her make a decision such as looking at report cards. Have you ever looked at your grades to decide how well you are doing in school?

So, there are different styles in making decisions. We make many decisions every day and can even use a combination of decision-making styles. In fact, there may be times when you may hear other people give you advice, but it just doesn't feel right for you. Has that ever happened to you in which someone was telling you to do something, but it did not feel right to do it? Or, maybe there was a time you needed advice from someone when the choice seemed too difficult to make. Has that ever happened to you? What was hard about it? Allow students to respond to these questions and emphasize their decision-making style: Intuitive (feels right), Dependent (relies on others), and Rational (analyze data). (5 minutes)

This activity is about making decisions. There is no right or wrong answer. You get to make a decision in predicting what a card will be. If you predict correctly, your team will earn points. If the prediction is not correct, your team will not earn points. The team with the most points wins the game. Remember, you can make your decision by listening to someone else, listening to your own gut feelings, or by looking at the scores that is on the board. We will practice with one student volunteer so everyone will know what to do.

Lesson

1. Write the instructions to *The Card Game* on the whiteboard. (5 minutes)

The Card Game

The possible predictions and the approximate odds are:
1. Pass (always collect)
2. Guess the color of the card (red or black; 1 out of 2 chances)
3. Guess the suit of the card (hearts, diamonds, clubs, or spades; 1 out of 4 chances)
4. Guess the card to be a deuce (1 out of 13 chances)
5. Guess the card to be a one-eyed jack (2 out of 26 chances)
6. Guess the card to be a joker (1 out of 53 chances)

Rewards: If the prediction is correct, the following points may be collected:
   Pass (Does not select a card) = 10 points
   Color (Red or Black) = 20 points
   Suit (Hearts, Diamonds, Clubs, or Spades) = 30 points
   Deuce = 40 points
   One-eyed jack = 50 points
   Joker = 100 points

2. The class will be divided into four groups/teams (the number of students in each group represents the number of rounds the game will be played so everyone has a chance to participate; the number of groups can be altered to fit the class size). Have the groups come up with a name for

their team and write the team name on the whiteboard. Within each group, have the students select who in their group will go first, second, and so on. (5 minutes)

3. To begin **The Card Game**, the Counselor will explain the information listed below on the whiteboard and how many rounds the game will be played (enough rounds so all students may actively participate.

a) The Counselor shuffles and spreads the cards on the desk.

b) One student from one group will walk to the desk and make a prediction about a card (color – red or black, suit – hearts, diamonds, clubs, or spades; deuce, one-eyed jack or joker) or "pass." During this time, students from his or her team as well as other teams can offer advice (or distraction) on which prediction (or pass) to make.

c) The Counselor writes the prediction (color – red or black, suit – hearts, diamonds, clubs, or spades; deuce, one-eyed jack or joker) or "pass" on the whiteboard.

d) The student selects the card (If "pass" is selected, the Counselor simply writes the point value on the board for passing and no card is selected).

e) If the prediction is correct, the points are added under the team name. For example, if a student predicts "Color – Red," and does indeed draw a red card. 20 points are added. If the prediction is incorrect, no points are added.

What is currently unfolding is the student's choice of listening to his/her self **(Intuitive)**, their team and/or the other teams **(Dependent)**, or reviewing scores and point values in making a prediction **(Rational)**.

f) The card is placed back into the deck and all cards are reshuffled before the next student from another group takes his or her turn.

g) At the end of round one, the Counselor briefly reviews the predictions and announces the scores.

4. Demonstrate a "practice" round with one student so the class understands what to do. The Counselor shuffles a deck of 53 cards (include one joker) and spreads them face down on the desk. A student comes to desk to select a card. Before drawing a card, the student makes a prediction about the card he/she is about to draw. (1 minute)

5. The next round invites another student from each team. Steps are repeated until all students have had the opportunity to actively participate. The Counselor tabulates the scores and reviews the predictions or decisions made during the game.

Processing Questions:

1. While playing this game, did you change the way in which you make decisions? (**Intuitive** is based on gut feeling; **Dependent** is relying on the advice from others; **Rational** is analyzing scores and probability data posted on the board; or a Combination of the styles).

2. If so, describe what influenced you? Maybe you were worried that you would not do well so you listened to the advice of others. Or you had noticed a trend of the scores posted on the board and thought your choice was the best logical decision to win the game. Or you felt that your answer was the best decision. What else?

3. What did you learn while watching your peers make decisions and then while you were making decisions? Were you satisfied with your answers? What would you do differently?

4. What decisions do you make at home or at school in which you use the same decision-making style and may or may not have the same influences? What might you do differently?

5. What have you learned about yourself from this activity? What else do you need to learn? For example, do you think it is ok to make a decision on your own? Is it ok to make a decision to do something when someone else says to do something else? When is it helpful to listen to the advice of others? What is it like to look up information by yourself and make a decision?

Cautions: Inform students that the use of a deck of cards for this activity is not considered gambling.

Next Possible Lesson Plan Topics: Learning to develop goals (career, personal and social domains), and Identifying steps to achieve goals (career, personal and social domains).

Credit/References

Buck, J. N., Wang, S. L., Daniels, M. H., & Harren, V. A. (1986). *WPS career planning program: Student handbook*, Los Angeles: Western Psychological Services.

About the Counselor:

Sandra Terneus is a Professor at Tennessee Tech University, Cookeville, TN. sterneus@tntech.edu

What is Conflict?
Lessons 1 and 2

Submitted by Jennifer H. Greene and Sandra M. Logan

School Level: Elementary.

Target Population: Grades 3 to 5.

Goals:
1. Learn about types of conflict.
2. Learn that conflict can be negative or positive.
3. Learn how to handle conflict.

ASCA Standards:

PS:A1.6 Distinguish between appropriate and inappropriate behavior
PS:A1.7 Recognize personal boundaries, rights and privacy needs
PS:A2.1 Recognize that everyone has rights and responsibilities
PS:A2.2 Respect alternative points of view
PS:B1.1 Use a decision-making and problem-solving model
PS:B1.3 Identify alternative solutions to a problem
PS:B1.6 Know how to apply conflict resolution skills
PS:C1.10 Learn techniques for managing stress and conflict.

Estimated Time: Two 30 to 45 minute lessons.

Materials: Whiteboard and markers or smart board; **Poster of Conflict Resolution Model** (adapted from Wittmer, Thompson, & Loesch, 2000).

Lesson 1

1. Counselor begins with: Conflict is something that we all experience. It can have profound negative or positive consequences in our personal lives and globally. Many positive changes such as the abolition of slavery came out of a situation of conflict yet there are many negative consequences also. What are some conflicts that occur at school? These conflicts can make a classroom feel less safe or can lead to positive changes.
2. Write the word **Conflict** on the board.
   a. Ask students what they know about conflict.

b. Record students' ideas around the word "conflict" in a word web. (Student can brainstorm individually or in groups) (10 to 15 minutes)

3. Facilitating a whole class brainstorming session, have students make a list of examples of conflict in each of the following settings: school, home, community (local/national/ international). Write all ideas on the white board.

a. Encourage students to think of both positive and negative ideas. Emphasize results or consequences of conflict.

b. Help students to build on existing knowledge about conflicts they may have studied such as the civil war and the American Revolution. If students have not studied those conflicts, a book about the civil war could be utilized or counselor could focus more on personal conflicts, such as those conflicts that may occur in the classroom.

c. Make connections between ideas (i.e. conflicts at school, conflicts at home, global conflicts, conflicts that led to positive changes, etc.). For instance, discuss with students how conflict at home can occur when children are not honest with parents. Or, in school, children may encounter conflict when they do not agree with another student's decision. (8 to 10 minutes)

4. After brainstorming connections, allow students to volunteer to identify which ideas are negative (circle in one color marker) and positive (circle in a different color marker) (8 to10 minutes)

5. Process with these questions: (5 to 10 minutes)
✓ Are more of the ideas about conflict negative or positive?
✓ Why do you think that is?
✓ Does conflict have to be negative?
✓ What makes conflict negative or positive?

6. Summarize that Conflict can be either positive or negative. We often think of conflicts as a bad thing but it does not have to be. Next time we will work on some positive ways to handle conflict at school or at home.

Lesson 2

1. Review the last lesson on conflict by asking students what they remember about conflict and, if necessary, reminding students of the examples they brought up during the last lesson. Ask them if conflict is a good thing or a bad thing. If they have forgotten, remind them that there can be both positive and negative consequences of conflict and that conflict is not necessarily a bad thing. (3 to 5 minutes)

2. Ask students to think more specifically about conflicts that happen at school by asking, "What conflicts have you been involved in or have you seen here at school?" (8 to 10 minutes)

3. Teach students the steps in "Conflict Resolution" model (adapted from Wittmer, Thompson, & Loesch, 2000) using the poster. (3 to 5 minutes)

4. Have two students volunteer to role-play resolving a conflict using the model (provide an easy conflict scenario such as deciding who's turn it is on the swing at recess). Allow the class to help with the solutions or anytime the two get stuck.
   - If students are reluctant to volunteer, the counselor and teacher can go first or the counselor can role play with one student.
   - It is more likely that there will be too many volunteers, which will lead into the next step. (8 to 10 minutes)

5. Allow the class to practice the "Conflict Resolution" model in groups of 2 or 3 with made up conflicts, such as the one's listed in the chart (at the end of the lesson), or with student generated conflicts.
   Some classes may have groups that the students already work in, if so use those. Other-wise, counting off can work to divide students into groups. (1 minute)

6. Process activity with these questions. (8 to10 minutes)
   ✓ How did it work to practice solving a conflict?
   ✓ What was easy? What was difficult about this?
   ✓ Would it be harder or easier if you were mad?
   ✓ What have you learned?
   ✓ What would you do differently next time you are in a conflict?
   ✓ What did someone else say that you liked and you might want to borrow as a skill sometime?

7. Summarize the two lessons by saying something such as, "As we've discussed, conflict is not necessarily a bad thing. Sometimes conflict has positive results such as the abolition of slavery or changes to unfair laws. Here at school, we can make conflict positive by using the conflict resolution model that you just practiced." (1 to 2 minutes)

Cautions: For schools that have refugee students, political conflict may have touched their lives more directly. This lesson may need to be adapted depending on their experiences. Other children's lives also have been directly impacted by conflict. As mentioned, refugee students lives may have been directly impacted by political turmoil, students may have a parent in the military who has left for war, or students may have experienced conflict in their home through domestic violence or divorce.

Though this lesson normalizes the experience of conflict, it is important to monitor students who may need to meet individually after the lesson. The first author worked in a school with many refugee students and none were triggered by this lesson.

References

Wittmer, J., Thompson, D. W., & Loesch, L. C. (2000) *Classroom guidance activities: A sourcebook for elementary school counselors.* Minneapolis, MN: Educational Media Corporation.

About the Counselors:

Jennifer Greene is a Doctoral Student at University of Central Florida. Previously, Jennifer was a School Counselor at an international school in Georgia that offered the International Baccalaureate Primary Years Programme to refugee, immigrant, and American born students, jengreene@knights.ucf.edu

Sandra Logan is a Doctoral Fellow at University of Florida in Gainesville. Previously, she was an Elementary and Middle School Counselor in Southern California. Also, she has served as President of the Orange County chapter of the **California Association of School Counselors.** Logan.here2help@gmail.com

Conflict Resolution Model
(adapted from Wittmer, Thompson, & Loesch, 2000)

Step 1: Decide who is going to talk first

   Hint – whoever is more upset or flip a coin

Step 2: The first talker shares their side of the story

Step 3: The first listener repeats back what they heard

   Repeat steps 2 and 3 as needed for understanding

Step 4: Switch roles and repeat steps 2 and 3

Step 5: Decide what the problem is.

Step 6: Brainstorm solutions to the problem

Step 7: Agree on a solution if possible.

   If no agreement, go back to step 6 or compromise

92

Role Play Scenarios

Your two best friends have been hanging out without you and you just found out they had a sleepover and didn't invite you	You want to play soccer at recess, but your friends want to play tag.
You shared your food from lunch with your friend and now he won't share his with you.	In order to finish your group project, you need to color it. But, the other group won't share the markers.
You need to use a dictionary but they are all being used and no one will share.	You would like to use the swings at recess but other students using the swings are taking a long time.
Another student hanging up his coat knocked yours off and didn't even pick it up.	A friend borrowed a book from you and when she gave it back, the pages are all wrinkled.
A classmate bumped into you while you were illustrating a story and ruined your pictured.	Someone keeps kicking you under the table at lunch. It must be on purpose because they didn't say sorry.

Getting Ready for Middle School: Lessons 1 and 2

Submitted by Sandra M. Logan

School Level: Elementary.

Goals: Students will be able to:

1. Identify at least three differences between elementary and middle school.
2. Discuss thoughts and feelings associated with transitioning to a new school environment.
3. Identify at least three strategies that were suggested in order to succeed in middle school/junior high.

ASCA Standards:

A:A1.1 Articulate feelings of competence and confidence as learners

A:A1.2 Display a positive interest in learning

A:A1.5 Identify attitudes and behaviors that lead to successful learning

A:A2.3 Use communications skills to know when and how to ask for help when needed

A:B2.1 Establish challenging academic goals in elementary, middle/jr. high and high school

PS:A1.4 Understand change is a part of growth

PS:C1.11 Learn coping skills for managing life events.

Estimated Time: 35 to 40 minutes.

Materials: Whiteboard & markers (or overhead projector or SMARTboard); pens, (1 per student), Handout *How to Succeed* (Logan, 2014) (1 per student), and Video *Middle School Transition* (Freymuth, 2009), student homework assignment, *Getting Ready for Middle School Summer Calendar* (Channing Bete, n.d.).

Special Directions: If students may feed into more than one middle school, research ahead of time the unique characteristics of each school. For instance, one middle school may offer particular electives, sports or academic programs, or after-school programs that another may not. Be able to provide students with answers or know of a person to direct them to.

Lesson 1

1. School Counselor begins with: *Today, we are going to talk about getting ready for middle school. This is an exciting time for some students, but rather stressful for others. Transitioning to a new school means learning a new environment with new people and new expectations. I am going to have you share some of your concerns about transitioning to middle school and we are going to hear firsthand from some middle schools who can give you some advice.* (3 minutes)

2. Distribute handout *How to Succeed in Middle School* (Logan, 2014) to students. Begin by having students brainstorm on their own about what thoughts or activities make them excited? What about nervous? *Please write your name on your paper and take about three minutes to write down what parts of middle school are you excited about? What aspects are you nervous about? Also, feel free to write any questions you may have and hopefully I will be able to answer them for you today.*

(Very common themes are about being at a new school, new people, multiple teachers, changing classes, bell schedules, using lockers, changing into gym clothes, extracurricular activities, and of course, homework expectations.) (5 minutes)

3. After students have written about their initial thoughts about middle school, use the whiteboard to brainstorm and have students volunteer to their ideas with the class.

   Now that you have written down some of your ideas, do I have someone who wants to share with me ONE thing that you have written down? (Try to get at least 5 unique ideas).

   Write them on the whiteboard. (7 to 10 minutes)

4. Students will view video "*Middle School Transition*" (Running time is approximately 8 minutes, 30 seconds). Since it is an online video, queue the video prior to the beginning of the lesson to avoid the potential of any commercials.

   Now, we are going to watch a video about how to get ready for middle school. You will be hearing from students who are currently in middle school. It is my hope that they will give you a better ideas of what to expect next year. After the video, we will discuss what you saw.

5. After viewing the video, ask students about their observations.
   Ask Processing Questions:
   * What did you notice the students from the video mention about homework?
   * Describe how middle school is different from elementary school.
   * Who did they mention you can talk to if you are having difficulties adjusting to middle school life?
   * What was some of the advice they recommended to you?
     (5 minutes)

6. Return to the handout and have students complete the rest of the questions. (5 to 7 minutes)

7. End the lesson by reminding students that it is okay to feel nervous and excited. They will have time to adjust to their new environment and have trusted adults that they can ask for help. Also, encourage students to visit the school counselor if they are having trouble adjusted to middle school in any way. Share with students that you will be visiting one more time to further discuss planning and preparation for the transition to middle school. Tell them you will be coming for another session after they complete the handout. Hand out that handout?

Lesson 2

1. School Counselor begins with: *During our last lesson, we watched a video and discussed your excitement and fears with transitioning from elementary to middle school. The video demonstrated various activities that will be new experiences for you. Today, I'm interested to hear from each of you about how your homework assignment went. By the end of our lesson, it is my hope that we can plan for some activities that will help support your transition.*

2. Ask students to raise their hands to be called and share one thing they remember from the last lesson. Paraphrase students' answers, which will mostly likely revolve around their apprehensions with this transition. (5 minutes)

3. Using the PBS Kids website, review some of the changes that will occur in middle school.   (10 minutes)

    http://pbskids.org/itsmylife/school/middleschool/article2.html

While reviewing the website, make sure to emphasize that while there will be more work, there will also be more unique opportunities such as having a locker and participating in elective courses and extracurricular activities.

4. Have students take out their handout *How to Succeed in Middle School* (Logan, 2014), which was distributed during the last lesson, as well as their homework assignment. Read aloud the writing prompt that was provided to students for homework. (10 minutes) *Taking what you have learned about middle school, write one paragraph about how you feel about middle school/junior high and what steps are required or necessary to be successful? Who might you talk to if you need help?*

Do not require all students to share, allow those that are interested in sharing. If minimal participation occurs, encourage students to share by stating that they are probably not the only one with similar thoughts.

5. Transition the lesson to brainstorming ways to get ready for middle school during the summer. Write student suggestions on the whiteboard. *Let's brainstorm some activities that might take place during the summer that can prepare you for middle school.* (10 minutes)

6. Distribute *Getting Ready for Middle School Summer Calendar* to each student. Encourage students to use some of the ideas presented in class today, as well as to take the calendar home and collaborate with their parents. Provide students with the following examples: *July 21st through 25th is sports team training; August 12th & 13th are orientation days, 8am-11am; Pick up supply list & student from school August 15th.*

7. Conclude lesson by emphasizing to students that they are about to transition to a new school, new setting, with new people. It will take time to adjust. But, with time management and organization, they will learn how to succeed in middle school.

Cautions: Some students may have a negative connotation about how "scary" middle school is (due to sibling or other influences like the media). Some students may feel overwhelmed after the presentation—be available to meet with students on individual concerns.

Credit/References

Freymuth. (2009, April 15). Middle School Transition [video file]. Retrieved from
http://www.teachertube.com/viewVideo.php?video_id=43265

Supporting Resources:
http://pbskids.org/itsmylife/school/middleschool/
This website is visually appealing & kid friendly. Includes a book list for fiction/non-fiction books about transitioning from elementary school.
http://shop.channing-bete.com/onlinestore/storeitem.html?iid=166684
If school funds are available, this is a great, inexpensive summer planning calendar for students getting ready to enter middle school/junior high.

About the Counselor:

Sandra Logan is a Doctoral Fellow at University of Florida in Gainesville. Previously, she worked as an Elementary and Middle School Counselor in Southern California. Also, she has served as a volunteer and executive board member to many professional organizations, including President of the Orange County chapter of the **California Association of School Counselors**. Logan.here2help@gmail.com

Name:_____

How to Succeed in Middle School

Soon you will be leaving elementary to enter middle
school. What are your thoughts about starting middle
school? Are you excited? Anxious? What questions do you have?

_____

_____

_____

_____

After our class discussion and viewing the video, what are 5 "new" things that you have
learned about middle school?

    1.

    2.

    3.

    4.

    5.

What are two strategies that will help you be successful in this new environment?

    1.

    2.

How have your thoughts changed?

_____

_____

_____

_____

Homework Assignment:

Taking what you have learned about middle school, write one paragraph about how you
feel about middle school/junior high and what steps are required or necessary to be
successful? Who might you talk to if you need help?

(Logan, 2014)

Understanding How We Work in a Group: The Balloon Tower Challenge

Submitted by Christy W. Land and Jolie Ziomek-Daigle Ph.D.

School Level: Elementary/Middle.

Target Population: Upper elementary to lower middle school.

Goals: Students will:

1. Define cooperation and teamwork and identify individual roles within a group or team.
2. Participate in a team-building activity to help identify various roles within a group.
3. Discuss the importance of individual contributions to their small groups and to their classroom as a whole.
4. Be able to answer identify roles and behaviors to work cooperatively as part of a group or team.

ASCA Standards:

A3.2 Demonstrate the ability to work independently, as well as the ability to work cooperatively with other students
PS:A1.9 Demonstrate cooperative behavior in groups
PS:A2.6 Use effective communication skills.

Estimated Time: 30 minutes.

Materials: Balloons (12 balloons per group), masking tape (one roll per group), **Cool Runnings** (Turtletaub, 1993) info DVD, DVD player and television, and index Cards (1 index card per student).

Lesson

1. The Counselor should begin with: We are going to watch a short video clip that demonstrates teamwork. As you watch this video clip, please think about what this clip is demonstrating- is this team working together successfully?

2. Show the video clip from the movie **Cool Runnings** (DVD **Start Time** 52:45 DVD **Stop Time** at 53:16). The video clip will demonstrate unsuccessful teamwork. The video clip reveals teamwork that was uncooperative and without clearly defined group rules. (2 minutes)

3. The Counselor will introduce the topic of teamwork/cooperation. The group leader will ask "What is cooperation/teamwork? Did the video clip demonstrate good teamwork? Why or why not? Why is teamwork/cooperation an important concept to think about as students? Why is it important that each individual contribute to their groups or teams?" (3 minutes)

4. Ask the students to share some of their own experiences in working with groups or being part of a team. Did everyone on the team/group contribute and work cooperatively together? What worked well in their past group experiences? What could have been done differently? (Focus on the following themes for positive group work: helping, everyone participates, common goals, hard work.) (5 minutes)

5. The students will participate in a team building challenge called Balloon Tower. Divide students into groups of 3 or 4 and provided ten balloons and one roll of masking tape. Students will be instructed that they are only allowed to use the supplies provided. It will be explained that the students will have two minutes to plan how they will build their tower and that no talking will be allowed during the challenge. Counselor says "In your small groups you will participate in a team building challenge, called Balloon Tower. The challenge is to see what group can build the tallest balloon tower made out of balloons and masking tape. Your group may use no other supplies other than balloons and masking tape that are given to you. If someone in the group talks, a balloon will be taken away by the Counselor. As you work in groups, notice your role and how people contribute.

6. You will now have two minutes to plan in your group how you will achieve the challenge". (2 minutes)

7. The students will complete the challenge: to build the tallest tower with only the supplies given. (7 to 8 minutes)

8. One member of each group will bring their balloon tower to the front of the room and the balloon towers will be judged collaboratively to determine which balloon tower is the tallest by the class and the winner of the challenge will be announced by the Counselor. (3 minutes)

9. Ask the students to discuss what worked well in their challenge groups and what could have been done differently.
   ✓ What roles within the group did the students play?
   ✓ Did the group work cooperatively together?
   ✓ What worked well within the groups?
   ✓ What were some challenges that the groups faced?
   ✓ How did the plans change as the group built?
   ✓ Did everyone in the group agree with the plans?
   ✓ If your group lost a balloon, how did that feel?
   ✓ How did you feel about your finished balloon tower?
   ✓ What did you learn from participating in this team building challenge?
   ✓ Why is teamwork/cooperation important as students?
   ✓ How can students demonstrate cooperative behavior when working with a group or team?
   (Focus on the following themes for positive group work: helping, everyone participates, common goals, hard work.) (3 to 4 minutes)

10. Show the video clip from **Cool Runnings** (DVD **Start** 88:11 DVD **Stop** **89:20)** that demonstrates cooperative teamwork where each group member is contributing. The group will discuss the differences from the first clip to the second clip. What did they observe as successful teamwork in this clip? (5 minutes)

11. As a "ticket out of the door", students are asked to write how they contributed cooperatively to their group during the balloon tower activity on an index card and one example of how they will contribute positively to their classrooms on the back of the card. (2 minutes)

School Counselors Share Their Favorite Classroom Guidance Activities

12.   Facilitator can give the notecards to the classroom teacher to display on a bulletin board as reminder of how students can contribute positively to their classroom.

Cautions: Students with sensory processing issues may be sensitive to the popping of the balloons.

Adaptations: Facilitators may use an alternative video clip to demonstrate uncooperative and cooperative group and team work. Alternative video clips include:

Gold Recruitment (2011, December 19). *Teamwork.* Retrieved May 20, 2013 from: http://www.youtube.com/watch?v=gGyP5iK9wAI.

Novan NG (2012, March 3). *The Power of Union is Strength.* Retrieved May 20, 2013 from: http://www.youtube.com/watch?v=jop2I5u2F3U).

Shilpamht7 (2012, February 10). *Teamwork an Inspirational 2D Movie.* Retrieved May 2013 from:
http://www.youtube.com/watch?v=_fxtwWk.NNsY

Credit/References

Lesson was adapted from Jones, A. (2002). *More team-building activities for every group.* Richland, WA: Rec Room Publishing.

Turteltaub, J. (Producer) & Turtletaub, J. (Director). (1993). *Cool Runnings* (Motion Picture). United States. Bueana Vista Home Entertaiment.

About the Counselors:

Christy Land, Ed.S., LPC is a Professional School Counselor at Hightower Trail Middle School in Marietta, Georgia. Christy.land@cobbk12.org

Jolie Ziomek-Daigle, Ph.D., LPC, is an Associate Professor and School Counseling Program Coordinator at University of Georgia. jdaigle@uga.edu

Homeroom Quilt

Submitted by Mike Behm, Annemarie Cervoni, Ann Linder, Amy See, Jennifer Stahl, Margaret Sullivan and Maureen Brett

School Level: Elementary/ Middle/High.

Target Population: At the beginning of the year for classes of students who will be together all year.

Goals: To foster a sense of unity and camaraderie amongst homeroom students while expressing individual creativity.

ASCA Standards:
PS:A1.1 Develop positive attitudes toward self as a unique and worthy person
PS:A2.3 Recognize, accept, respect and appreciate individual differences.

Estimated Time: 30 to 40 minutes.

Materials: 4"X 4" pieces of cloth (one per student), assorted colors of fabric markers and paints, assorted embellishments (buttons, sequins, ribbons, etc.), fabric glue. (Newspaper to put beneath the fabric in case the markers or paints bleed through.)

Lesson

1. Announce to the students that they will create a "Homeroom Quilt" to represent each person in the homeroom. Once assembled, the quilt will be hung in the classroom for the entire year. Instruct students to be creative when designing their individual square.

2. Pass out a fabric square to each student.

3. Direct them to write their names clearly and boldly on the square.

4. Then ask them to create a design to represent themselves using color, patterns, words, sayings, drawings, etc. Show what materials are available for decoration.

5. Once individual squares are created, they should be set aside to dry.

6. Once dry, they will be assembled on a large mounting cloth to be hung in the homeroom.

Processing Questions:
✓ What does your square say about you?
✓ What is one thing you learned about another student that you didn't know before?

Cautions: Be sure to set aside time for clean up at the end of class. It is also important to make sure all tools and materials are being used safely.

Adaptations: May use different materials, depending on age of students.

About the School Counselors:

Mike Behm, Annemarie Cervoni, Ann Linder, Amy See, Jennifer Stahl and *Margaret Sullivan* make up the Guidance Department at Orchard Park High School in Orchard Park, NY. *Maureen Brett* is a School Counselor at Lancaster Middle School in Lancaster, NY. Mbrett@lancaster.wnyric.org

I Can Study, You Can Study, We Can Study!

Submitted by Joy Rose and Sam Steen

School Level: Middle.

Goals: Students will:

1. Identify their academic strengths and assets that and learn how these can improve their study habits.
2. Examine their current study habits, learn new ways to study effectively and recognize the positive effect that good study habits can have on their grades.
3. Develop the skills necessary to persevere in order to maximize their academic achievement.

ASCA Standards:

Personal/Social Development:
PS:A1.1 Develop positive attitudes toward self as a unique and worthy person
PS:A1.10 Identify personal strengths and assets
PS:B1.11 Use persistence and perseverance in acquiring knowledge and skill
Academic Development:
A:A1.1 Articulate feelings of competence and confidence as learners
A:A1.4 Accept mistakes as essential to the learning process
A:A1.5 Identify attitudes and behaviors that lead to successful learning
A:A2.2 Demonstrate how effort and persistence positively affect learning
A:B2.3 Develop and implement annual plan of study to maximize academic ability and achievement.

Estimated Time: 45 minutes.

Materials: Paper, pens, scissors (enough for students to share), **Study Skills Handout** (Falco, 2008).

Lesson

1. Explain to the students that in this session we will learn more about ourselves and more about each other through brainstorming and role-play. We will also talk about our own study habits and how they can be improved. The major purpose of this lesson is to make sure we are

achieving at our full academic potential by studying hard, trying our best, and asking for help when we need it.

2. Assign students to groups of 3 or 4 based on their seats in the classroom. Instruct the students to brainstorm with their group what good study habits versus poor study habits would look like. (5 minutes)

3. After the students have examples of both scenarios, have the groups take turn role-playing one of their scenarios for the rest of the class. Ask the student observers to determine if what they are seeing is an example of good or poor study habits. Use the role-plays to start a discussion about the students' own study habits. Use these questions to facilitate the discussion:
   ✓ What did you see your peers doing that was a poor study habit?
   ✓ What did you see your peers doing that was a good study habit?
   ✓ Give an example of one thing you would have done in the situation that your peers did not do.
   ✓ Have you ever experienced a similar situation? If so, how did you respond? (15 minutes)

4. Ask for volunteers to share some aspects of their current study habits and have a volunteer make a list of these on the board. Promote honesty during this activity by allowing it to be a safe place for students to share that they may not have any study habits that they currently use. (10 minutes)

5. Once the discussion is complete, have students complete the **Study Habits Checklist** (Falco, 2008). As students discuss the study habits that they currently have, be sure to present them with the following suggestions of ways to improve: (5 minutes)

- Set aside a regular time and place to study. (Examples: in the living room right after school, in your bedroom for an hour before bed, etc.)
- Don't try to study when you are tired or hungry. If necessary, grab a snack and then take a nap.
- Study in a place that is free from distractions.
- Set goals for yourself. Consider breaking up your work into small chunks and take short breaks while you study.
- Prioritize by making a list of what you need to get done, and start with the most important thing on your list. This will allow you to spend the most time on the most time consuming assignments.
- Give yourself plenty of time to review the material. In other words, don't wait until the last minute to start studying.

- Study with a friend. Studying with a friend may help you understand the information as you talk it out with each other. When studying with a friend be sure to consider; not copying each other's work exactly, taking turns choosing the time and place, focusing on the work and not the friend, and being patient with each other.
- Ask for help if you don't understand something. Ask your teachers, family members, or other trusted adults that may be able to provide clarity on something you are working on.

Processing Questions: (10 minutes)
✓ What did you learn about your study habits?
✓ Which of your current study habits do you think are effective?
✓ Which of your current study habits might need improvement?
✓ What are some of the barriers or things you do that keep you from developing or using good study habits?
✓ What's one new habit you can commit to trying?
✓ How can we help each other to improve our study habits both in school and at home?

Adaptations: This lesson could be adapted to focus on a particular school subject by altering the questions to make them applicable solely to that subject. For example; what are your current study habits for Math class?

Next Possible Lesson Plan Topics: Organization, Time Management, Asking for Help and Self-Advocacy

Credit/References

Falco, Lia D. (2008) *"Skill-builders": Enhancing middle school students' self-efficacy and adaptive learning strategies in mathematics.* (Doctoral dissertation). Retrieved from Proquest, UMI. (3303631).

About the Counselors:

Sam Steen, Ph.D. is an Associate Professor in School Counseling at George Washington University, Washington DC. slsteen@gwu.edu

Joy Rose is an 8th Grade Counselor at Columbia Heights Educational Campus, Washington, DC. joy.rose@dc.gov

Name:_____

Study Habits Checklist (Falco, 2008)

Directions: Read each statement carefully and circle the response that is true for you.

1. I set aside a regular time for studying every day.	YES	NO
2. I give up if an assignment is difficult.	YES	NO
3. I study best with the stereo or TV on.	YES	NO
4. I waste time because I am not organized.	YES	NO
5. I enjoy learning.	YES	NO
6. I focus entirely on my work when I study.	YES	NO
7. I study before I do anything else.	YES	NO
8. I could get better grades.	YES	NO
9. I get distracted when I study.	YES	NO
10. I have trouble finding enough time to study.	YES	NO
11. Good grades are important to me.	YES	NO
12. I try to find a quiet place to study.	YES	NO
13. I spend too much time on some things and not enough on others.	YES	NO
14. I tend to put off studying.	YES	NO
15. I get tired/sleepy when I study.	YES	NO

A Chain is Only as Strong as Its Weakest Link

Submitted by Jillian Boals

School Level: Middle.

Target Population: Grade 6.

Goals: Students will:
1. Be able to relate the saying "A chain is only as strong as its weakest link" to school and the classroom.
2. Learn about themselves and their classmates.

ASCA Standards:

PS:A1.1 Develop positive attitudes toward self as a unique and worthy person
PS:A1:10 Identify personal strengths and assets
PS:A2:3 Recognize, accept, respect and appreciate individual differences.

Estimated Time: 35 to 45 minutes.

Materials: Crayons, markers, or colored pencils; multiple colors of construction paper cut into strips, **Chain Link** handout (Boals, 2012), **Animal Traits** handout.

Introduction:

1. Hand out a piece of paper that says "A chain is only as strong as its weakest link". Ask the students if they have ever heard the saying and to define what the saying means. (i.e., one weak link can ruin a chain because then the chain is not so strong - will break). (2 to 3 minutes)
2. Ask the students how they can relate this saying to the classroom. Direct the conversation to how each student in the class represents a chain link and if one starts to fall it will bring down the rest of the class. Ask for specific behaviors that would cause the chain to "break" (i.e., talking when not supposed to be, bullying, fooling around in class, not doing their work). (2 to 3 minutes)
3. Discuss how the class could bring up and support the person who might be having trouble or is being seen as the "weak" link. Probe the students for specific actions to support the "weak" link (i.e. encourage

classmates to stay on track, support the victims not the bully, help students who need it). (4 to 5 minutes)

4. Explain to students that the class will create their own chain link that will hang in the classroom to remind them to always remain a strong chain. Show an example chain link (one you made representing yourself) so students can visually see what they will be creating in the activity. (1 to 2 minutes)

5. Pass out a construction paper strip and an **Animal Trait Sheet** to every student. (Some of the traits may need to be defined as there are words the students may not know.) (1to 2 minutes)

6. Explain that the students are going to each pick an animal that best describes them based on the traits listed next to each animal. (1 to 2 minutes)

7. Instruct students to decorate their chain link with their name on one side and their animal with the traits on the other. Have the students include at least three listed traits on the side with the animal. Students can draw the animal as well as write it. Students can be creative in decorating their chain link. (1 to 2 minutes)

8. While students to decorate their chain, circulate to answer any questions and make sure students are on task. (15 to 25 minutes)

9. Each student will come up to add their link to the chain. Start with the teacher and/or counselor as the middle link as they are the center that holds the class together. Have each student bring their link to the front one at a time and share what animal they are and some or all related traits. Connect each link to the chain by stapling the ends into a circle after passing it through the previous link. Alternate the name and animal sides being on the outside to represent both. Add chains to each side of the middle link evenly. You can alternate colors so the chain has more variety. (10 to 12 minutes)

10. Display the chain in the classroom as a constant reminder to stay a strong chain.

Processing Questions:

✓ How can we relate this activity to classroom rules, expectations, or behaviors?

✓ Why is it important to have a variety of "animals" in the class?

✓ What animals can help each other?

✓ What traits do we have and/or that we can borrow from other animals to help us

  o Work together in class?

  o Be respectful of others?

o Keep our classroom neat?

Cautions: If students are having trouble picking an animal, help them choose one if you know the student well. If you don't know the student well, ask the teacher or their peers if they could help the student choose an animal that would fit them.

Adaptations: Instead of using the animal traits, students could just come up with their own traits they bring to the classroom, or have them pick a character trait that represents them.

Credit/References

Animal traits were adapted from an activity on the Business Training Works Inc. website (www.businesstrainingworks.com)

About the School Counselor:

Jillian Boals is the 5th to 8th grade School Counselor at Global Concepts Charter School, Buffalo, NY and a graduate of the School Counseling Program at University at Buffalo, SUNY. jboals@globalccs.org

A CHAIN IS ONLY AS STRONG AS ITS WEAKEST LINK.

ANIMAL TRAITS (Adapted from Business Training Works Inc. www.businesstrainingworks.com)

Alligator - Maternal and vengeful
Ant - Group minded, patient, active, and industrious
Antelope - Active, agile, and willing to sacrifice
Armadillo - Safety oriented and cautious
Badger - Courageous, aggressive, healing and energizing
Bat - Regenerative and long living
Bear - Industrious, instinctive, healing, powerful, leader, protective of the world, and strong
Beaver - Determined, strong-willed, constructive, and protective
Bee - Organized, industrious, productive, wise, social, celebratory, and enthusiastic about life
Buffalo - Sacred and strong
Butterfly - Metamorphic and transformative
Cat - Protective, detached, sensual, mysterious, magical, and independent
Cheetah - Swift, insightful, and focused
Cow - Nurturing and maternal
Coyote - Intelligent, stealthy, tricky, and mischievous
Crane - Solitary, just, enduring, independent, intelligent, and vigilant
Crow - Law enforcing, shape shifting, changeable, creative, spiritual, energetic, and just
Deer - Intellectual, gentle, caring, kind, subtle, graceful, feminine, gentle, and innocent
Dog - Noble, faithful, loyal, trainable, protective, and guiding
Dolphin - Kind, prudent, capable of deep emotion, wise, and happy
Dragon - Enduring, wise, powerful, and fiery
Dragonfly - Flighty, carefree, and strongly imaginative
Eagle - Divine, sacrificing, intelligent, courageous, spiritually illuminated, healing, and daring
Elephant - Strong, powerful, and wise
Elk - Strong and agile, proud, independent, pure, and noble
Falcon - Adventurous, passionate, and leading
Fish - Graceful
Fox - Cunning, agile, quick-witted, diplomatic, wild; feminine in its magic of camouflage, shape-shifting and invisibility
Frog - Cleansing, transformative, sensitive, medicinal, undiscernibly beautiful and powerful
Gazelle - Aggressive
Goose - Self-demanding, reliable, prudent, rigid, vigilant, parental, and productive
Hawk - Informative, intuitive, victorious, healing, noble, cleansing, visionary, and protective
Horse – Independent, enduring, mobile, terrestrial, powerful, and free
Hummingbird - Pompous, timeless, healing, and combative
Jaguar - Chaotic and shape shifting
Lion - Family-oriented, strong, energetic, courageous, and protective
Lizard – Conservational and visionary
Llama - Comforting to others
Lynx - Discrete, protective, and guiding
Moose - Headstrong, enduring, steadfast, and wise
Mouse - Observant, orderly, organized, and detail oriented
Opossum - Diversionary, strategic, and deceptive
Otter - Playful, friendly, dynamic, joyful, helpful, and generous
Owl - Deceptive, clairvoyant, insightful, informative, detached, wise, changeable, and silent
Ox - Sacrificing and self-denying
Peacock - Immortal, dignified, and self-confident
Porcupine - Innocent, companionable, and trustworthy
Rabbit - Fearful, timid, nervous, humble, intuitive, and balanced.
Raccoon - Curious and clean
Raven - Introspective, courageous, self-knowing, healing, protective, tricky, and magical
Salmon - Proud, intense, confident, wise, inspiring, and rejuvenating
Seahorse - Confident and graceful
Seal - Loving, desirous, imaginative, creative, and dreamy
Shark - Predatory, enduring, and adaptable
Skunk - Noticeably present, and strong
Snake - Impulsive, hardheaded, transformative, healing, energetic, and wise
Squirrel - Organized and gathering
Stag - Leader, regenerative, giving of bounty, beauty, and mystical signs.
Swan - Graceful, balanced, innocent, soulful, loving, beautiful, self-possessed
Tiger - Strong, brave, powerful, and energetic
Turkey - Generous, life-giving, and self-sacrificing
Turtle - Nurturing, shy, and protective
Weasel - Strong, energetic, ingenious, and stealthy
Whale – Wise and giving
Wolf - Loyal, persevering, successful, intuitive, trainable, ritualistic, and spirited
Woodpecker - Sensitive, protective, and loyal

Ready..Set..Goals!
Submitted by Sam Steen and Joy Rose

School Level: Middle.

Goals: Students will:
1. Learn about short and long term goals.
2. Learn how to set S.M.A.R.T. goals for themselves, related to academic achievement.
3. Explore and discover the strategies necessary for reaching the goals that they set for themselves.

ASCA Standards:

Academic Development:

A:B2.1 Establish challenging academic goals in elementary, middle/jr. high and high school

A:B2.5 Use problem-solving and decision-making skills to assess progress toward educational goals.

Estimated Time: 45 minutes.

Materials: large stars cut out of construction paper, markers or colored pencils, colored index cards, hole puncher, and yarn.

Lesson

1. Share with students that in this lesson we will be discussing short-term and long-term goals. We will learn what these are and then we will set goals that we would like to achieve this school year. Ask for student volunteers to share how they would define short-term goals. One definition for short-term goals is *ones that you will achieve in the near future (e.g., in a day, within a week, or possibly within a few months).* Next, have students share how they would define long-term goals. One definition for long-term goals is *ones that you will achieve over a longer period of time (e.g., one semester, one year, five years, or twenty years).* Once the definitions have been explained and are understood by all, introduce students to the idea of creating S.M.A.R.T. goals. If necessary, the counselor should review the definition of each term of the S.M.A.R.T. goals.

S- specific (what exactly do you want to accomplish?)
M- measurable (how will you demonstrate that the goal has been met?)
A- attainable (what steps will you take to reach the goal?)
R- realistic (is your goal with-in your reach?)
T- timely (by when will you achieve your goal?) (5 minutes)

2. Ask students to brainstorm individually ONE short-term academic goal and ONE long-term academic goal that they would like to achieve over this school year. Remind students that we want to try and set S.M.A.R.T. goals for ourselves. Allow students time to think on their own and then discuss with two of their peers seated nearby. (5 minutes)

3. Give each student a cut-out star to write down the goals that they came up with. Have them write their long-term academic goal on one side and their short-term academic goal on the other side. (5 minutes)

4. Give students 4 or 5 colored index cards that have been cut in half. Ask them to write one strategy on each that will represent a step towards reaching their goal. Students can discuss with each other some possible strategies. (5 minutes)

5. After students have written their goals and the steps/strategies they think are necessary for reaching their goal, collect all stars and index cards. Pass out 1 star to each student making sure that no student receives their own star. After mixing up the index cards, display them on the floor or on a table. Ask students to select the steps that they think are needed to reach the goal that they were given. They can also create new steps for the goal they are working with if they think more are needed. After all students feel they have the steps required to reach the goal they are working with, have each student identify their goal and which steps/strategies they had written down at the start of the activity. Discuss with the students any differences the observed when working with each other's goals. (15 minutes)

6. After the conclusion of the class, using yarn in order to connect the index cards to the star, hang them up in your office for display if students are willing.

Processing Questions: (10 minutes)

✓ What was it like for you to set specific goals for this school year?
✓ How did you go about choosing the steps it would take to reach your goals?
✓ What can we do, as a class, to help each other be successful in reaching our goals this year?
✓ How should we go about checking in about our goals and progress?
✓ Who can you talk to about your goals with in school in the future?

Cautions: Some students may prefer that their goals not be displayed.

Adaptations: The conversation could be adapted to focus on personal goals, career goals, as well as more specific academic goals.

Suggestions on How to Integrate into Core Curriculum: This activity could be integrated by having students focus their goal-setting on specific subject areas. For example, in math the students could set goals based on the math standards. After taking their first test in the class, the teacher can share with students how they performed on each standard that was addressed on the test and students can set goals regarding how they hope to perform on those standards on the next test. The teachers could then be given the goals for their classroom, and to follow-up with student progress throughout the year.

Next Possible Lesson Plan Topics: Perseverance When Our Goals Become Hard to Reach, Asking for Help (self-advocacy), How Do Our Goals Effect Our Classroom Behavior?

About the Counselors:

Sam Steen, Ph.D. is an Associate Professor in School Counseling at George Washington University, Washington DC. slsteen@gwu.edu

Joy Rose is an 8th Grade Counselor, Columbia Heights Educational Campus, Washington, DC. joy.rose@dc.gov

School Counselors Share Their Favorite Classroom Guidance Activities

Character Traits and Qualities: Lesson 1 and 2

Submitted by Annette McClure

School Level: Middle.

Goals: Students will:
1. Learn about character traits.
2. Identify their top five character strengths and weaknesses.
3. Identify how they actively behave their top five character strengths and/or weaknesses in their words, attitudes and behaviors.
4. Recognize how character traits/qualities are reflected or presented in their attitudes and behaviors with individuals.
5. Take action to change character trait weaknesses into a character strength which influences students to learn and apply self-monitoring behavioral skills.

ASCA Standards:

PS: A1:1 Develop positive attitude toward self as a unique and worthy person
PS: A1.8 Understand the need for self-control and how to practice it
PS: A1.10 Identify personal strengths and assets.

Estimated Time: Two lessons 45-minutes each.

Materials: SMART Board, chalk board or flip chart; **Character Trait Worksheets** (McClure; 2014), notebook; pencils or pens; poster board or 8x11 white construction paper; crayons, colored pencils, or I-Pads to create video productions.

Lesson 1

1. To begin this activity, invite students into a discussion about character traits. Ask the students to identify someone they like to be around, someone they trust, a favorite person such as a parent, sibling, extended family member, teacher, coach, or etc. Write several on board.

2. Ask those students who provided the examples to describe why they like this person. Guide the responses by interjecting character traits or qualities from the character trait list. Write the student's response under the person they identified.

This will help students begin to recognize the meaning of the phrase *character trait* and the words *quality* and *quality* in correlation with others and themselves. It will also help them communicate the quality in relation to the following question.

3. Ask the students "What they think a character trait is?"

4. Ask the students to help you write a definition on the chalk or white board. Be sure to applaud the student definition; however, correct any misnomers in their definition by explaining to the students that ***a character trait is an quality or quality that describes a person.***

5. Further explain that character traits are also based on qualities we value and need. To help clarify this for the students:
   a. Ask students to consider the examples on the board.
   b. Ask them, why the character trait or quality listed might be of something they value within themselves or others?
   c. As them why the character trait or quality listed might be of something they need for themselves or from others? (10 minutes)

6. You can build on your students' understanding of how character traits are based on qualities we value and need by elaborating on the examples. For instance, utilize visualization to help students picture the value and/or need through storytelling or narrative.

The following is a sample scenario that you may copy and print to handout to your students. **<u>BE SURE to change the red italicized words so students do not know the answers.</u>** Note: You may personalize this activity by creating your own narrative.
   a. Have the students follow along as you read the narrative.
   b. Have the students circle what they believe are character traits and/or qualities in the scenario.
      ANSWERS: 24 character traits/qualities.

Scenario

Three 8ᵗʰ grade students, Mike, Sarah, and Tim, are waiting at school for their parents to pick them up. They are tired from their school day. Their parents are usually *punctual* when picking them up from school; however, today, their parents are late.

Another student, Lisa, who is a ninth grader, has driven up in a car. She has parked by the curb where the students are waiting for their parents. Lisa has her school permit so she drives her mother's car to school.

Lisa asks Mike, Sarah, and Tim if they want a ride home. Sarah says "No, I am going to wait for my mom to get here". Tim says, "Why? Lisa has a car and we can get home now"! I am tired of waiting around"! Sarah replies, "Lisa has her school permit which means Lisa is not supposed to be driving anyone else home". Mike is *impatient*. He says, "I want to be home now. I don't care if Lisa only has her school permit."

Sarah asks, Mike and Tim, "Do you want Lisa to get a ticket?" Lisa chimes in, "I won't get a ticket. No one will see us"! *Politely*, Sarah refuses the ride and tells Mike, Tim and Lisa that she will wait for her mother. Tim has thought about what Sarah has said. Sarah was *observant*. Tim believes Sarah has *courage* to say no. He thinks about what is mother and father would say. His parents would ask him if he had made a *responsible* choice.

Mike was *impatient*. He was *determined* to get home. Mike made the decision to have Lisa drive him home. He opened the door to Lisa's car, *fearlessly* got in the car, and shut the door behind him. As Lisa put the car into drive, Mike yelled out the window to Tim and Sarah, "Hey, see you two on the flip-side". I will be home and you two will still be here waiting for your parents!" Lisa drove off, stopping at the stop sign. She signaled to turn right and with wave to Sarah and Tim, Lisa and Mike were off in the direction of Mike's home. Mike turned to Lisa and said, "I don't have the *tolerance* to sit and wait!"

Sarah and Tim looked at each other and Sarah shook her head as she said to Tim, "I hope Lisa doesn't get stopped by a police man with Mike in her car". If she does, she won't be able to drive for a while". "Yeah", Tim responded, "That would stink"! "My parents would ground me if I didn't have the *integrity* (synonyms: *reliable*, *honest*, *trustworthy*) to follow the rules"! About three minutes after Lisa and Mike had left, Tim and Sarah's mothers appeared and pulled up to the curb, close to where Sarah and Tim were standing. Tim and Sarah said goodbye to each other as they walked to the cars.

When Sarah got into her mother's car, her mother said, "I am sorry I was late! Thank you for being so *patient*"! Sarah responded, "It is okay mother. I knew you would get here as soon as you could or you would have father get me".

At that same time, after Tim had gotten into his mother's car, Tim was explaining to his mother how Lisa had given Mike a ride home. "Mom", he said, "Lisa, only has her school permit." Tim's mother, hugged Tim, and *gently* said, "Tim, I *appreciate* that you made the *responsible* choice to wait here at the school for me." "I would have been so worried when I arrived and found you were not here. I would have been scared that something bad had happened to you". Tim answered, "Mom, even though I know I can *depend* upon you to be here after school to pick me up, I was tired. I am not going to lie Mom, I thought about getting a ride home from Lisa but Sarah *respectful* pointed out that Lisa only had her school permit and Lisa could get into trouble giving us a ride home. *Thanks* Mom for saying you *appreciate* that I made the right choice!"

Tim's mom made a right at the stop sign to go home. As Tim and his mother were nearing their street, Tim spotted Lisa and Mike pulled over at the curb with a police car behind them. A police man was talking with Lisa and Lisa was crying.

Tim looked at his mother and exclaimed with *optimism*, "Mom maybe the police man will just give her a warning this time." Tim's mom shook her head and said with *concern*, "Whether Lisa gets a ticket or not, I hope she lets her parents know what happened." Tim agreed.

7. By utilizing the funnel approach, students learn the connection between event, character trait/quality, behavior, and outcome and what the individual is "in control of". Here are some processing questions to help students funnel the learning information.

✓ Why is punctual something we value? In our scenario, why would it be important for the three students to remember that their parents are most often punctual?

✓ Mike is impatient; however, ask the students why Mike needs to be patient. (Mike needs to be patient because his parents are most often punctual and may arrive at any moment. Being impatient, Mike doesn't take the time to think through his choices.)

✓ Sarah answers politely. What if Sarah answered impolitely?

✓ How is being polite something we value? Or something we need?

✓ Sarah was observant. What was Sarah observant about?

✓ Was being observant something of value? (Yes, Sarah knew Lisa only had her school permit.)

School Counselors Share Their Favorite Classroom Guidance Activities

✓ Why would it be of value for Sarah to have courage to say no?
✓ Tim's parents value responsibility. Why would being responsible be of value?
✓ Mike's impatience influenced his decision to let Lisa give him a ride home. Mike has determination. Is having determination of value?
✓ Is Mike's determination something that is good or bad?
✓ How is Mike's fearlessness of value? Is that good or bad?
✓ Why is tolerance something of value?
✓ Why might you need others to be tolerant?
✓ What is integrity? Is it good to have integrity? What value does having integrity show? (It shows others that we are trustworthy, honest, and reliable. We mean what we say; and do what we say we will do.)

There are ten more character traits in the scenario. If time permits, go through the remaining ten. Create your own examples. (15 minutes)

8. Guide students into discussing attitudes and behaviors. You may ask what does attitude mean? ***Attitude is how you use your character trait/quality.*** To elaborate, you may say "When someone uses their voice loudly, that might be seen as showing attitude". (Students may challenge you here because sometimes when an individual is loud, it may be for other reasons such as someone being deaf. An easy way for us, as facilitators or teachers to remember the concept about attitude being how we use our character trait/quality, is to reflect about temperament. ***Temperament is attitude.*** Temperament isn't about being smart or talented, it refers to how we use our voice and our character traits/qualities in how we relate with other individuals. Ironically, temperament is also a character trait/quality.

9. After a short discussion on attitudes, guide students into a brief discussion about "what are behaviors". Behaviors are idiosyncrasies, quirks or habits that can be either good or bad. Behaviors are what we do (our actions). Provide students an example of both good and bad behaviors.

Good behaviors:	*Bad behaviors:*
Doing your homework	*Spitting*
Making your bed	*Not doing your chores*
Taking out the trash	*Not doing your homework*
Going to school	*Skipping school*
Wearing a coat	*Lying*
Helping others	*Talking back to parents/adults*
Telling the truth	*Gossiping*

10. Direct discussion to how character traits/qualities are reflected or presented in our attitudes and behaviors with other individuals. To simplify this for students, describe a situation to help students visualize how being kind can be reflected in an individual's attitude and behavior. I have provided several examples here.

"If I say I am kind, but I push others out of the line to get to the front of line, am I behaving kindly?"

More examples:

- "If I describe myself as having the character trait of being punctual but I am always late to class, am I behaving punctual?"
- "If I describe myself as having the character trait of being neat but my homework has scribbles and crossed out marks all over it, does my work show I am neat?"
- "If I describe myself as having a character trait for being honest, but I lie every day, am I behaving honestly?"
- "If I describe myself as having a character trait for being patient, but when playing games with friends, I demand them to hurry up because it is my turn, am I behaving with patience?"

(You may make up your own descriptors to show how we express our character traits/qualities through our behaviors and attitudes.)
(10 minutes)

11. Ask for volunteers to share what information they learned about character traits. (5 minutes)

Lesson 2

1. To begin, ask students to tell you what they remember from Session I. You may utilize processing questions such as those that follow:

✓ "What they think a character trait is?"
✓ "What is the definition is for character trait?
    (Write definition on chalk or white board. *A character trait is a quality or quality that describes a person.*)
✓ "What else character traits are based on? *Character traits are also based on qualities we value and need.*
✓ "What does attitude means? *Attitude is how you use your character trait/quality. Our attitude is reflecting our temperament. Temperament is not about being smart or talents, it refers to how we utilize our voice and character traits/qualities combined when we relate and/or communicate with other individuals.*

✓ Remind students that behaviors are what we do. Ask the students for a few good and a few bad behaviors. Write their suggestions on the chalk or white board.

✓ Ask students how character traits/qualities are reflected or presented in our attitudes and behaviors? *You may use the examples in Step 8 from Session l.*

2. Handout **Character Trait Worksheets** for Parts 1 & 2 (McClure; 2014). Go over the directions for activity. Use your personal character traits/qualities to provide examples on the chalk or white board. (10 minutes)

3. Have students number off and gather into small groups. Utilizing Handout, have students complete both worksheets individually. Explain to students that once they have completed worksheets, they may discuss their findings with group. Group members may offer suggestions to each other at how to change a character weakness to a character strength.

NOTE: Observe and listen to each groups discussion; redirecting back to topic if necessary. Listen for negative criticism among students; redirect negative criticism to positive criticism. (25 minutes)

4. Bring groups back together. To process lesson, ask for volunteers to:
   a. Summarize their findings for character strengths and weaknesses
   b. Ask them to share how they present their strengths in their attitude and behavior.
   c. Ask them to share what they have learned from the two lessons.

5. Summarize lesson. Ask your students to reflect on their findings and to be observant of character traits/qualities for next lesson's discussion. (10 minutes)

6. **BONUS:** The bonus is for students to *practice* turning one identified character trait/quality weakness into a strength. Encourage students to practice changing the character trait/quality weakness to character trait/quality strength for a month. Have students write about what they begin to notice about themselves and what they begin to observe and notice from other individuals when they display the character trait/quality weakness as a character trait/quality strength.

For example: I am not good a practicing patience. I challenge myself daily to practice patience. I reflect on how effective I was in displaying patience. More importantly, and subsequently, I begin to notice how having patience positively influences my relationship with other individuals.

NOTE: Encourage those students that participate in the bonus to write about their experience in one month. Ask students to share their findings with the class at later date. For those students that write about their experience, offer a "free bonus" for an assignment of equal value.

Cautions: Some students might require help developing sentences as well as integrating knowledge. Time limit may increase depending on students' needs and discussion.

Adaptations: Activity may be adapted for varying learning styles such as having younger students create a visual of their self-displaying a character trait and/or quality. Role-plays may be developed to help middle and/or high school students practice utilizing character-traits and/or qualities.

Credit/References

This lesson is modified from cognitive-behavioral material I created for a 12-week group for the Nebraska Probation program RISE-Rural Improvement for Schooling and Employment. For more information visit the website at: http://www.probation.rise.nebraska.gov/.

Next Possible Lesson Topics: Leadership, how to overcome obstacles and/or challenges, developing actions plans, trust, setting and obtaining goals, managing differences, developing values, how to make good decisions, communication, and motivation.

About the Counselor:

Annette has over 28 years of experience working with both youth and adults ages 4 to 65 years as a Certified Nurse's Aide, Daycare Provider, CCD (Sunday school) Teacher, substitute Teacher, Family Service Provider, Community Treatment Aide, Mental Health/Alcohol & Drug Counselor-in-Training and a Child Family Services Specialist. She is a provisionally licensed Mental Health Practitioner. annette.mcclure@doane.edu

Character Traits Handout (McClure, 2014)
Part 1

The following worksheet has a list of character traits. 1.) **Look up all the character traits or qualities. 2.) Using a separate sheet of paper, write the character trait or quality. 3.) Beside each character trait or quality, write the definition.**

Adaptable	Appreciative or Appreciation
Attentive	Available
Caring	Committed or Commitment
Compassionate	Concern
Confident or Confidence	Considerate
Consistent	Contentment
Cooperative	Courageous
Creative	Decisive
Deference	Dependable
Determined	Diligent
Discrete	Efficient
Fair	Faith
Fearless or Fearlessness	Flexible
Forgiving	Friendly
Generous	Gentle
Gracious	Giving
Honest	Humble
Integrity	Joyful
Kind	Love
Loyalty	Meek
Merciful	Observant
Optimism	Patience
Peaceful	Perseverance
Persistent	Persuasive
Prudence	Punctual
Purposeful	Resourceful
Respect	Responsibility
Security	Self-Control
Sincerity	Submissiveness
Tactful	Temperance
Through	Thrifty
Tolerance	Trustworthy
Truthfulness	Virtue

Part 2: Complete all five directions.

1. Review the list and circle 5 of the character traits that you think best describes your character traits/qualities strengths.
2. Write a sentence for each of your 5 character traits/qualities showing how your behavior and attitude displays your character traits/qualities as a strength.

Example: Character Trait/Quality strength-**CIVIL**
Civil means "displaying accepted social behavior such as being polite, not rude".
My sentence: I _will continue to be_ **civil** when in the lunch line or waiting for my turn.

7. _____

8. _____

9. _____

10. _____

11.   _____

3. Write Review the list and put an "X" on the 5 character traits that you think best describes your character traits/qualities weaknesses.

4. Write a sentence for each of your 5 character traits/qualities showing how your behavior and attitude displays your character traits/qualities as a strength.

Example: Character Trait/Quality weakness-**Punctual**
Punctual means, "arriving on time".
My sentence: I _will practice being_ **punctual by being on time for my classes.**

1. _____

2. _____

3. _____

4. _____

5. _____

Teaching Students to Ask for Help

Submitted by KaMeshia Baskin,
Rebecca Hoover, and Kerrie R. Fineran

Target Population: Middle.

Goals: Students will learn:
1. Who to ask for help and how to ask for help.
2. What steps to take when they have a problem they cannot solve themselves.
3. Skills that they have to be a helper.

ASCA Standards:

Standard B: Students will make decisions, set goals and take necessary action to achieve goals.

Estimated Time: 50 minutes.

Materials: *The Helping Model Handout* (adapted from Dougherty, 2005; Parsons & Kahn, 2005) (one for each student and Counselor); leader-created scenarios in which students may need to ask for help (these can be adapted to the needs of the classroom. An example scenario is outlined below), short movie clip featuring an adolescent with a problem (e.g., *Mean Girls, Cyberbully or Degrassi High)* (optional).

Lesson

1. Introduce the activity to students by saying, "Has anyone ever had a problem that you weren't sure how to handle or who to even go to for help?" You may ask students to think about a time when they experienced this or ask students to share examples with the group, depending on time. Continue by saying, "Today we're going to talk about how to ask for help and how to discern who might be a good person to ask for the help you need. We will talk about a step by step guide for how to ask an adult for help. We will also consider when, where, and how to seek help for solving problems and making decisions." (2 to 3 minutes)

2. Show a movie clip of a child in need or in trouble to begin the lesson. (optional) (5 minutes)

3. Next, define consultation, consultant (could also identify as "helper"), and consultee (could also identify as "help seeker") for the students. (5 minutes)

4. Discuss characteristics of a good consultant/helper and a good consulting relationship (this can be in brainstorm form with the students). Group leaders may want to ask students to think about the characteristics of person that they trust and of whom they have asked for help before. Characteristics to consider might be knowledgeable, experienced, good listener, dependable, etc. (5 minutes)

5. Invite students to brainstorm ideas on ways characters in the clip (or in the examples that students identified earlier if not using a media clip) could have asked for help and solved their problems. Ask students to consider which specific adults the consultees/ help seekers might have gone to go to for help such as counselors, teachers, etc. Also consider asking them what they learned about whom not to ask for help. (5 minutes)

6. Discuss *The Helping Model Handout* with students and go through the process of how to ask for help. (10 minutes)

7. To complete the lesson, have students practice asking for help within small groups with different scenarios. Break the class up into groups of 3-5 students. Hand out scenarios for each of the groups to process and practice who and how to ask for help. Ask the students to consider different options and weigh the pros and cons of each option. (10 minutes).

Example Scenario: Becky is upset because she found out that her best friend has been spreading a rumor about her. She feels betrayed by her friend and wants to confront her, however, she does not know what to say. Becky is not sure who to go to or how to ask for help solving this problem. What are some of Becky's options?

128

Processing Questions/Conclusions:

- ✓ What could be the effects of choosing the wrong person for advice?
- ✓ How would you know when you need to seek help or assistance from an adult?
- ✓ Has anyone ever asked you for help or advice? What was that like?
- ✓ How can you see yourself using this model in the future?
- ✓ How can you use what you learned to eventually become a consultant/helper and assist others when they have problems?

Cautions: Caution students to always seek the help of an adult if they or someone they know has suicidal thoughts or they become aware of any other dangerous situation. A good time to discuss this is during the processing time, when asking the question, "How would you know when you need to seek help or assistance from an adult?"

Adaptations: This model could also be used with students to set goals. Counselors can use the model to teach students how to set goals, implement plans that are created during consultation, and evaluate the plan to determine its effectiveness.

References

Dougherty, M. A. (2005). *Psychological consultation and collaboration in school and community settings.* Belmont, CA: Thomson Brooks/Cole.

Parsons, R., & Kahn, W. (2005). *The school counselor as consultant: An integrated model for school-based consultation.* Belmont, CA: Thomson Brooks/Cole.

About the Counselors:

KaMeshia Baskin and *Rebecca Hoover* are Graduate Students and School Counseling Interns at Indiana University-Purdue University, Fort Wayne.

Kerrie R. Fineran is an Assistant Professor and Coordinator of School Counseling at Indiana University-Purdue University, Fort Wayne and a licensed School Counselor. finerank@ipfw.edu.

The Helping Model
(adapted from Dougherty, 2005; Parsons & Kahn, 2005)

Stages	Purpose
Entry- allow the consultant/helper to get a general feel for the problem	Make contact with perspective consultant/helper Ask politely for their assistance (use appropriate social skills) Provide information and details about the problem to the consultant/helper
Diagnose- provide information, define the problem, set goals and brainstorm possible solutions	Provide information to consultant/helper Explain the problem to the consultant/helper Provide multiple examples of the problem Communicate desired solution to the problem Consultee/Seeker can also provide information, suggestions, and potential solutions Work with the consultant/helper to pick a plan that best fits the consultee/seeker's needs
Implementation- Choose an intervention, formulate a plan, implement the plan and evaluate the plan	Follow through with the advice given Other stakeholders may get involved such as parents, friends, siblings, teachers, school administrators, and members of the community
Disengagement-evaluate the process of consultation, wind down	Decide if plan is working- if not, reevaluate If working, reinforce and discuss problems that may arise in the future Thank the consultant/helper for their help

Vocabulary:
- **Consultant/Helper**: A knowledgeable person who provides experience or expert advice to those who need help.
- **Consultee/Seeker**: Person seeking the advice or help of knowledgeable adult.
- **Consultation**: The exchanging of ideas, experiences, and advice between two or more people.

(definitions adapted from Dougherty, 2005)

Introduction of School Counselors and Middle School Needs Survey

Submitted by Tracy Rabey, Denise Scheig, Marla Varrone, and Maureen Brett

School Level: Middle.

Goals: To introduce the Pupil Personnel Staff and identify students who may need support.

ASCA Standards:

PS: A2.6 Use effective communication skills
PS: B1.3 Identify alternative solutions to a problem
PS: B1.5 Demonstrate when, where and how to seek help for solving problems and making decisions
PS: C1.5 Differentiate between situations requiring peer support and situations requiring adult professional help.

Estimated Time: 20 Minutes.

Materials: **Needs Survey** - 1 for each student, pen or pencil.

Lesson

1. Counselors should introduce themselves to the students. If this is a group of new students, describe what and where the counseling department is and the services they offer.
2. Counselor begins with: "The counseling department is available for any student that has any concern about school, home, or themselves. We can work with students on academic and organization skills, coping with difficult issues at home or with friends, and we are always available to talk with you if you're struggling with something on your own. Sometimes, like today, we will come into your classroom to facilitate different activities. Other times (if your school provides group counseling) we provide group counseling if a set of students struggling with similar issues. Lastly, counselors can meet individually with students who are having trouble in school."

3. Counselors will pass out the **Needs Survey** to students. State that it is to be kept completely confidential so please no sharing answers and no looking at anyone else's paper. Tell them it is voluntary survey and that if they choose to fill it out, only the counselors will see what they have written. The survey will give counselors information about possible issues that students may be struggling with, and they will use it to see what they can to do help. (If doing this in small groups, take students to the guidance office to make them feel more comfortable and ensure confidentiality.

4. Explain each question, differentiating between what is normal and what is cause for concern. For example with number 1: Feeling angry sometimes is normal, however if you often find yourself getting angry about things and are unable to control it, you should mark this as a concern. Complete this with the three designated areas of Self, Home/Family, and School.

5. Explain that the fourth section is to tell the counselor a little bit more about the student.

6. Tell the students that the bottom section is very important. If there is anything on the survey or that is NOT listed on the survey that you'd like to talk about with your counselor, please indicate that on the bottom. If there is nothing, please write "none".

7. See students individually for the areas of concern that they indicated and determine the appropriate course of action.

Cautions:
Immediately after receiving the surveys, the counselor should scan through them to identify high risk students. The students that indicated urgent areas of concern should be seen before those with lower-risk concerns.

Adaptations:
This may also be used at the high school level. Questions may be simplified and condensed to be appropriate for elementary students as well.

About the School Counselors:
Tracy Rabey (trabey@lancaster.wnyric.org), *Marla Varrone* (mvarrone@lancaster.wnyric.org), *Denise Scheig* (dscheig@lancaster.wnyric.org), and *Maureen Brett* (mbrett@lancaster.wnyric.org) are School Counselors at Lancaster Middle School in Lancaster, NY.

NAME: _____ DATE: _____

LANCASTER MIDDLE SCHOOL
Local Counseling Needs ● Middle School Survey
NOTE: THIS SURVEY IS VOLUNTARY

☐ I have concerns about **MYSELF**

☐ Anger	☐ Eating Disorder	☐ Sadness	☐ Drug/Alcohol Use
☐ Friendship	☐ Stress	☐ Self-harm	☐ Overall Health/Weight
☐ Other (Explain on lines)			

_____

☐ I have concerns about **HOME/FAMILY**

☐ Fighting	☐ Divorce/Seperation	☐ Loss of a loved one
☐ Sick Family Member	☐ Drug/Alcohol Use	☐ Other (Explain on lines below)

_____

☐ I have concerns about **SCHOOL**

☐ Fighting	☐ Grades	☐ Attendance
☐ Bully Issues	☐ Dropping Out	☐ Other (Explain on lines below)

_____

☐ I am happy to be a student at LMS!
☐ I am happy to be me!
☐ I have no concerns at this time, but will contact my counselor if necessary.
☐ I am involved in one or more groups/organizations. *Please List:*

_____
_____

☐ I have something I would like to discuss with my counselor.

I would like to see my counselor   ☐ ASAP (Emergency)   ☐ Non-Emergency

_____
_____

COUNSELOR FOLLOW-UP
LANCASTER MIDDLE SCHOOL
Local Counseling Needs ● Middle School Survey

Puzzling Communication

Submitted by Ashley Kilgore, Ashley Freels, and Kerrie R. Fineran

School Level: Middle.

Goals: Students will:
1. Learn to differentiate between verbal and nonverbal communication.
2. Be able to describe verbal (speaking) and nonverbal communication (listening and behaviors).

ASCA Standards:
PS: A2.7—know that communication involves speaking, listening, and nonverbal behavior.

Estimated Time: 40 minutes.

Materials: Four "25 to 50" piece puzzles (2 pairs of identical puzzles) (difficulty of the puzzle should be related to the age of the students) with several pieces removed from one set of the puzzles. These sets will be used for the second portion of the activity. For 25 piece puzzles, remove 4 pieces and for 50 piece puzzles remove 10 pieces. Note: if group size is more than 20, use an additional set of puzzles.

Lesson

1. Begin with: "The purpose of this activity is to introduce you to the topic of communication. By participating, you will be able to describe the differences between verbal and nonverbal communication and how they enable us to interpret messages from others."

2. Continue: "I am going to divide you into 2 groups. We go around the room and count off by 2 (by 3 if there are three groups) to split into our groups." After splitting in into groups, say: "Each group will be given a puzzle and will have three minutes to work as a group to complete as much of the puzzle as possible. You may talk to and consult with each other in your small group." (The first puzzle given to groups should include all the puzzle pieces).

3. After 3 minutes, the school counselor asks the following processing questions:
- ✓ How did your group members communicate with each other to put together the puzzle?
- ✓ How difficult was it for you to understand your group members?
- ✓ Who can tell me some of the different ways of speaking used in your group? (examples: volume, tone of voice). (7 to 8 minutes)

4. For round two, each group should be given a different puzzle (missing pieces puzzle) and instructed "Please do not speak with each other as you try to complete this puzzle for three minutes but you may communicate nonverbally."

5. The school counselor then asks the following process questions:
- ✓ How did you "talk" with your group members without speaking out loud?
- ✓ What was it like for you to have to work together without speaking?
- ✓ With the second puzzle, your group was missing several pieces of the puzzle just like you were missing a piece of communication, speaking.
- ✓ Who can name some types of nonverbal behaviors? (7 to 8 minutes)

6. Final Processing Questions: (10 minutes)
- ✓ What did we do? Why do you think we did it?
- ✓ What was it like to do it?
- ✓ Why it is important for us to be able to communicate with others?
- ✓ In what ways can you make sure you understand what others are communicating to you? How can you make sure other people understand what you are trying to communicate to them?
- ✓ How can you apply what we learned about communication to your life?
- ✓ What is one change you can make in your communication style? Commit to something that you do not do now but think is pretty attainable goal for you to achieve.

Cautions: The goal is not for the students to be able to complete the puzzle but to focus on the process of working together. Therefore, be sure to choose a puzzle the will not be easily completed within three minutes.

Adaptations: Assign one student from each group to wear a blindfold or earplugs during the activity. After each round, ask group members what they did to help this member participate in the activity. More puzzles can be utilized depending on the numbers of students you want to have in each group. It could also be useful to have various "puzzle stations" around the room that each have different rules and have the groups rotate to the various stations. For example, one station could involve trying to complete the puzzle blindfolded, another where students can only communicate with one another in writing, and another where students can only use one hand each to complete the puzzle.

About the Counselors:

Ashley Kilgore and *Ashley Freels* are Graduate Students at Indiana-University Purdue University, Fort Wayne and are both currently School Counseling Interns.

Kerrie R. Fineran is an Assistant Professor and School Counseling Coordinator at University Purdue University Fort Wayne, and is a licensed School Counselor. kilgoreashleye@gmail.com.

Getting Help: The Art of Asking Questions

Submitted by Lia D. Falco, Tyler Williams, and Kathleen Conner

School Level: Middle.

Goals:
1. Improve self-efficacy, and increase students' self-reflection and metacognition as they learn to recognize the need for help.
2. Reinforce students' ability to overcome threats to self-worth when asking for help.
3. Increase feelings of autonomy through instrumental help-seeking behaviors.

ASCA Standards:
A:A1.1 Articulate feelings of competence and confidence as learners
A:A2.3 Use communication skills to know when and how to ask for help when needed
A:B.1.4 Seek information and support from faculty, staff, family, and peers.

Estimated Time: 45 to 50 minutes.

Materials: **Getting Help** (Falco, 2008) worksheet and example "problem-scenarios" for each group.

Lesson

1. (5 minutes) Begin lesson with a class discussion, asking students to share their thoughts about getting help and the feelings they experience when asking questions in class. The counselor should ask the following questions:
   ✓ "How many of you feel comfortable asking questions during class?"
   ✓ "Can you think of a time when you wanted to ask a question in class but didn't?"
   ✓ "What prevented you from asking a question when you needed to?"
2. (2 minutes) The counselor should help students process their responses to the questions by reflecting back the common themes. For example, the counselor might say, "It sounds like many of you refrain from asking questions because you don't want to feel stupid or

embarrassed, or you can't seem to find the right time to ask, or you don't know how to ask the right question."

3. (3 to 5 minutes) The counselor should then explain that these feelings are very common, and that almost everyone has avoided asking a question at some point during their life. The counselor should summarize by saying, "The important thing to remember is that knowing when and how to ask questions might be the most important thing you'll ever learn in school. Remember that everyone has different strengths and abilities, and thinking about your strengths as a learner can make you feel more confident when you are asking questions. Asking questions helps *everyone* learn – not just the person who asked. Today, you will learn how to ask 'instrumental questions.' Instrumental questions are the kind of questions that help you the most because the person you are asking will have to give you *more* information. It's like getting more for your money. Later, you will hear examples of instrumental and non-instrumental questions."

4. (3 to 5 minutes) The counselor should introduce the activity by explaining that there will be three things to do for the rest of the lesson. First, there will be a brainstorm. Next, students will work in small groups to practice asking questions. Last, the small groups will share their ideas with the whole class.

5. (3 minutes) Ask students to brainstorm out loud their strengths as learners. Examples of strengths are: fast reader, good listener, good at memorizing, being organized. If they have trouble getting started, ask students to share what they think their classmates' strengths are. After students are done brainstorming, the counselor should help them process by asking, "Was it easy or hard to think of strengths? How did if feel when you did this?"

6. (15 minutes) The counselor should divide class into small groups of 4 to 5 students. Going around the room, have the students call out a number from one to four or five. Then, have all the "Ones" sit together; all the "Twos" sit together; all the "Threes" sit together, etc., until everyone is in a small group. Next, the counselor should distribute a "problem-scenario" to each group. The counselor should instruct the groups to work together using their worksheets to describe the problem in the scenario, the feelings/emotions of the person experiencing the problem, and possible questions to ask in order to get help solving the problem.

7. (15 minutes) When groups finish, ask each group to share their "problem scenario" with the class, along with the questions they created to help solve the problem. The counselor should facilitate discussion by giving feedback about the questions each group generated, pointing out when students generate an "instrumental question." When pointing out examples of instrumental questions, the counselor should briefly explain how the question helps you learn more:

- Not instrumental: "I don't understand" (teacher might simply repeat the same information)
- Instrumental: "I don't understand why you did ..." (teacher will explain the steps)
- Not instrumental: "Can you do problem 17?" (teacher might just do the problem for you)
- Instrumental: "Can you show me how to start problem 17?" (teacher will get you started, but you will finish and probably remember how to do it again)

End the lesson by emphasizing the importance of getting help when you need it. The counselor should validate help-seeking behaviors as an important strategy for managing the learning process. For example, the counselor can conclude by saying, "Most people can't learn everything the first time they are taught. In order to really understand something, it is essential to ask questions. Sometimes, you might not ask a question when you really need to. Today, you learned new ways to ask questions that will hopefully make you feel more confident so that you will ask questions to you and your classmates learn more."

Cautions: This lesson should be given in the context of improving study skills. Because this activity requires a certain degree of trust and collaboration that other lessons might not, outcomes will be better if students have an established rapport with the counselor.

Adaptations: Different "problem scenarios" for other learning contexts or subjects. Or students create their own scenarios.

Suggestions on How to Integrate into Core Curriculum: This activity could be integrated into a larger unit on study skills and/or prior to the introduction new math or science concepts in math or science classes. For example, a teacher might be introducing algebra for the first time in a 6th grade math class. Prior to the start of a new math unit, the counselor could deliver this lesson and discuss with students the importance of using their new skills as they begin the new unit with their teacher.

Next Possible Lesson Plan Topics: Study skills (e.g., time management and test preparation), Goal-setting (setting attainable academic goals). These skills can and be specific to the subject area (e.g., math or science).

Credit/References

Falco, L. D. (2008). *"Skill-builders": Enhancing middle school students' self-efficacy and adaptive learning strategies in mathematics."* Doctoral dissertation. UMI Proquest Disserations, 3303631.

Karabenik, S. A., & Newman, R. S. (Eds.). (2006). *Help seeking in academic settings: Goals, groups, and contexts.* Mahwah, NJ: Lawrence Erlbaum Associates.

About the Counselors: *Lia D. Falco*, Ph.D., is an Assistant Professor of Practice, and *Tyler Williams* and *Kathleen Conner* are M.Ed. Candidates in the School Counseling Program in the Department of Disability and Psychoeducational Studies Department at the University of Arizona. Dr. Falco also is a certified School Counselor and former Middle School Counselor. ldf@email.arizona.edu

Mr. Williams is a School Counselor at Sahuarita High School, AZ.

Ms. Conner is a School Counselor at Lauffer Middle School in Tucson, AZ.

Possible "problem-scenarios"

- Gabriel missed a few days of school last week because he was sick. His parents picked up his homework for him, and he did most of it before coming back to school today. There were some things he didn't understand because he wasn't in class, and now he is even more behind today because the whole class has moved on to a new chapter.
- Amelia has always been really good at math and gets good grades. She got off to a good start this year, but lately the class seems to be moving kind of fast, and everyone else seems to be understanding things better than she is. Sometimes her teacher skips steps when showing the class how to solve new problems.
- Alex usually feels comfortable asking questions in class. Today, his teacher said something that he didn't understand, so he raised his hand and said, "I don't understand." When his teacher explained it again, Alex was still confused.
- Rachel's class is learning to solve algebra equations. Rachel thought she understood everything the teacher covered last week, but when it came time to take the quiz Rachel couldn't remember the steps and didn't do very well. The test is at the end of the week.

School Counselors Share Their Favorite Classroom Guidance Activities

Getting Help Practice Worksheet

Name:_____

Directions: Read over your "problem-scenario" with your group, and answer the questions on the worksheet. Remember to use your "feeling" words to describe emotions.

1. What makes this situation a
    problem?_____
    _____
    _____
    _____
    _____

2. How do you think this person is
    feeling?_____
    _____
    _____
    _____
    _____

3. What can this person do to solve the
    problem?_____
    _____
    _____
    _____

4. Give one or two examples of questions this person can ask to get
    help._____
    _____
    _____
    _____
    _____

Choose Your Own Ending

Submitted by Sonji D. Gregory, M.A. PCC-S

School Level: Middle/High.

Goals: Students will:
1. Learn to identify potential consequences using real-life situations.
2. Learn problem solving skills, brainstorming strategies, and alternative action steps for making informed real life decisions.
3. Assess the likelihood of negative choices that produce negative consequences.

ASCA Standards:

Standard A: Students will acquire the knowledge, attitudes and interpersonal skills to help them understand and respect self and others.
PS:A1.6 Distinguish between appropriate and inappropriate behavior
PS:A1.8 Understand the need for self-control and how to practice it
Standard B: Students will make decisions, set goals and take necessary action to achieve goals.
PS:B1.2 Understand consequences of decisions and choices
PS:B1.3 Identify alternative solutions to a problem
Standard C: Students will understand safety and survival skills.
PS:C1.7 Apply effective problem-solving and decision-making skills to make safe and healthy choices.

Estimated Time: 45 minutes to an hour.

Materials: One or more pre-selected age appropriate news articles from a reputable news source. The article(s) need to address a news event without giving away the ending. Favorite articles can be laminated for use again in future classes. Be sure to keep the ending a surprise. The ending should be consistent with the goal of the exercise. For example you may want to avoid an article where the student gets away with a crime. The news event should not be so well known as to spoil the ending.

Article Example (with link):
http://www.nytimes.com/2011/02/02/us/02bully.html?_r=0

The above article is about seven students that bullied a young boy outside his school. The students were eventually arrested. In this example you will see that it would be important for the counselor not to read the title because it would tell the students that the seven boys were eventually arrested. The article also mentions the arrest in a couple of the paragraphs throughout the story. The counselor would need to copy and paste the article into a Word Document. Remove all references to the conclusion of the story. The counselor will read the removed sections of the article at the end of the exercise. By preparing the revised article ahead of time, the counselor will prevent accidently revealing the ending.

Special Directions: The counselor should prepare several alternative endings prior to presenting the activity to the students. These endings are used to assist the groups if they get stuck while brainstorming endings. Use your examples sparingly to generate more ideas for the students. Do not use the true ending as an example. Examples of alternative endings for the above article: 1. The seven boys were given detention 2. The seven boys became more popular at school with their friends 3. The seven boys were given a warning. 4. The seven boys were never located and got away with it.

Lesson

1. The counselor gives very little introduction to the students. "This is a real news article and this event actually occurred. As you listen to me read the article think about how this event might end. If you have heard this news story before and already know the ending please raise your hand and I will read another article. It is key that no one knows the ending."
2. The counselor will read news article (not including the ending) to the entire class. (10 minutes)
3. Students are then asked to brainstorm different possible endings to the article with one other classmate. Students should be encouraged to use their own life experiences to generate ideas. One of the students will write down the ideas for their pairing. (15 minutes)
4. The counselor will then ask all the students to return to the large group discussion and share outcomes. The counselor will write down all outcomes suggested on the whiteboard. The counselor can add

additional prepared endings at this time if they are not mentioned by the students. After the students have chosen several possible endings, the counselor will ask the students to share which outcome they believe is most likely. The counselor should encourage the students to explain why they think one ending is more probable than some of the others. (15 minutes)

5. After the students discuss the possible endings, the counselor can read the real ending to the story. (5 minutes)

6. Processing Questions (15 minutes)

✓ Do you think that the individual(s) thought about the possible consequences before the incident occurred? Why didn't the individual(s) make a different choice?

✓ Do you think the same consequence would happen to you if you made the same decision? Why or Why not?

✓ What strengths do you possess that would assist you in making a better choice? Who else could influence your decision in either positive or negative ways?

✓ What could the individual(s) have chosen to do differently? How would this have changed the way the news story ended?

Cautions: This article must be selected specifically for the group it will be used with and should deal with subjects that are age appropriate and contextually appropriate for a school setting. Some articles may contain language that needs to be edited.

Adaptations: The counselor can offer several possible endings for the children instead of asking the students to generate various endings to make the activity considerably shorter.

About the Counselor:

Sonji D. Gregory M.A. PCC-S is an Adjunct Professor in Counseling Program at Malone University and a Ph.D. Student at Regent University. sonjgre@mail.regent.edu

Group Cohesion Web

Submitted by Jessica Eisenman

School Level: Middle/High.

Target Population: Grades 6 to 12.

Goals: Students will:
1. Increase their awareness of their own actions and the actions of others.
2. Become aware of how the actions of themselves and others can affect the climate and cohesion of a group setting.
3. Distinguish between positive and negative behaviors in a group.
4. Recognize the connection between actions and consequences.

ASCA Standards:

PS:A1.6 Distinguish between appropriate and inappropriate behavior
PS:A1.8 Understand the need for self-control and how to practice it
PS:A1.9 Demonstrate cooperative behavior in groups
PS:B1.2 Understand consequences of decisions and choices.

Estimated Time: 45 minutes.

Materials: One large ball of yarn, large paper and writing utensil or chalkboard.

Lesson

1. Counselor begins with: We will be participating in an interactive activity. We need to develop (or review) our classroom rules. Ask a student recorder to record the group rules on the large paper or chalkboard. The following are examples of group rules:
2. Take turns speaking.

3. Follow directions given by the School Counselor.
4. Show respect for others by listening when they are speaking and being aware of your facial expressions and comments. Only make positive, constructive comments when it is your turn.
5. Counselor then says: Group cohesion emphasizes connectedness among members which leads to feelings of unity and safety. Cohesion is defined as "togetherness" and "interconnectedness."
6. Ask students what this means to them. Highlight answers such as "we all affect each other" and "we are all connected."
7. Counselor says: The purpose of this activity is to demonstrate how we are connected and can influence each other.
8. Ask students to discuss the positive ways in which individual behavior can affect the entire group, such as arriving to class on time, completing homework, raising a hand to speak, actively participating, asking questions, etc.
9. Instruct the students to stand in a circle.
    a. Describe to the students that each person will take a turn catching and tossing the ball of yarn while holding onto one piece of it.
    b. Holding a ball of yarn, identify one positive thing that you contribute to the classroom before tossing the ball of yarn to a student. (If students appear uncomfortable verbalizing positive self-statements, suggest that they identify something nice about the person who they throw the ball to next.)
    c. Then, hold the end of the yarn tightly in your hand while tossing the ball of yarn to someone across from you in the circle. (You should still be holding the end of the yarn at this point and the other person should catch the ball of yarn, creating a line, or connection between you.)
    d. The other person states positive one thing they contribute and then passes the ball of yarn to another person, while holding onto it. (The result is a yarn line between you and the person you threw it to, and that person and the person he/she threw it to.) (If students have difficulty identifying positive contributions to the group, solicit input from other group members or provide examples.)

10. After everyone has taken a turn, the result is a web, or a net-looking form between all of the group members. Discuss with them how our choices and behaviors not only impact ourselves, but the class as a whole, as well. Describe how each student is capable of making positive and negative choices.
11. Lead a discussion about group cohesion, how each member has the potential to impact others in a positive way, and how when we are all respectful, we can form a tight-knit group.
12. Then ask several members to drop their end of the yarn. The result is a weakened web. Assist group members in identifying what type of behaviors, comments, attitudes, and assumptions may weaken the group cohesion. Give specific questions and what comments you would want to highlight.
13. Ask for a volunteer to gather the yarn from each member and instruct students to return to their seats.
14. Ask these processing questions:
✓ How do you feel as a member of this class? What types of behaviors have influenced your feeling? What level of support do you feel (on a scale of 1-5)?
✓ What are the benefits of having a cohesive class? What behaviors lead to group cohesion?
✓ How does it affect you when the group cohesion is weakened?
✓ What can each one of us do to strengthen or cohesion? (Record on large paper or chalkboard.)
15. End with a positive comment that emphasizes positive behaviors that lead to cohesion.

About the Counselor:

Jessica Eisenman is currently the Program Director of School-Based Behavioral Health Services (a collaboration between Family Service & Children's Aid Society and Oil City Area School District) and also a Ph.D. Student in Counselor Education and Supervision from Regent University. She is a certified School Counselor in Pennsylvania and licensed Professional Counselor in Pennsylvania with an MA in School Counseling from Edinboro University, PA. jessei1@mail.regent.edu

Time Quadrants

Submitted by Hilary Parsons, MEd, LPC

School Level: Middle/High.

Goals: Students will:
1. Identify how four quadrants apply to self.
2. Prioritize daily activities.

ASCA Standards:
C:A2 Develop employment readiness
C:A2.1 Acquire employability skills such as working on a team, problem-solving and organizational skills
C:A2.8 Understand the importance of responsibility, dependability, punctuality, integrity and effort in the workplace
C:A2.9 Utilize time-management and task-management skills.

Materials: 4 different color highlighters/markers per student (red, blue, yellow and orange), board and writing utensil for counselor, *REAL SCHEDULE* Handouts (Parsons, 2014), *TIME QUADRANTS* Handouts (adapted from Covey, 1998) Handout, and *IDEAL SCHEDULE* Handouts (Parsons, 2014).

Estimated Time: Pre-Group assessment activity: 10 minutes; lesson, 60 minutes.

Special Directions: Prior to the lesson, ask students to complete *REAL SCHEDULE* and bring to classroom guidance lesson. (If students have difficulty completing and returning the handout, complete it one-on-one or make time to complete during group.) In person or through written direction, inform students: *"Where does all your time go? Using your REAL SCHEDULE, complete step 1 and write down what you do this week. Be as accurate as possible. If you planned to wake-up on Sunday at 9AM to start your homework, but you really got up at 10AM and watched TV for an hour, write that. Bring to the classroom guidance lesson."*

Lesson

1. Counselor begins with: *"Time is like a suitcase; you can pack a lot in when things are organized (Covey, 1998). This activity will teach you how to be effective with time management, so you can pack more into your day. We are going to learn how to work smarter, not harder. Sometimes it's tough to prioritize what to do and when to do it. Prioritize means asking yourself, 'What do I tackle first?'"*

   "When you're not sure what step comes first, ask yourself these two questions, 'Is this urgent?' and 'Is this important?' The way we manage our time falls into one of these 4 Quadrants or realms: Firefighting, quality time, distractions and time wasting (Covey, 1998)."

2. Pass out **TIME QUADRANTS HANDOUT.** Draw a box split into four quadrants on the board. You will fill in the quadrants as you explain them below. The students will fill in their personal behaviors in each quadrant on their handout as you discuss them. Answer questions as you explain and discuss the quadrants:

FIREFIGHTING	QUALITY TIME
DISTRACTORS	TIME WASTERS

a. Discuss Quadrant 1: *"Using the TIME QUADRANTS HANDOUT (adapted by Covey, 1998), let's look at **Quadrant 1 Firefighting: URGENT & IMPORTANT** [write in top left quadrant on board]. This is the crisis quadrant where you have to put out fires. This is the most stressful quadrant to spend your time. For example, if you procrastinate and don't start a project until 8:00PM the night before it's due, that is urgent (it's due tomorrow) and important (it's worth 50% of your grade). Because spending a lot of time in Quadrant 1 can be stressful, we want to limit our time here. In the long run, it can cause poor health like high blood pressure, headaches, stomachaches, muscle tension and poor sleep. When do you find yourself in Quadrant 1? How does your body feel when you are stressed out?"*

Solicit relevant examples from students and write on board in Quadrant 1. Themes include procrastination, upcoming test, unexpected trip to hospital, and late for practice (Covey, 1998).

b. Discuss Quadrant 2: "*Let's look at __Quadrant 2 Quality Time: IMPORTANT BUT NOT URGENT__ [write in top right quadrant on board]. Quadrant 2 is where we prioritize and have excellent time management skills. This is where we want to spend most of our time. Students who spend time here are less stressed because they plan ahead and set goals rather than waiting until the last minute. If an essay is due in a week, a person in Quadrant 2 will break a large project up into little bites. Quadrant 2 is filling up the gas tank before you are on empty. It's where you practice before a big game or musical performance. When do you find yourself in Quadrant 2?*"

Solicit relevant examples from students and write on board in Quadrant 2. Themes include making time for long-term projects, applying for jobs/college, exercise, relationships, planning ahead, relaxing, working with a tutor, and asking a teacher for help (Covey, 1998).

c. Discuss Quadrant 3: "*Let's look at __Quadrant 3 Distractors: URGENT BUT NOT IMPORTANT__ [write in bottom left quadrant on board]. This is where we welcome interruptions and have difficulty prioritizing. If you get a text message while you're doing homework, it's tempting to drop everything and respond. It might feel urgent; however, it's not as important as finishing your homework. Another example is if you have a paper due Monday, and your friend calls Friday night and asks you to help with their minor problem. You decide to help them and avoid your own work in the process. What are some more examples of distractions in Quadrant 3?*"

Solicit relevant examples from students and write on board in Quadrant 3. Themes include difficulty saying no to interruptions, reputation for being people-pleaser, lack of discipline, and feeling walked all over by others (Covey, 1998).

d. Discuss Quadrant 4: "*Let's look at __Quadrant 4 Time Wasting: NOT URGENT AND NOT IMPORTANT__ [write in bottom right quadrant on board]. This is where excessive TV watching, mindless hours on the computer and an absurd amount of video gaming time are spent. Notice I said excessive. Of course you need time to relax in your day, I'm not going to tell you never to watch TV or play video games because your brain needs time to unwind. But when these activities are excessive, then you're in Quadrant 4. What activities get you stuck in Quadrant 4?*"

Solicit relevant examples from students and write on board in Quadrant 4. Themes include excessive TV, browsing the Internet mindlessly, shopping to distract, endless time on phone, and irrelevant reading (Covey, 1998).

3. Break into small groups and have students complete the questions on the second page of the *TIME QUADRANTS HANDOUT*:

✓ Where (in what Quadrant) do you spend more time than you would like to?

✓ For those of you that have shared they spend too much time procrastinating, what are the problems with spending too much time in Quadrant 1 (e.g., increased stress level, increased anxiety, increased flight or flight response, increased somatic complaints)?

✓ When was the last time you were in Quadrant 2? What did you do to get there (e.g., study environment, support of teacher, tutor, parent, caregiver, friend)?

4. Ask students to take out the *REAL SCHEDULE HANDOUT* they completed prior to group, *"Now that we understand the 4 Quadrants, it's time to identify in which quadrant you spend the most time. Using the REAL SCHEDULE, follow the directions on the handout starting with Step 2."* (20 minutes)

   a. Pass out the markers (red, blue, yellow and orange) and review Step 2 instructions as a group.

   b. Processing Questions: Once students have completed the sheet, break into pairs and answer the following questions from the handout.

   c. Then process the questions as a large group with the following emphasis: *"In life, there are things you can control which are called 'controllables' (like turning in homework on time) and things you can't control (car breaks down). What 'controllables' are present in your life that you want to get a handle on? How will you make that happen?"*

   "What did you learn about where you spend your time as you look at your REAL SCHEDULE?"

   Themes include procrastination, time wasters, working smarter with time, identify what activities are within the student's control."

   d. In a large group, brainstorm changes that need to be made to their future schedule.

5. Pass out *IDEAL SCHEDULE HANDOUT*. Tell students: "*On your IDEAL SCHEDULE, follow the directions and write how you want to spend your time this week. Be realistic with your time. Start with the important tasks. Make at least one change from what you usually do that you think will help.*" Review Step 1 instructions as a group.

  a. In pairs, talk about what is not urgent that could be moved or eliminated. "*What is in Quadrant 1 that can be preplanned so it's not a crisis? Give them directions of what to look at and what to do. Use pairs or some groups to help problem solve or identify problem areas that students might not be able to do on their own.*"

✓ What is one schedule change you can make this week that will help you?

✓ Look at your **REAL SCHEDULE** and find a place where you were in Quadrant 1. What can be preplanned this week so it's not a crisis?

✓ Ask you partner to look at your **REAL SCHEDULE** and **IDEAL SCHEDULE.** What coaching do they have for you?

✓ What might get in the way of following your **IDEAL SCHEDULE** this week? What problem solving can you do ahead of time?

  b. More Processing Questions as large group after you complete the handouts (10 minutes):

✓ What did you learn today? How will it be helpful in school and in future jobs?

✓ How might your good time management make your parents/caregivers/teachers/friends feel?

✓ What did you learn from someone else that you might use?

✓ What can you commit to for next week? What can you do differently based on what we talked about this week?

Credit/References

Covey, S. (1998). *The 7 habits of highly effective teens.* New York: Franklin Covey Co.

About the Counselor:

Hilary J. Parsons, LPC works at Cleveland Clinic Children's, Center for Pediatric Behavioral Health, ADHD Center for Evaluation and Treatment. She is a Doctoral Student in Counseling and Human Development Services at Kent State University. Jparson2@kent.edu

TIME QUADRANTS HANDOUT (adapted from Covey, 1998)

Directions: Fill in what you do in each Time Quadrant then answer questions.

1. URGENT & IMPORTANT **CRISIS & FIREFIGHTING**	**2. NOT URGENT, BUT IMPORTANT** **QUALITY TIME**
• *Procrastination* • *Putting out fires* • • •	• *Prioritizing & Setting Goals* • *Planning* • • •
3. URGENT, BUT NOT IMPORTANT **DISTRACTIONS**	**4. NOT URGENT & NOT IMPORTANT** **TIME WASTING**
• *Trouble saying no* • *Responding to texts at the wrong time* • • •	• *Video games for hours* • *Too much TV* • • •

1. Where do you spend more time than you would like?
2. What are the problems spending too much time in Quadrant 1? How does it affect your stress level? Your body? Your relationships?
3. When was the last time you were in Quadrant 2? What did you do to get there (e.g., study environment, support of teacher)?

_____'s Real Schedule: What I actually did this Week

<u>Complete before lesson:</u> Write what you did this past week in the time blocks (e.g., practice, procrastinate on a paper, played video games). Be as accurate as possible. If you planned to wake-up on Sunday at 9AM, but you REALLY work up at 10AM, write what ACTUALLY happened.

	Mon	Tues	Wed	Thrs	Fri	Sat	Sun	example
:00AM								Wake up / LATE!
:00AM								School
:00AM								
0:00AM								
1:00AM								
2:00PM								Crammed for Test
:00PM								Test
:00PM								Study Hall & Texting
:00PM								Practice
4:00PM								
:00PM								
:00PM								
:00PM								Dinner Homework
:00PM								TV
:00PM								
0:00PM								Computer
1:00PM								Homework

Q1 red <u>red</u> Firefighting	Q2 <u>blue</u> Quality
Q3 <u>yellow</u> Distractor	Q4 <u>orange</u> Time Waster

<u>Complete during class:</u> Using your red, blue, yellow and orange markers, outline the boxes of your activities with the appropriate Quadrant color.

School Counselors Share Their Favorite Classroom Guidance Activities

<u>Pair up with a partner and ask each other the following questions</u>. Write down your answers.

1. In which Quadrant do you spend the most time?

2. What healthy or unhealthy patterns do you notice in your schedule? Would people who know you agree?

3. Is how you're spending your time working or not working for you? *(Hint: If you are stressed out a lot, your schedule is not working!)*

4. When do you spend time in Quadrant 2? How can you spend more time there?

5. What did you learn from doing this activity?

_____'s Ideal Schedule:
What I will do this week...

	Mon	Tues	Wed	Th	Fri	Sat	Sun
7:00AM							
8:00AM							
9:00AM							
10:00AM							
11:00AM							
12:00PM							
1:00PM							
2:00PM							
3:00PM							
4:00PM							
5:00PM							
6:00PM							
7:00PM							
8:00PM							
9:00PM							
10:00PM							
11:00PM							

Complete during lesson. Create a schedule for this week with the following guidelines:
Write out blocks of time: sleeping, eating, personal grooming, classes, practices, job
Write down when you are going to study using these guidelines:

o Tackle difficult subjects when you are the most fresh.

o Do you study best in morning, afternoon, or night? When is your energy the highest?

o Your hardest subject requires the most time.

o Don't put two similar subjects together, such as English and History.

o Save your easiest subject for last.

School Counselors Share Their Favorite Classroom Guidance Activities

Pair up with a partner and ask each other the following questions. Write down your answers.

1. What is one schedule change you can make this week that will help you?

2. Look at your **REAL SCHEDULE** and find a place where you were in Quadrant 1. What can be preplanned this week so it's not a crisis?

3. Ask you partner to look at your **REAL SCHEDULE** and **IDEAL SCHEDULE.** What coaching do they have for you?

4. What might get in the way of following your **IDEAL SCHEDULE** this week? What problem solving can you do ahead of time?

Discovering Our External Assets

Submitted by Laura Colavito, Kathryn Moore, and Joy Rose
Other Contributors: Jabari Henley-Edwards

School Level: High.

Target Population: Grade 9.

Goals: Students will be able to:

1. Identify potential sources of support both in and out of the school setting that will assist them through their high school and future collegiate careers.
2. Recognize the sources of support that are already present in their lives.
3. Identify extracurricular activities that they might be interested in joining.
4. Explore the value of participation in such activities.

ASCA Standards:

PS:A1.10 Identify personal strengths and assets
PS:C1.6 Identify resource people in the school and community, and how to seek their help.
A:C1 Relate school to life experiences
A:C1.2 Seek co-curricular and community experiences to enhance the school experience
C:A1 Develop career awareness
C:A1.8 Pursue and develop competency in areas of interest
C:A1.9 Develop hobbies and vocational interests.

Estimated Time: 45 to 50 minutes.

Materials: Whiteboard, markers, paper, pencils, and *Discovering External Assets Questionnaire* (Colavito, Moore, & Rose, 2014), list of extracurricular activities, and list of outside resources.

Lesson

1. Tell students: "In today's lesson we will be talking about potential activities and supports that are available to you inside and outside of school." Begin with a whole group discussion with the following questions:

   ✓ What are some extracurricular activities you are involved in?
   ✓ What are some benefits of being involved in activities outside of school?
   ✓ Who is one person, within our school, that is a support to you currently?
   ✓ Who is one person within our surrounding community (or beyond) who is a support to you currently?

   Emphasize that these can be any type of activity or group that students enjoy; encourage students to think broadly about various types of support. (3 minutes)

2. After the discussion, define internal and external assets with the group. Ask students if anyone can provide a definition. One common definition for *internal assets* is: aspects within oneself that are strengths (e.g., sense of purpose, personal power). *External assets* are defined as: aspects outside of oneself that enable them to be successful provided by the family, school, and/or community. Explain to students that this lesson will focus on external assets, including specific sources of support. (3 minutes)

3. Next, have students turn and talk to the person on their right to brainstorm a list of individuals/organizations who could serve as support networks inside the school and within the surrounding community. *Examples*: school counselors, teachers, advisors, mentors, family, religious organizations, sports teams, and extracurricular clubs. (5 minutes).

4. Have students regroup as a class and share the list/ideas they came up with. (5 minutes)

5. Next, have students turn and talk to a different peer, to brainstorm and list ways to get involved at the school or in the community through extracurricular activities, sports, or clubs that they might be interested in. *Examples:* volunteering at local community organizations, religious groups, athletic teams, school-sponsored clubs, and student government. (5 minutes).

6. As a large group, have students share their ideas with the class and record this list on the whiteboard. If there are other ways to get involved at the school that the students have not identified, add those activities as well. If there are any students who are already involved in some of the activities mentioned, invite them to share their experiences. (10 minutes)

7. Explain to students the benefits of participation in activities. Tell the students: "Participating in activities both in and out of school provides many benefits including the opportunity to expand your social circles, learn more about your interests, become a part of the school community, and enhance your college applications." Discuss potential barriers that might deter students from connecting with individuals within and outside of the school. Tell the students: "Sometimes students are hesitant to take advantage of these opportunities for a variety of reasons. For example, some students are nervous about joining a club or activity that they have never done before. Others are worried that they will not have time to participate due to school and home obligations. Many students would like to get involved in activities, but don't know how to start." Have students share any relevant experiences and discuss ways of overcoming those barriers. Ask the students: "Would anyone like to share a reason that has prevented you from joining a club or activity? What are some ways that we could overcome those barriers?" (10 minutes)

8. Students complete the **Discovering External Assets** questionnaire (Colavito, Moore, & Rose, 2014). Ask students to complete independently, while thinking about how they can utilize these resources to help them reach their goals. (5 minutes)

Adaptations: A related topic could focus more on the barriers that prevent students from participating in extracurricular activities. Using a similar group format, students could be instructed to make lists of potential barriers and discuss ways of overcoming them.

Credit/References

Lesson adapted from: Griffin, D., Shi, Q., & Steen, S. (2011). Supporting students of color on campus. In T. Fitch & J. Marshall (Eds.), *Group work and outreach plans for college counselors* (pp.111-122). Alexandria, VA: American Counseling Association.

Search Institute. (2006). *40 Developmental assets® for adolescents* (ages 12-18). Retrieved from Search Institute website: www.search-institute.org/system/files/40AssetsList.pdf.

About the School Counselors and Contributors:

Laura Colavito is a 9th grade School Counselor at Millbrook High School in Raleigh, NC and received her graduate degree in School Counseling in May 2013 from George Washington University. lcolavito@wcpss.net

Kathryn Moore is a 10th grade School Counselor at School Without Walls Senior High School in Washington, DC and received her graduate degree in School Counseling in May 2013 from George Washington University. kathryn.moore@dc.gov.

Joy Rose is the 8th Grade Counselor at Columbia Heights Educational Campus in Washington, DC and received her graduate degree in School Counseling in May 2012 from George Washington University. joy.rose@dc.gov

Jabari Henley-Edwards received an M.A. in Education in May 2012 from George Washington University. Jb71824@gmail.com

Discovering External Assets Questionnaire
(Colavito, Moore, & Rose, 2014)

1. What are some extracurricular activities you could become involved in?

2. What are some benefits of being involved in activities outside of school?

3. List at least one person, within our school, who is potentially a support to you currently.

4. List at least one person within our surrounding community (or beyond) who is potentially a support to you currently and could continue to be a support in the future.

5. List one person within our school who may potentially be a support to you throughout your high school career.

Create A School
Submitted by Tina R. Paone, Ph.D.

School Level: High.

Goals: Students will:
1. Establish skills of working together towards a common goal.
2. Gain an understanding of compromise as they work together and find they must agree with one another to move forward.
3. Gain an understanding of why certain rules exist in their schools/society.

ASCA Standards:
PS:A2.1 Recognize that everyone has rights and responsibilities
PS:A2.2 Respect alternative points of view
PS:A2.6 Use effective communications skills
PS:B1.1 Use a decision-making and problem-solving model
PS:C1.2 Learn about the relationship between rules, laws, safety and the protection of rights of the individual.

Estimated Time: 45 minutes.

Materials: Paper, crayons, markers, and other craft materials (e.g., buttons, yarn, glitter, shells, rocks, etc...).

Lesson

1. Introduction: Today we are going to discuss a dilemma. School counselor will determine with class if they know what a dilemma is. The term dilemma will be defined. Emphasize that dilemmas are difficult situations that tend to not have an easy answer. Moral dilemmas are situations that allow you to look at things from a number of different angles. These moral dilemmas often question different players in the situation. For example, how will my decision affect me? How will my decision affect others?

How will my decision affect the world around me? Who do I need to take into account when making this decision? In this next example, a moral dilemma about the dress code at school will be presented. The dilemma is not asking you to change the dress code, just consider all the different perspectives that could be affected by this. (5 minutes)

2. School counselor reads this dilemma: "There is a dress code where you attend middle/high school. You do not agree with some of the parts of the dress code and you feel that you should be able to wear what you want. You know that if you wear something that is against the dress code, you will be punished. You want to organize the student body to protest the dress code by having everyone wear whatever they want".

3. Process the dilemma with the students by asking these questions: (5 minutes)

✓ What if people disagree with the protester's point of view?
✓ What would you do?
✓ Why would you make that decision?
✓ What in your life can you relate closely to this situation?
✓ What other events or situations are similar to this situation?
✓ Can you think of some examples that would cause you to think differently from what you would do in this specific example?
✓ What is the most important thing you consider when making decisions like this?
✓ Whose feelings do you consider when making tough decisions?

4. When we look at this dilemma, we can see that there are many different ways in which you can respond. Sometimes when it comes to rules in school, there are many that exist and others that could be added to create an ideal school. What would your ideal school look like? What type of rules would you have? In a few minutes, you will have an opportunity to figure that out.

5. Split students up into small groups of six (or smaller depending on your class size) by having them count off in sixes or appropriate number. Have students move to various places in the classroom where each of the groups can process with the group members and not be infringing upon another group.

6.Once in small groups, explain to the students that they are going to work together to develop their ideal school that the six of them agree upon. The goal of the activity is to have them work together, communicate with one another, and learn that sometimes they must compromise for the group to work as a whole.

o Indicate to students that they can create whatever they want in the school (food, rules, transportation, etc.).

o They must also choose collectively, how to inform the other groups in the class about their school once it is created.

o Allow them to use paper, crayons, markers, and other craft materials to represent their school. Students get to decide how they would like to represent their school and what type of artifacts they create. For example, one group might decide to create a school mascot using various craft materials, where another group might decide to create a map of their school, and another might decide they want to create a student handbook. Ultimately, the students get to decide how this artifact will look. (30 minutes)

7. Once the groups have completed their task, have small groups report back to the other groups about their schools and what they created.

8. Process with students what it was like to create an ideal school:

✓ How did you decide what your school would be?

✓ What influenced you to make your decisions about your school?

✓ How does what you do in the school affect those around you?

✓ What types of things do you see in your ideal school that you would like to see here at your current school?

✓ How can you make positive changes here at our school?

✓ How was this activity for you?

✓ What feelings came up for you during this activity?

Credit/References

This activity was created as part of my dissertation, *The Comparative Effectiveness of Group Activity Therapy on the Moral Reasoning of At-Risk High School Students.*

About the Counselor:

Dr. Paone is currently an Associate Professor and Chair of the Department of Educational Leadership, School Counseling, and Special Education at Monmouth University in West Long Branch, NJ. Previously, Dr. Paone was a High School Counselor. tpaone@monmouth.edu

Strategies for Success
Submitted by Donna Neary and Theresa A. Coogan

School Level: High.

Goals: Students will:
1. Understand time management by assessing how their time is spent, drawing connections to implications this has on academic achievement, and identify areas for change/improvement
2. Understand how to identify and set long and short term goals with an academic focus
3. Become aware of their current priorities as determined by how they spend their days as illustrated on the **Time Management Tool** worksheet

ASCA Standards:

A-A1: Improve academic self-concept
A-A2: Acquire skills for improving learning
A-B2: Plan to achieve goals
A-C1: Relate school to life experiences
I-A-5: Individual counseling, group counseling and classroom guidance programs ensuring equitable access to resources that promote academic achievement; personal, social and emotional development; and career development including the identification of appropriate post-secondary education for every student.

Estimated Time: 90 minutes.

Materials: **Time Management Tool Worksheet** (Neary & Coogan, 2014), pencils.

Lesson

1. Example of an introduction to students: "We want you to be able to take charge of your learning and feel confident about your decisions in school and preparing for after high school. This is a lifelong learning piece that everyone practices. If you can start now, it will be skills that

you can take with you throughout the rest of your life. Let's explore some of the different ways we can be successful in school and also identify some of the possible barriers to success and ways to address them effectively. Two of the most helpful strategies that people use regardless if they are in high school, college, or the workforce include time management and goal setting skills." (10 minutes).

2. Counselor facilitates a discussion with the class concerning what is needed to be academically successful students and test taker. Target questions to use when facilitating this discussion with the group include:
   ✓ What does "time-management" mean to you?
   ✓ Provide an example of a way you used time management when you were at your middle school to be successful.
   ✓ Thinking about being a high school student now, in what ways might you need to adjust your time management plan that you used in middle school? (20 minutes)

3. Counselor distributes the **Time Management Tool**. Counselor says: "We've now had a chance to brainstorm and discuss what "time-management" is and what that looked like for you as a middle school student and how that might need to change as a high school student. As you continue in your high school career, you're opportunities to be in charge of your own learning will continue to increase. We want to be sure you have a skills to assist you to be successful throughout high school as well as after you graduate. We're going to focus now on an activity that can assist you with identifying and practicing helpful study skills by concentrating on time-management." (10 minutes)

4. Students complete the **Time Management Tool Worksheet**. Counselor and Teacher float around classroom while students are taking the tool to assist with any questions as needed. If possible, recommend also having a projected copy of the same worksheet on display. Each student independently completes their own worksheet. (10 minutes)

5. Counselor works with students to take steps to identify and create short term goals and long term goal. The counselor says: "Now that you've had a chance to reflect on the specific time spent during one week day (e.g., 24 hours), let's see how we can use that information to help us identify a plan for you to be successful when we think about time-management and study skills. Let's think about creating some goals that can be helpful to each of you. When we think about goals, it's important to know there are 2 main types: short term goals and long term goals."

6. Counselor provides information and example about how to set goals, short and long term. All goals share four main characteristics: specific deadlines for completion; specific objective goal; realistic to achieve; and provides a challenge, yet still attainable. The short term goals take place in a shorter time frame (e.g., 1 day to 1 month, commonly) and will often be used to work towards the long term goal. There can be several short term goals as a part of one long term goal. Here are examples of short term and long term goals that illustrate the four characteristics noted above in each individual goal as well as how the short term goals can connect to the long term goal:

   a. Short Term Goal #1: In order to receive an A on my next Math test, I will study my math notes and readings 15 more minutes every day.

   b. Short Term Goal # 2: In order to increase my Math grade by a half-letter grade by the end of the quarter, I will complete all homework assignments throughout the rest of this quarter.

   c. Long Term Goal : To receive an A- or higher in Math at the end of this academic year. (20 minutes).

7. Counselor says: "Now we've discussed what goal setting looks like and shared an example with you. We'd like to ask each of you to use your own the time-management sheet that you've created to create one short term goal that will be completed by the end of the quarter, and one long term goal that will be completed by the end of this academic year in this class. You can work on this as homework and will turn this into your teacher as a homework assignment. If you'd like to schedule a meeting with your School Counselor to continue discussing your strategies for success after this assignment, please contact us. Use the examples of the short term and long term goals that we provided you with to assist you. Remember that both of the goals you create need to include the four characteristics and the short term goal should be connected to assisting you with your long term goal. (20 minutes).

Processing Questions:

✓ What did you learn today?

✓ What was most important for you? Why?

✓ What did you learn from someone else that you might use?

✓ What can you commit to for next week? One time you can do differently based on what we talked about this week. commit to something that you do not do now but think is pretty attainable (don't set yourself up for failure).

✓ Take these examples of questions and make them specific to the goals of your activity so tie them to time mgmt. strategies, what is working right now for the students, what is not, and what new strategies based on this discussion they might want to try?

Cautions: Students may need additional guidance and assistance with goal-setting if this is the first time they are learning about how to set academic goals. A follow-up session could be created if this is a need for the population. Counselor should discuss the expected engagement level with the Teacher as this activity is based on a collaborative delivery of the lesson. If the Teacher cannot be present, another Counselor is recommended to be present to assist.

Adaptations: Break the activity into two 45-minute lessons with time management being one lesson and goal setting being a second. Additional homework questions could be included to expand the students' self-reflection:
✓ What have you learned by completing this time management worksheet that will help you become more successful?
✓ Which one of the activities on your time management worksheet is hindering your success to reach your goals?
✓ From completing this worksheet, what have you learned about your priorities?
✓ What percent of your time should be focused on school?
  If more time was available (e.g., block scheduling or multiple sessions), students create their short term and long term goals as a part of the activity.

About the Counselors:

Donna Neary is currently a School Counselor at Brockton High School; Brockton, MA. She has been a School Counselor since 1991. donnaneary@bpsma.org

Theresa A. Coogan, Ph.D. is an Associate Professor and School Counseling Programs Director in the Department of Counselor Education Bridgewater State University in Bridgewater, MA. theresa.coogan@bridgew.edu

Time Management Tool (Neary & Coogan, 2014
(adapted from: Brockton High School Guidance Department, 2010)

How do you Spend your Time during the Week?

Directions: Think about what your typical weekday looks like and fill in the hours per day you spend on the activities mentioned below. Use 30 minute increments to help. You can indicate any notes in the "notes" column. After you've completed this first step, go back and identify for each activity is that something you *must* do every weekday, something that you *should* do every weekday, or something that you *want* to do every weekday.

Task/Activity	Hours Per Day (30 min increments)	Notes	Must/Should/Want
Get Ready for School (e.g., dress, shower)			
Commute to/from School			
Attend School	6.5 hours		
Prepare and eat Breakfast			
Prepare and eat Lunch			
Prepare and eat Dinner			
Sleep			
Nap			
Complete Homework and projects			
Study for tests and quizzes			
Review notes or read textbooks			
Complete household chores/family obligations (e.g., Babysitting, cleaning)			
Work or Volunteer			
Extracurricular activities with school (e.g., team sport, clubs)			
Extracurricular activities non school related (e.g., lessons, club sports)			
Using the Internet or cell phone, non-school related (e.g., Facebook, Twitter, Emailing, Texting)			
Using the Internet or cell phone, school related (e.g., research for class or project)			
Play computer or video games			
Watch TV or Movies			
Hang out with Friends			
Hang out with Family			
Other:			

CAREER EXPLORATION AND PLANNING CLASSROOM GUIDANCE LESSONS

School Counselors Share Their Favorite Classroom Guidance Activities

Amazing Grace: Her Dream Comes True

Submitted by Carol O. Cleveland,
Sheila M. Austin, and M. Carolyn Thomas

School Level: Elementary.

Target Population: Grades K to 4.

Possible Classes to Be Integrated: Reading or Story Time.

Goals: To help students:

1. Decrease the effects of role limitations of gender and ethnic stereotyping.
2. Strengthen their belief that they are unique and can choose a variety of roles for themselves.
3. Increase their exploration of nontraditional and traditional roles.
4. Empower them to believe that their dreams are possible.

ASCA Standards:

C:A1.2 Learn about the variety of traditional and nontraditional occupations
PS:A1.1 Develop positive attitudes toward self as a unique and worthy person
PS:A2.4 Recognize, accept and appreciate ethnic and cultural diversity.

Estimated Time: 45 minutes.

Materials: Hoffman, M., & Binch, C. (1991). **Amazing Grace**. New York: Dial Book for Young Readers.

Special Directions: Bibliocounseling is the therapeutic use of literature as a healing or developmental tool where the child interacts with the character(s) through the process of identification, catharsis, insight, and universalization. The child identifies similarities with the character and feels less different, shares emotions with the character, learns from the character's growth, and realizes that others face similar problems. Books such as **Amazing**

Grace are powerful instruments in helping children learn the career competencies of developing a positive self-concept, discarding role limitations caused by gender and cultural biases, and exploring a variety of roles not previously considered.

Lesson

1. For higher grades, the teacher may assign **Amazing Grace** as reading homework. For Kindergarten and Grade 1 students, the Counselor reads the book to or with the children. The counselor should create an intimate setting so each student can clearly hear the story and see the pictures. Students who read the book as an assignment are told they will be asked to share their thoughts and feelings about Grace in either small groups or as a class activity.

2. In small groups of 5 to 7 members, students are given a worksheet with the following incomplete sentences, and asked to finish the sentences, one at a time, and share their personal answers with the group: (20 minutes)

✓ When Grace was told she could not be Peter Pan, she must have felt...........

✓ When Grace was told she could not be Peter Pan, I felt.............................

✓ Nana was trying to teach Grace that...............................

✓ I liked Grace because.................................

✓ Grace and Nana taught me that ....

3. **Processing Questions**: The children are then given a second worksheet with the following questions, and asked to answer the questions and share their answers with the group: (25 minutes)

✓ What have you dreamed of being when you get older?

✓ Who helps you believe in your dream?

✓ Have you ever been told you could not have a role or consider a job because of your gender or culture?

   o If so, how did you feel?

✓ Since getting to know *Grace,* how have you changed what you think of yourself?

✓ If you had a friend who was afraid to play a role or hope to be a certain kind of worker, what would you tell your friend?

Cautions: Counselors should work with teachers in deciding which grades are appropriate for the book and the questions as reading levels and maturity may vary greatly in elementary grades.

Adaptations: This exercise could be modified to use in classroom guidance with larger groups, be extended to two sessions, or number of questions or incomplete sentences could also be reduced or modified to fit the time required. The counselor may also use a form of technology to project the pages of the book for all to see.

How to Integrate into Core Curriculum:
Ask the teachers to include bibliocounseling with **Amazing Grace** and other books in their lesson plans. By involving the teachers, this and similar exercises can become integral career development components of the comprehensive guidance and counseling program.

Next Possible Lesson Topics:
Choose other children's books that help teach any of the career development competencies outlined in the *ASCA National Standards for Students* or *The National Career Development Guidelines: Competencies and Indicators for Elementary School Students.*

Credit/References

Gladding, S. T. (2011). *The creative arts in counseling* (4th Ed.). Alexandria, VA: American Counseling Association.

About the Counselors:

Carol O. Cleveland is an Elementary School Counselor at J. Larry Newton School in Fairhope, AL. whcleveland@zebra.net

Sheila M. Austin is Professor and Dean of the School of Education at Auburn University Montgomery in Montgomery, AL. saustin1@aum.edu

M. Carolyn Thomas is Professor of Counselor Education at Auburn University Montgomery in Montgomery, AL. mthomas@aum.edu

Chicken Man: Making the Best of all Jobs: Lessons 1 and 2

Submitted by Carol O. Cleveland,
M. Carolyn Thomas, and Sheila M. Austin

School Level: Elementary.

Target Population: Grades K to 4.

Possible Classes to Be Integrated: Reading or Story Time.

Goals: The goals *are* to help students:
1. Learn that every job is important and worth doing well.
2. Develop a positive attitude toward all work and learning.
3. Increase their openness to learning new skills.
4. Understand the interrelatedness of jobs.
5. Strengthen the value of responsibility and keeping commitments.

ASCA Standards:
C:A2.7 Develop a positive attitude toward work and learning
C:A2.8 Understand the importance of responsibility, dependability, punctuality, integrity and effort in the workplace
C:C1.2 Explain how work can help to achieve personal success and satisfaction.

Estimated Time: Two lessons of 30 to 45 minutes each.

Materials: **Chicken Man** by Michelle Edwards (2008).

Special Directions: Bibliocounseling is the therapeutic use of literature as a healing or developmental tool where the child interacts with the character(s) through the process of identification, catharsis, insight, and universalization. The child identifies similarities with the character and feels less different, shares emotions with the character, learns from the character's growth, and realizes that others face similar problems.

Lesson 1

1. For higher grades, the teacher may assign **Chicken Man** as reading homework. For Kindergarten and Grade 1 students, the Counselor reads the book to or with the children. The counselor should create an intimate setting so each student can clearly hear the story and see the pictures. Students who read the book as an assignment are told they will be asked to share their thoughts and feelings about Grace in either small groups or as a class activity.

2. In small groups of 5 to 7 members, students are asked to answer the following questions, one at a time, and share their personal answers with the group:
   ✓ Why do you think the hens laid more eggs than ever before?
   ✓ What was it about Chicken Man that made the hens and roosters so happy?
   ✓ Why did other people think they always wanted Chicken
   ✓ Man's jobs, no matter what job he had?
   ✓ What was it about Chicken Man that made him good at whatever job he was given?

3. After the students have answered the questions, the counselor summarizes their responses and points out similarities among the group members. Students might mention that the chickens were happy because Chicken Man liked them and enjoyed taking care of them, so they laid more eggs and that Chicken Man's positive attitude about any work made him good at whatever job he was given.

4. The counselor ends with a statement that uses the students' responses about positive work values and the importance of all jobs to prepare them for the second session. Students are told the group will apply the lessons learned about Chicken Man to their own school and home jobs.

Lesson 2

1. Ask students to return to their same group as in the previous lesson. The counselor paraphrases the summary at the end of Session 1.

2. The counselor then gives the students the following list of incomplete sentences and asks them to complete the sentences and share their responses with the group.
   a. The chickens liked Chicken Man because.................

b. I want to be like Chicken Man in the following ways....................

c. The jobs or school lessons I do not like are................

d. If I become more like Chicken Man, I would change........... about myself so I could do better at the things I may not like doing.

e. When Chicken Man kept his promise to visit his friends in the **coop and everyone was happier, I felt**...........................

After the students have shared their responses, the counselor summarizes the responses, pointing out the importance of positive attitudes about all work, dependability, responsibility, and satisfying personal needs through work.

Cautions: Reading levels and maturity vary greatly in elementary grades. Counselors should work with teachers in deciding which grades are appropriate for the book and questions.

Adaptations: The counselor could also use technology to project the pages on the book for all the students to see.

Next Possible Lesson Plan Topics: Choose other children's books that help teach any of the career development competencies outlined in the *ASCA National Standards for Students* or *The National Career Development Guidelines: Competencies and Indicators for Elementary School Students.*

Credit/References

Edwards, M. (2008). **Chicken Man**. Montgomery, AL: Junebug Books.

About the Counselors:

Carol O. Cleveland is an Elementary School Counselor at J. Larry Newton School in Fairhope, AL. whcleveland@zebra.net

M. Carolyn Thomas is Professor of Counselor Education at Auburn University Montgomery in Montgomery, AL. mthomas@aum.edu

Sheila M. Austin is Professor and Dean of the School of Education at Auburn University Montgomery in Montgomery, AL. saustin1@aum.edu

Create a Career Caricature: Lessons 1 and 2

Submitted by Jennifer Ross-Menelli and Melissa Luke, Ph.D.

School Level: Elementary.

Target Population: Grades 2 through 5.

Goals: Students will identify:
1. At least two skills and strengths they possess.
2. Identify at least one specific career of interest.
3. Articulate at least one connection between their skills and interests, and future careers options.

ASCA Standards:

C:A1.2 Learn about the variety of traditional and nontraditional occupations

C:A1.3. Develop an awareness of personal abilities, skills, interests and motivations

C:B1.2 Identify personal skills, interests and abilities and relate them to current career choice

C:C1.3 Identify personal preferences and interests influencing career choice and success

C:C2.1 Demonstrate how interests, abilities and achievement relate to achieving personal, social, educational and career goals.

Estimated Time: Two 40-minute sessions.

Materials: Two-sided **Paper Doll** template, markers, crayons and/or colored pencils, and whiteboard or flip chart paper.

Lesson 1

1. Begin with this introduction to the activity saying, "In this activity, we are going to talk about the different strengths and talents that you have that can help you decide what career you want when you are older. To begin, I want us to think about Christopher Columbus, the famous explorer, for a few minutes. What kinds of interests do you think he had? What kind of activities do you think he liked to do? Perhaps he liked to be outside and explore nature or maybe he enjoyed learning about the ocean. Can you think of specific skills he needed? He definitely needed to know how to read a map and use a compass.

The things that Christopher Columbus was interested in and the activities that he liked to do led him to develop the skills necessary to be an explorer. His career, or job, was an explorer." (5 minutes)

2. The counselor asks for a volunteer to define an "interest," a "strength," and an "activity." Differentiate the three by illustrating the differences with an interest is the broadest and reflects an affinity; an activity is a behavior that may reflect an interest, but it is something that can be observed; and a strength is skill that is positively evaluated by self or others. To do this, the counselor will ask "How is an activity different from an interest?" The counselor will tell the students that an interest is something that you like to do or something that you want to learn more about. A strength is something that you are good at. An activity is something that you participate in at home, at school or in the community. (3 minutes)

3. The school counselor will tell the students that our interests help us choose the activities we do. The counselor might say: "I am interested in science (interest) and I am good a good reader (skill) and so I am reading all of the **Magic School Bus** books (activity). What are some of the activities you are interested in?" (2 minutes)

4. The school counselor will pass out the creative caricature template. Instruct students that on the front side of the paper caricature, they will draw themselves, and their interests and strengths. For example, a student might draw herself with a fishing rod, a puppy, a computer and a violin. This student likes fishing and playing with her puppy and is good at using the computer and playing the violin. (10 minutes)

5. At the bottom of the paper, instruct the students to write out what interests and strengths they represented in their drawings. If time is a concern, suggest that the students only draw one interest and one strength. (5 minutes)

6. Ask for a few volunteers to share their drawings and their identified interests and strengths. Emphasize the connection between their interests and strengths and possible future careers choices as they talk. (7 minutes)

7. To process this activity, ask questions such as:
   ✓ What was this activity like for you?
   ✓ Can you identify something you learned about yourself? About a classmate?

School Counselors Share Their Favorite Classroom Guidance Activities

✓ How did it make you feel to think about your interests and strengths?

✓ What similarities/differences did you notice between your interests and strengths and that of your classmates?

✓ In what ways might interests and skills be similar? How are they different?

✓ Can you think of any examples of when you have observed your classmates' described interests and strengths?

✓ How might you explain your career caricature to you parents/caregiver? (8 minutes)

8. The school counselor should summarize and end the session by stating, "We learned a lot about our interests and skills today. We learned the difference between skills, activities and interests and we learned all about the skills and interests of our classmates. Thank you for sharing! As you grow older, your strengths and interests will grow with you and will help you choose your future careers and jobs."

9. The school counselor should collect the career caricatures from each student as they will be used in the second session.

Lesson 2

1. Pass out the students' career caricatures from the first session. Review the student's strengths and skills as discussed in the previous session. Invite the students to share their career caricatures with the class and share with the class one strength or interest. Tell the students that our strengths also help us choose the careers/jobs we choose to do when we're adults. For example, on my career caricature, I drew a calculator, numbers and all of my books neatly stacked. I am interested in math and I am very organized and so I might want to be an accountant. Or, I like to run around and climb trees and I am good at helping people and so I might like to be a fireman or firewoman. Or, I like to build with Legos and I am good at figuring out puzzles so I might like to be a computer programmer. (5 minutes)

2. Tell students that there are many different types of careers available to them. On a whiteboard or flip chart, write out the following list of different career fields: Business; Creative; Nature; Fixing, Building, Technology: Helping. Ensure that there is enough room around each career field to write different types of jobs. Read the different types of careers to the students and after reading each career path, have students call out a different type of job or career within the specific category. Write down or invite a student to write down the different jobs suggested by the students. (10 minutes)

- Business Path: People who like to work with numbers and be organized
  - Possible careers- business owner or accountant
- Creative Path: People who like to draw, write or perform
  - Possible careers- Author, Dancer or Artist
- Nature Path- People who like to work outdoors with plants and animals
  - Possible careers- Veterinarian, Farmer, Naturalist or Park Ranger
- Fixing, Building and Technology Path- people who like to figure out how things work and build things
  - Possible careers- Construction, Computer Programmer, Biologist, Astronomer or Web Site Developer
- Helping Path- People who like to work with people to help make things better for others
  - Possible Careers- Doctor, Teacher, Fireman, Policeman, Counselor or Nurse

3. Ask the students to identify examples of the strengths and interests that are needed for a few of the suggested careers. For example, an interest in animals and science and a strength in patience might be necessary to be a veterinarian. Write down the students suggestions near the suggested careers. (5 minutes)

4. Tell the students that they are now going to think about their own strengths and skills and what careers might be natural extensions of these and therefore of interest to them. Instruct students to flip their paper over and to brainstorm how their interests and strengths might fit into a career. For example, a student who drew a computer and Legos might think about being a computer game developer. Or, a student who drew a fishing pole and animals might think about being a marine biologist. Students can write down their thoughts on the side of the paper or can just think quietly for a few moments. After a few moments of thinking, ask the students to draw themselves in a career that matches their interests and strengths. (10 minutes)

5. Ask for a few volunteers to share their drawings. Ask the volunteers to tell the class how their strengths and interests relate to the career they drew themselves in. The school counselor then asks other students to offer additional ideas for how the interests and strengths may relate to the activities and career choice. (5 minutes)

6. The school counselor should spend whatever time is left, but at least 5 minutes, processing the activity. Try to allow as many students to talk as possible, carefully using group counseling skills such as linking, reframing, and reflection. To process this activity, ask questions such as: (5 minutes)

- ✓ What was this activity like for you?
- ✓ What did you notice happening in the room as we completed the activity? (This is an opportunity for the school counselor to use immediacy, and make process observations of what took place.)
- ✓ Can you identify something you learned about yourself? About a classmate? About us as a group?
- ✓ What was it like to think about what you might be when you grow up?
- ✓ What are some other ways we might learn about different careers?
- ✓ Even though we talked about how interests and strengths can lead to a career of interest, what other ways do you think people select a career?
- ✓ Related, do you think all people in a certain career have the same interests or strengths? Explain.
- ✓ Can anyone think of other careers that might be related to some of the careers identified by classmates?
- ✓ What is something you might do to develop a skill that is related to your chosen career of interest?

7. The school counselor should conclude the session by stating, "We spent some time talking about our interests, strengths and careers and jobs we might want when we get older. Thank you for sharing! It can be exciting to think about our future and I hope you enjoyed thinking about your future career. Bring your career caricature home, and share with your all the parts of your caricature and where you see your future career."

Cautions: Be attentive to gender-neutral language and/or to switch back and forth between the gender pronouns, as children can be particularly sensitive to gendered socialization associated with career choice. The school counselor may even want to address this during the activity if s/he notices examples of students' beliefs and assumptions about gendered careers surfacing. Additionally, the school counselor needs to attentive to the different learning abilities of the students and may need to adapt the lesson accordingly, such as providing more comprehensive explanations of concepts or questions.

Next Possible Lesson Plan Topics: How the skills and strengths of the students translate to success in school.

About the Counselors:

Jennifer Ross-Menelli is a Graduate Student in Mental Health Counseling at Syracuse University. JLRoss03@syr.edu

Melissa Luke, Ph.D. is an Associate Professor, Interim Chair, and Coordinator of School Counseling at Syracuse University. Previously she was a High School Counselor. mmluke@syr.edu

My Career Caricature

My Interests:

_____
_____
_____
_____
_____
_____

My Strengths:

_____
_____
_____
_____
_____
_____

My Career Caricature

I might want to be a:

_____

Drive of Your Life: Lessons 1, 2, 3, and 4

Submitted by Sandra M. Logan and Jennifer Greene

School Level: Middle.

Target Population: Grade 7 and above.

Goals: Students will:
1. Understand the relationship between the world and work.
2. Be able to identify personal attributes that contribute to their success.
3. Be able to identify at least 3 careers of interest to them.
4. Understand the relationship between education and specific careers.

ASCA Standards:

C:A1.3 Develop an awareness of personal abilities, skills, interests and motivations
C:B1.2 Identify personal skills, interests and abilities and relate them to current career choice
C:B1.5 Use research and information resources to obtain career information
C:B2.1 Demonstrate awareness of the education and training needed to achieve career goals
C:C1.1 Understand the relationship between educational achievement and career success
C:C1.3 Identify personal preferences and interests influencing career choice and success.

Estimated Time: Four 45-minute lessons, best conducted as 1 lesson per day for 4 consecutive days. (If counselor is not available for all lessons, a teacher can facilitate lessons # 2 & 3).

Materials: Computer with access to the internet & printing capabilities (including Flash player & headphone capabilities), writing utensils, **Drive of Your Life** worksheets (Logan & Greene, 2014).

Lesson 1

1. Begin with: *Over the course of the next week, our focus is on participating in lessons that will allow you to explore career possibilities and the pathways towards your career goals. We will be utilizing an online program called Drive of Your Life. This program will help you to begin thinking about your personal attributes and your future.*

2. Have students turn to a nearby partner and tell one another 5 things that they are good at or their strengths. The counselor may need to offer examples of strengths (e.g., being a good writer, a good listener, has empathy, has good hand-eye coordination, is organized)

3. On page 1 of the Drive of Your Life handout, have students fill in 3 personal strengths and 3 things that they really enjoy doing (explain that they do not have to be good at them, but rather simply enjoy doing them).

4. Brainstorm with students about different types of careers and record them on the board.

5. Explain to students the importance of knowing yourself and pursuing a career that involves one's strengths and areas of interest. State that they will be participating in an online career exploration program that helps them to match their strengths and interests with particular careers.

6. Have students go to the webpage, www.driveofyourlife.org
   a. Walk students through the registration and information portion.
      i. Have students select 'student' for type of user
      ii. Select 'Register'
      iii. Select 'At school' for their location
      iv. Select 'Outside Indiana' for their specific location
      v. Proceed to select the appropriate state, city, and school name
      vi. Select grade level from drop down menu
      vii. Type student's first name, middle initial, last name, as well as teacher's prefix and full name.
      viii. Students are to select a username that is at least 6 characters, as well as a password that is at least 6 characters.

    ix. Once step 8 is completed, a pop-up window will state:
      STOP...Write down your username and password in a safe place.
      If you forget, you will need to start over.

  b. Have students write down their user name and password on their form.

7. Collect forms and bring to the next lesson. It may be helpful to create a master list of all students' usernames and passwords, just in case students lose theirs.

8. Conclude lesson by saying: *Now that you have set up an account, our next lesson will focus on assessing your personal strengths and qualities. You will be able to begin building parts of your car so that you can take part in your career journey.*

Lesson 2: Customize Your Ride

1. Begin the lesson by asking students: *What do you remember about our last lesson?* Emphasize that as one begins to recognize their own strengths and areas of interest, they can begin to explore careers that may best suit them.

2. Have students log onto webpage and type in their information

3. Upon successfully logging in, the following message will appear:
    Most of today's careers involve some education or training after high school. Drive of Your Life helps you find careers that interest you and understand what it will take to prepare for those careers. You absolutely can achieve your dream job...so start here.

  a. *STEP ONE: THE ONE & ONLY YOU*
    There is no one just like you. You have unique strengths and talents. In this section, you will answer a series of questions about your likes, interests, and abilities. Each question will have 4 possible answers. There is no right or wrong answer, so just click the one closest to how you feel.
    Remember to answer honestly with your own personal likes and dislikes—not what you think others like or don't like. Your answers will guide the rest of Drive of Your Life, so it's important to say how you feel.

School Counselors Share Their Favorite Classroom Guidance Activities

b. *STEP TWO: A CAR FOR THE ONE & ONLY YOU!*

You also will have the opportunity to design a car to take you exploring a variety of career and educational options. As you answer each section, you will get to customize that car. Eventually, you will earn your Driver's License—a list of classes to take in high school that will prepare you for your career. Print this license and keep it to guide your class scheduling in high school.

Explain that as the students work through the program, they are able to build and drive their own car. They will earn parts of the car as they progress in their personal and career exploration. In the next lesson, they will get to drive this car to several destinations (careers).

c. **Customize Your Ride** module involves a 48-question survey, completed 8 questions at a time, using a 4-point Likert scale (*No Way, Not Exactly, All Right, I Can Go For That!*). At the end of each section of 8 questions, students get to create another aspect of their car.

   i.   Pick your car type
   ii. Pick the color of car
   iii. Pick color of underbody lights for car
   iv. Pick wheels for car
   v.   Pick custom design paint for car
   vi. Pick steering wheel type

The questions are broken into sections to prevent students from disengaging from the process.

d. Remind students to work through these slowly, reading each question. The most honest answer is probably the one you think of first, go with that and don't over analyze. There are no right or wrong answers; simply one's preferences.

e. At the end of the survey, students are presented with the results of their personal style. Their style will be summarized and 3 personality traits will be provided. For example, results may be: *Ongoing, Structured, & Creative.*

f. On their worksheet, have students list their 3 traits and write 1-2 sentences about how they perceive this trait or an example of how each trait is seen in their lives.

g. Their last step for the day will be to customize their license plate. Remind students that they need to be appropriate.

h. Have students log out of system and let them know that they will continue their "drive" next session.

Lesson 3: Plan Your Trip

1. Begin the lesson by reviewing what students worked on last time. Have them take out their worksheet and look it over. Ask students to share what traits that they have identified about themselves.

2. Have students log onto webpage and type in their username and password. (If students cannot remember, reference their master list.)

3. Direct students to look at the key explaining how each symbol represents a different level of education required for that career. For example, the graduation cap picture with a black hat represents "No high school experience," whereas the yellow graduation hat with a '5' on it represents "5 years of schooling beyond high school."

4. Then have students look through the career options that would most suit them (according to survey). Explain how to look through these, sort by level of education, and then select 5 of the careers from the list for possible further research. Allow students to subjectively pick which of the careers most interest them. Write these 5 identified careers on pg. 2 of the **Drive of Your Life Worksheets**.

5. Have students stop at this point, turn off computers, and demonstrate on your computer how to navigate through the 'jump in and drive' section.

6. Upon beginning this section, students will see the following message appear:

Now that you've picked careers that interest you, it is time to learn what they involve. First, answer some multiple choice questions and earn points. Then, visit the different careers that interest you to learn about a typical day on the job. FastFacts will show you if there is a high demand for that career, the usual salary it pays and the education you need to do the job.

The next step is the most important—print your driver's license. This is your plan for high school—the classes and diploma type that will help you prepare for your future. You will also see information on colleges. Printing the license will get you bonus points on your Drive! Remember—everyone needs education. There are lots of options. Use the information from Drive of Your Life to help figure out what you might want to do and how much education you will need. Good luck! Explain how you can earn money for answering questions correctly, which can be used to purchase accessories for your car (all student start with $2,000). For example, students could be asked about which of the following careers is suited for athletes? Then students are to select the appropriate answer. Correct answers earn $500, while incorrect answers deduct $200.

7. At the end of the class period, have students log out of system and let them know that they will continue their "drive" next session.

Lesson 4: Jump in and Drive

1. Explain that today we will be driving the car, stopping in at various career destinations as it was illustrated at the end of the last lesson..

2. Have students log onto webpage and type in their username and password. (If students cannot remember, reference their master list.) It is suggested that you walk around and monitor students' progress, as they will be completing them the process at various paces

3. Out of the 5 careers, students are to select their top 3 careers based on their personal interest and fill out specified information on pages 3 to 5 of **Drive of Your Life** handout. Students identify which categories they would like to write data about. The categories are:
   i. Typical tasks performed
   ii. Hazardous conditions
   iii. Physical demanding
   iv. Working outside
   v. Working with others
   vi. Working with computers
   vii. Skill set

viii. Next steps

4. Then, they will complete the *Fast Facts* section for each selected career. Students will be working independently so expect to problem-solve and monitor their progress. It may be necessary to assist students in selecting their top careers as well as completing the handout correctly.

5. Student must review both the *Typical Day* and *Fast Facts* sections to move forward in the game.

6. Have students 'finish drive' by reviewing each of their identified careers.

7. Once students have reviewed their careers, they will be given the opportunity to print their driver's license. For example,

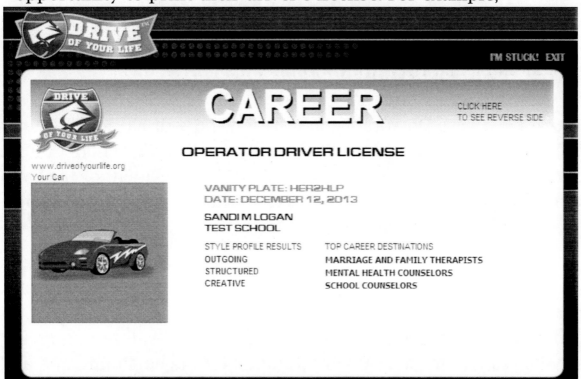

8. Wrap up the lesson by encouraging students to use the website on their own and further explore other careers.

Cautions: Make sure all computer/laptops being used met the specification necessary. Consult with the IT Help sheet. https://www.driveofyourlife.org/ithelp/IT%20Help%20Sheet%20Mar%2020

10%20version.pdf. Be prepared for students to have various levels of technology competence—some students may need more time than others. Perhaps even a prior lesson on computer usage depending on the experience of students.

Adaptations: For ELL students or students receiving special education services allow for extra time and additional adult assistance. Utilize more visuals and examples for both ELL students and students with special needs.

Credit/References

www.driveofyourlife.org

About the Counselors:

Sandra Logan is a Doctoral Fellow at University of Florida in Gainesville. Previously, she worked as an Elementary and Middle School Counselor in Southern California. Also, she has served as a President of the Orange County chapter of the **California Association of School Counselors.** Logan.here2help@gmail.com

Jennifer Greene is a Doctoral Student at University of Central Florida. Previously, Jennifer worked as a School Counselor at an international school in Decatur, Georgia. This school offered the International Baccalaureate Primary Years Programme to refugee, immigrant, and American born students. jengreene@knights.ucf.edu

Name: _____

Teacher: _____

Grade: _____

Drive of Your Life: Career Exploration

www.driveofyourlife.org

User ID: _____

Password: _____

3 Personal Strengths:

1.

2.

3.

3 things I enjoy doing:

1.

2.

3.

Lesson 1

School Counselors Share Their Favorite Classroom Guidance Activities

My Personal Style is:

1. _____   2. _____   3. _____

   1. I am _____ because

   2. I am _____ because

   3. I am _____ because

Possible Careers:

1.

2.

3.

4.

5.

Top 3 Careers

For Typical Day, read all; choose 3 of the following to write down information about:

Typical tasks performed	Working with others
Hazardous conditions	Working with computers
Physically demanding	Skill sets
Working outside	Next steps

Career #1: _____   <u>Typical Day</u>

1._____

_____

_____

2._____

_____

_____

3._____

_____

_____

<u>Career Fast Facts</u>

Annual and hourly wage:

Preparation:

3 helpful high school courses:

Career #2: _____   <u>Typical Day</u>

1._____

_____

_____

2._____

_____

_____

Career #2: _____ <u>Typical Day   (cont.)</u>

3._____

_____

_____

<u>Career Fast Facts</u>

Annual and hourly wage:

Preparation:

3 helpful high school courses:

Career #3: _____ <u>Typical Day</u>

1._____

_____

_____

2._____

_____

_____

3._____

_____

_____

<u>Career Fast Facts</u>

Annual and hourly wage:

Preparation:

3 helpful high school courses:

The Power of YuGiOh: Using Your Powers to Explore Careers

Submitted by Cory A. Brooks, M.S and Melissa Luke, Ph.D

School Level: Middle.

Goals: Students will be able to:

1. Identify at least one of each of the following: a personal belief, a skill, and an interest or motivation.
2. Explain the similarities and differences between a career related personal belief, a skill, and an interest or motivation.
3. Share ideas and reactions to classmates' career interest, including thoughts about type of related beliefs, skills, interests and motivations.

ASCA Standards:

C: A1.3. Develop an awareness of personal abilities, skills, interests and motivations
C: C1.3 Identify personal preferences and interests influencing career choice and success
C: C2.3 Learn to work cooperatively with others as a team member.

Estimated Time: 45 minutes.

Materials: Blank **YuGiOh Card** Handout; markers, colored pencils, or crayons; and lined paper and pen.

Lesson

1. Explain the activity as follows: Who knows what YuGiOh is? Has anyone here heard of this and could explain a little to others? Invite volunteer to speak, but if no one does, offer the following: YuGiOh is a strategic card game played by children and adolescents, in which they duel over cards that possess different powers, attributes, and defense in the YuGiOh fantasy world. (2 to 3 minutes)

2. Let's pretend that you were a character in YuGiOh who has never been created before. You can be whatever you like Wizard, Witch, Sorceresses, Fairy, Monster, or Magic Spell, etc.

3. Imagine what you would you look like, what magic or special power that you will have, what attack and defense level, and how you would use your powers. What are the goals or reasons you would need these powers and skills? Give them an example or two if they are not familiar with YuGiOh.

4. After you invent your YuGiOh character, think about how the special powers and skills will be manifested (or displayed). For example, if I were a Shape Shifter, my special power and skill would be to assume different forms. I could change my appearance whenever I wanted and others would have a hard time recognizing me. I might want to do this to blend in, to stay safe or hidden. What are some other ideas? (5 minutes)

5. Okay, once you have decided on your character, the special powers and skills, and why you might need or use them, you can begin to draw your character on the blank YuGiOh card. As the student draws his/her YuGiOh character, the professional school counselor circulates around the classroom and tracks and reflects on feelings associated with the child's drawing. Add a sentence or two about how to do this. Emphasizing that everyone has their own unique strengths. (2 to 3 minutes)

6. Students will be encouraged to give responses out loud. (If group is large students can write down responses and be called on.) (2 to 3 minutes)

7. During this time, the professional school counselor uses observation and occasionally links students' activities. Additionally, the school counselor may offer some process comments too, such as "It seems as if it's easier to decide what type of character you want to be, but harder to settle on one special power" or " There are so many special skills in this room right now, I can feel the tremendous power!" (10 minutes)

8. After the students finish their drawing, the professional school counselor helps students to share and explore in depth who he/she has invented, what magic and power spells will they have and how they would be used.

9. Additionally, the professional school counselor leads a discussion of the types of careers where similar types of interests, skills, and motivations may be necessary. For example, the school counselor might say "I noticed that Cory's character could read minds. Is there any job that you can think of that uses a similar skill? In what type of profession or job do people have to really understand how someone else thinks (almost any human service professional would benefit from this) but some typical responses might be police officer, teacher or counselor, advertiser. E.g. Healing Power- Doctor, Veterinarian, and/or Nurse. The professional school counselor can offer these and facilitate students' ability to discern how the special power might be useful in real jobs. (10 minutes)

Processing Questions: (10 minutes)

The client's YuGiOh character can provide valuable information about how he/she views themselves in the world. Potential process question could include:

✓ How is your YuGiOh character like you? How is it different? What would you emphasize when they answer?

✓ What is it about the special power that you selected that really appeals to you? How might your life be different if you had this skill?

✓ Pick one of the special powers or skills mentioned today (It doesn't have to be from your character), and explain a job or career that might use this same skill?

✓ What is the meaning behind your card? What do you like most about your power/spells?

✓ It's interesting to consider how all these special powers work in relation to each other, like what might happen if the characters you created were put together somewhere. What might happen in the YuGiOh game or even, in real life?

✓ How is your character related to you in real life? Do you wish you had powers in real life? How might your 'wish' help you think about possible future careers?

Cautions: This activity/intervention is fairly fast paced, moving sequentially through the outlined steps. On occasion, some students have a hard time keeping up with the next step. It can be useful in such instances to have the classroom teacher or a paraprofessional or volunteer parent work with the individual child while the school counselor moves on with the class. Related, the professional school counselor will need to save enough time at the end of the activity for appropriate processing. Without the processing, the meaning and potential benefit of the activity is lost. The school counselor will need to structure students' attention and thinking so that they can make the connections between the creative fantasy activity and their future career interests.

Adaptations: The focus could be shifted to communication skills; the activity could be useful for a variety of common presenting issues. This lesson plan can be helpful for kids with anger outbursts, or kids who shut down and withdrawal without talking because they are encouraged to express themselves artistically. The ability to reflect feelings associated with the character that the student has drawn may encourage the students who withdraw to begin to speak out. For the student who has anger outburst this lesson plan can encourage them to channel their energies differently by turning their weaknesses into strengths.

Suggestions on How to Integrate into Core Curriculum: The professional school counselor could collaborate with an English Language Arts teacher to relate this to characters in the literature that students have read. Additionally, the school counselor could make a connection to technology in lesson that follows by designing their YuGiOh characters on a computer based program.

Next Possible Lesson Plan Topics: An idea for a subsequent lesson involves building upon the YuGiOh character to make a card that represented a form of technology. The 'tool' cards would offer another way to identify career related abilities, skills, interests and motivations. As a culminating activity for the second lesson, students could attempt to 'play' a game of YuGiOh in small groups using the cards they made (school counselor could have additional cards to add for this purpose too, perhaps copies of those former students had created).

Credit/References

Adapted from *If I Were a Superhero* by Susan Kelsey http://www.gway.org/Websites/gway/images/Creative%20Interventions.pdf

Yami, P. (n.d.). *Blank Yu-Gi-Oh cards 3*. Retrieved from http://pharaoh-yami.deviantart.com/art/Blank-Yu-Gi-Oh-Cards-3-78325267

This classroom guidance lesson plan was inspired by the individual work Cory did with a student during his internship placement.

About the Counselors:

Cory Brooks, M.S., is a Middle School Counselor at Solvay Middle School in Solvay, NY and has worked with at -risk youth in urban education for the past several years. He is a recent graduate of Syracuse University. cobrooks@syr.edu

Dr. Luke is an Associate Professor, Interim Chair, and Coordinator of School Counseling, Syracuse University. Previously, she was a School Counselor and a High School Teacher. mmluke@syr.edu

Family Work Values: Tools from the Past: Lessons 1, 2, and 3

Submitted by M. Carolyn Thomas and Sheila M. Austin

School Level: Middle.

Goals: Students will:
1. Become aware of a family value that has persisted through one or more generations, and has had a positive effect on the family's achievement.
2. Learn from an older family member how that value may have helped overcome adversities, including discrimination.
3. Become aware of the relationship between values, attitudes and success.
4. Build a commitment to pass on the value to future generations.
5. Learn that all work has dignity.

ASCA Standards:

A:A1.3 Take pride in work and achievement
PS:A1.2 Identify values, attitudes and beliefs
PS:A1.12 Identify and recognize changing family roles
PS:B1.11 Use persistence and perseverance in acquiring knowledge and skills.

Estimated Time: Three lessons of 50 to 60 minutes.

Materials: Tools or cooking utensils of older relatives that may have been handed down for two or more generations. (See instructions at end of Lesson 1.)

Lesson 1

1. Counselor begins with an introduction to the relationship between values and success. Success is defined in terms of building a satisfying life for themselves and their families, and becoming contributing members of their communities. The acquisition of money is minimized as an indicator of success. A value is a belief or principle held by and individual that can be useful in achieving personal and family goals.

School Counselors Share Their Favorite Classroom Guidance Activities

2. Counselor says: "Tools or cooking utensils of an older relative of yours may have been handed down for two or more generations. These tools may represent a family value that has influenced success in your family, and helped your forebears overcome diversity. For example, an African-American student once brought an old hammer that had belonged to his grandfather. It was symbolic because the grandfather had to learn a myriad of skills to seek jobs to support his family. The hammer became the symbol of being willing to take on all kinds of work in a discriminating society in order to improve conditions for his family and future descendants. The student bringing the hammer to group cherished the hammer because it symbolized the value of striving in a difficult society and the dignity of all work. Another student brought a biscuit cutter her great grandmother had used to make biscuits. It was symbolic because the great grandmother had often sat her children and grandchildren in the kitchen and talked with them at length about life, true success, the value of all work, and acts of sharing and cooperation. The student continues to use the biscuit cutter, not merely to shape biscuits, but as an opportunity to teach her children the values that have contributed to generations of success. " (25 to 30 minutes)

3. The counselor asks students to discuss: (15-20 minutes)

✓ Can you think of an object that has been handed down in your family that seems to be cherished by an older family member? If so, what is it?

✓ If you know of such an object, what story have you been told about it?

4. Counselor then says: "If you cannot think of a special old tool in your family, you will get the opportunity in the homework assignment I am about to give you to ask a family member. Often these old home or kitchen tools may look banged up or of little value, and you may not have noticed them. When you interview your family member, you might discover why it has been kept, and why it is of such value."

5. Homework: Each student is asked to:

a. Identify an older family member they respect and interview so they can relate the story of the older relative at the next session. If an older family member is not available, the student may interview a respected teacher, neighbor or known member in the community.

Suggested questions for the interview might include:

✓ What about your years of work made you most proud?

✓ What motivated you to continue working, even during hard times?

✓ What values did you want to hand down to your children and their children?

✓ Is there a tool, cooking utensil, or piece of equipment that you got from your father or mother that represents a certain work value?

✓ If you give this symbolic object to your child, what story would you tell the child about it?

  b. Bring the object to the next lesson and be ready to tell the story about the older relative, and show how the value represented by the object has been handed down through the family. If the object cannot be brought to the group, the child can bring a photograph, drawing or description of the object.

Lesson 2

1. Counselor says: "Now that you have had the opportunity to ask a relative, valued teacher, or older friend about a home or kitchen tool that has been handed down in the family for two or more generations, you will share with the group what you discovered. As you listen to each member's story, try to see similarities in the stories. Also, look for deeper meanings in the stories to see why the tool is so important to the person. (5 minutes)

2. Ask students to relate their stories about the older relatives. This true story is built from the answers to the interview questions and from the stories of the older persons. (The time allotted for each student to share depends upon the number of students in the group. Small or subgroups can allow more time for each student. (15 to 20 minutes)

3. Process Questions: (15 to 20 minutes depends upon number of students in class or subgroups)

✓ How are you related to the older person, and what are the characteristics you like about this person?

✓ What is the tool or cooking utensil the person showed you or told you about that meant a lot to the person?

✓ What work or personal value did the older person say the object represented?

✓ What story did the older person tell you about the object?

4. The counselor provides closure to this session by using the children's stories to show similarities and deeper meanings, saying: "We can see meanings behind the tools in all your stories. Your family tools may be different, but the meanings are similar. You probably noticed how your family members have learned the value of hard work, how they have

overcome hard times, what makes a family close, and why learning a lot of different skills is important to success. Next session we will discuss specifically how these meanings have applied in your family, and how you can pass these values down to your children." (5 to 10 minutes)

Lesson 3

1. Counselor says: "Last session we talked about old tools and how the tools are symbols for home and work success values in your families. You talked about persistence, dependability, courage, family closeness, and overcoming hard times. Think about how your current family uses these values in their home and career work. Think about how you can use these values at school and in your home. Also, think about how you can pass on these values to your future family." (5 minutes)

2. Ask the following questions: (30 minutes)
✓ How have you seen this value used by your past family?
✓ How has your current family used this value?
✓ How can you use this value in planning a productive life?
✓ When you grow up, how can you make sure this value is passed on from you to your children and other family members?
✓ If you do not have the specific object you learned about from the older person with whom you spoke, what tool or utensil of yours can you use to teach a value and pass on to other relatives?
✓ What value(s) do you want to pass on?

3. Closure: (20-25 minutes)

The counselor summarizes the handed down values represented by tools, and shows the relationship between values and success based on students' responses to process questions. The students are also given the opportunity to share how they will use the value in their own lives. Finally, students are given the opportunity to plan how they will pass on the value to other relatives.

Counselor says: "You have shared how the value represented by your family tool has been used in your past and current family. You may also have recognized how family members have tried to teach you this value. You can play an important role in passing on these values to other relatives and future family members. When you were asked to identify the values and how you might pass them on, you gave several creative plans. As you learn to apply the values in school, family chores, volunteer work, friendships, and family relationships, you might discover more creative ways to perpetuate the value. Remember the tool, but more importantly, remember the value and meaning behind the tool. Those are the most important legacies your family has left you, and the most valuable gifts you can leave your children."

Cautions: Some children may be adopted, live with relatives or know little of their family. Adaptations can be made to prevent them from feeling badly. They can choose teachers or other important persons to interview, and the Counselor can make certain these students responding in groups do not feel different.

Adaptations: This three-lesson exercise could be extended over several weeks to reach more depth of discussion about work values, overcoming adversities, and commitment to future generations. Additionally, this exercise could be used with high school, college and graduate students.

How to Integrate into Core Curriculum: Language arts teachers could have the students write a story about the older person, the tool, or the role the value played in their families. Art teachers could get the students to make a drawing depicting the story. Students could also submit a poem or poster about family tools and work values for the annual National Career Development Association Poster/Poetry Contest each November; www.ncda.org

Next Possible Topics: Diversity, work values and social skills needed to overcome social problems such as poverty, discrimination, and gender bias.

About the Counselors:

M. Carolyn Thomas is Professor of Counselor Education at Auburn University Montgomery in Montgomery, AL. mthomas@aum.edu

Sheila M. Austin is Professor and Dean of the School of Education at Auburn University Montgomery, Montgomery, AL. saustin1@aum.edu

Now For Later

Submitted by Megan Beeching

School Level: Middle.

Goals:

1. Explore future career goals and assess how they relate to desired lifestyle.
2. Increase knowledge about how one's current choices are affecting their future goals.

ASCA Standards:

C:A2.7 Develop a positive attitude toward work and learning
C:C1.2 Explain how work can help to achieve personal success and satisfaction.

Estimated Time: 30 to 60 minutes.

Materials: Paper, drawing materials, *Now for Later* question sheets (Beeching, 2014).

Lesson

1. School counselor begins with: Have you ever thought about what you want in life when you are grown up? Today we are going to discuss our goals for the future and what we can start doing now to reach them.
2. Instruct students to fold their paper into four equal sections and label them "house," "career," "relationships," and "free-time." Students should then draw a picture of what these four areas of life will look like in the future. Have your own paper completed as an example, and share it with students. Tell students when they have their pictures completed, they will use their drawings to answer questions in a group. (15 minutes)
3. When students' pictures are complete, break them into groups of 5 to 7. Instruct them to share each of their drawings with their group and together complete one *Now for Later* worksheet per group. The worksheet allows students to analyze their life choices to see if they are on the right track to the future they see for themselves.
4. Discuss students' pictures and answers groups produced on the *Now for* Later worksheet as a class by asking students to share their

answers to the worksheet and asking these discussion questions:

✓ How are the pictures you drew in the boxes related? Does the type of career you have affect what type of home you can afford, etc? (Help students process inconsistencies in their planning. As an example, if they drew McDonalds in "career" and a mansion in "house" they need to know this is not realistic.

✓ What needs to happen this semester to steer you toward your future goals? This year? 5 years? 10 years? (Help students process the chain of cause and effect here. If their grades are not great, it will be less likely they can secure the post-secondary education needed for the career they want, and therefore the lifestyle they are after.)

✓ How will you use what you learned about yourself today to make changes in your life?

Adaptations: Students could cut pictures and images from magazines to create collages.

About the Counselor:

Megan Beeching is a graduate and Lab Mentor of the School Counseling program at Indiana University- Purdue University, Fort Wayne. megan.beeching@gmail.com

Now for Later (Beeching, 2014) (With Example Answers)

Students can produce any answers-these suggestions are to help facilitate conversation if needed

What are two academic choices students can make that will help them achieve the picture they see for themselves?
1. ___Study hard_____
2. _Pick challenging classes

Name two academic choices students can make that will hinder them from achieving the picture they see for themselves?
1. ___Drop out_____
2. Don't ask for help if I am struggling in a class

What two personal choices can students make now that will help them achieve the picture they see for themselves?
1. _Join clubs_____
2. _Pick positive friends_

Name two personal choices students make that hinders them from achieving the picture they see for themselves?
1. Use drugs/get in trouble
2. Have a lack of motivation

Identify two people you can speak with about academic choices.
1. _Guidance Counselor_
2. _Parents_____

Identify resources (e.g., people, books, websites) students can get information from to help their ideal future come true? 1. www.learnmoreindiana.org 2. www.triptocollege.org_____

School Counselors Share Their Favorite Classroom Guidance Activities

Now for Later (Beeching, 2014)

What are two academic choices students can make that will help them achieve the picture they see for themselves?

    1. _____

    2. _____

Name two academic choices students can make that will hinder them from achieving the picture they see for themselves?

    1. _____

    2. _____

What two personal choices can students make now that will help them achieve the picture they see for themselves?

Name two personal choices students make that hinders them from achieving the picture they see for themselves?

    1. _____

    2. _____

Identify two people you can speak with about academic choices.

    1. _____

    2. _____

Identify resources (e.g., people, books, websites) students can get information from to help their ideal future come true?

    1. _____

    2. _____

Identify how your school counselor can support students to do the right things now to reach their goals for later. Write your ideas below:

A Candy-Full Career

Submitted by Leslie Neyland and Christopher P. Roseman

School Level: Middle.

Goals: Students will:
1. Understand of the relationship between school performance and future career choices.
2. Learn to value their abilities as they discuss skills and talents related to school, home, and the community.
3. Learn how to seek out resources to successfully research and organize jobs based on their academic interests and personal abilities.

ASCA Standards:

A:C1.6 Understand how school success and academic achievement enhance future career and vocational opportunities

C:C1.1 Understand the relationship between educational achievement and career success

C:A1.1 Develop skills to locate, evaluate, and interpret career information.

Estimated Time: 40 minutes.

Materials: Different colored objects (e.g., M&M's, skittles, small food colored items, stones, erasers), large pieces of paper for each group, pen.

Introduction: Setting career goals is a great challenge throughout the adolescent years because it is an age with so much change and promise. While it may be difficult to envision a career at this age, it is not much different than trying to choose a favorite place to go on the weekend. It takes some discussion about where you want to go, what interests you most about a certain place, how you are going to get there, and how much fun it will be. Setting goals for choosing a potential career is much the same and by identifying your ideal job early and planning short-term steps to get there, you can achieve anything you want to do in life. This activity will help you to begin to think about careers based on some of your interests.

Lesson

1. To begin, pour multicolor objects into a bowl.
2. Ask each student to take as many, or at minimum, six objects (candy, etc.) as they like from the bowl. If candy, ask them not to eat right away. (5 minutes)
3. For each item they took, they will have to answer a question, depending on color. For example, you can designate: (10 minutes)

• Red: Favorite hobbies
• Green: Favorite things to do with a friend
• Yellow: Favorite movies
• Orange: Favorite classes
• Brown: Positive characteristic about themselves
• Blue: Things they are good at

The facilitator will then call out the color topic and everyone will go around the room sharing 1 answer per piece of candy/object.

Example: if you chose two red pieces of candy, you will name two favorite hobbies. Continue to go around the room until each color topic has been shared. After a participant has shared, they may then eat their candy.

4. The facilitators can then process the activity with the participants.
   ✓ What was it like to do this activity?
5. Ask questions that relate answers to hobbies, things to do, movies, what they are good at, and classes and careers.
   ✓ Do you like to do things with people or alone?
   ✓ Do you enjoy building things?
   ✓ Are you good with computers?
   ✓ What movies have you watched that inspire you?
6. Ask questions that relate answers positive characteristics to job skills and good work ethic.
   ✓ Are you good at reading, writing, math, speaking, and/or listening?
   ✓ Do you consider yourself creative, a good problem-solver, or a leader?
   ✓ Do you feel you are honest and responsible?
   ✓ What similarities did you notice in your answers?
   ✓ Similarities in other's answers?

7. Ask specific questions that tie their answers to interest clusters and then careers.
   - ✓ Do you like to help people who are sick?
   - ✓ Have you ever written computer programs?
   - ✓ Do you like to bake/sew, repair cars, or build things out of wood?
   - ✓ Do you like to write or play an instrument?

Thoughts about similarities in answers can be discussed along with differences. (15 minutes)

8. Based on the responses to the processing questions, organize the students in pairs or groups of three based on similar traits and career interests to have a discussion of qualities employers look for in employees.

9. Ask students in small groups to make a list of their positive characteristics and qualities they like about a friend on large piece of paper. (5 minutes)

10. Ask students in groups to discuss qualities employers look for in employees. (5 minutes)
   - ✓ What do you think is the most important quality for a specific career?
   - ✓ Which classes are important to be successful in a specific career?

11. Students will be given homework to create a list of 3 careers that interest them. Each student will be asked to learn as much as they can about the careers they are interested in by asking people who work in a career field of interest, and researching in the library and on the Internet.

Cautions: Keeping students focused on task and not having them more interested in the candy itself.

Credit/References

http://www.group-games.com/ice-breakers/mm-game.html

About the Counselors:

Leslie Neyland, MA is currently a Doctoral Counseling Student at the University of Toledo. Leslie.Neyland@rockets.utoledo.edu

Christopher P. Roseman, Ph.D., PC-CR, NCC is an Assistant Professor in Counselor Education Program at the University of Toledo. Christopher.Roseman@utoledo.edu

I Can Lead

*Submitted by Bria Booker, Heather Reynolds,
and Kerrie R. Fineran*

School Level: Middle/High.

Goals:

1. Develop an awareness of personal leadership beliefs and personal leadership qualities.
2. Identify skills necessary in becoming effective leaders.

ASCA Standards:

A:A2.4 Apply knowledge and learning styles to positively influence school performance
A:A3.3 Develop a broad range of interests and abilities
A:A3.4 Demonstrate dependability, productivity and initiative
A:A3.5 Share knowledge
A:C1.3 Understand the relationship between learning and work
A:C1.6 Understand how school success and academic achievement enhance future career and vocational opportunities.

Estimated Time: 30 to 45 minutes.

Materials: 6 quotes printed on separate pieces of paper that vary in viewpoints regarding leadership (more or fewer quotes depending on space and class size), tape, printed sheets with chosen processing questions (optional).

Some Possible Quotes:
- "My responsibility is getting all my players playing for the name on the front of the jersey, not the one on the back." *Unknown*
- "If your actions inspire others to dream more, learn more, do more and become more, you are a leader." *John Quincy Adams*
- "Don't necessarily avoid sharp edges. Occasionally they are necessary to leadership." *Donald Rumsfeld*
- "Education is the mother of leadership." *Wendell Willkie*
- "Leadership is influence." *John C. Maxwell*
- "Leadership is the art of getting someone else to do something you want done because he wants to do it." *General Dwight Eisenhower*

- "It is better to lead from behind and to put others in front..." *Nelson Mandela*
- "Effective leadership is not about making speeches or being liked; leadership is defined by results not attributes." *Peter Drucker*
- "Innovation distinguishes between a leader and a follower." *Steve Jobs*
- "The quality of a leader is reflected in the standards they set for themselves." *Ray Kroc*

Examples of quotes can be found on websites such as:
100 best quotes on leadership:
http://www.forbes.com/sites/kevinkruse/2012/10/16/quotes-on-leadership/
Brainy Quote: http://www.brainyquote.com/quotes/topics/topic_leadership.html
Good Reads: http://www.goodreads.com/quotes/tag/leadership

Prior to Lesson:

1. Find quotes about leadership that exemplifies various meanings or beliefs.
2. Choose a selected number of quotes to print largely on paper.
3. Tape the quotes on the walls around the room allowing space between the quotes so that students have room to stand by the quote of their choice.
4. Select which processing questions you would like to use and print them on paper, allowing room for students to write answers/notes. The group leader could also present processing questions by writing them on the board or including them in an electronic presentation format (such as PowerPoint).

Lesson

1. Explain to the students that you are going to discuss beliefs about leadership and skills needed to be an effective leader. The counselor may say, *"Today we are going to talk about an important topic: leadership. As we begin, I'd like for you to think about the characteristics of leaders you have observed both in school and out of school."* The group leader could also ask alternate beginning questions such as *"What characteristics exemplify an effective leader"* or *"What leadership qualities do you as an individual have?"* The group leader may just have students think about this quietly (approximately 2 minutes) or brainstorm/share as a group (5 to 10 minutes)
2. Invite students to walk around reading the quotes that are taped on the walls in various places in the room. Ask students to stand by the quote that best represents their personal views on what makes a good leader.

Say, "*at this time you will notice that there are various quotes hanging on the walls around the room.* (you may choose to read these quotes out loud to the students at this time). *Please walk around and read all the quotes quietly to yourself. Think about what each quote means and what it implies about leadership.*" (3 to 5 minutes)

3. Then say "*after you have read each quote, decide on which quote best represents your views on effective leadership. Stand by that quote.*" 4. Allow time for them to pick their quote. You may wish to discourage talking at this time, and instead play music (patriotic tunes may be appropriate such as "The Stars and Stripes Forever," the official March of the United States of America (US Code, Title 36 Chapter 10) or "America, The Beautiful"). (1 to 2 minutes)

4. Students will be clustered in groups around specific quotes. The group leader may choose to process in one of two ways: Small group processing with reporting to the large group later or full group discussion. Say, "*in the small groups you have created by choosing the same quote, choose one person to be the 'recorder' and one person to be the 'reporter.' Now, we will spend some time discussing the quotes you chose and the recorder should jot down notes as the group discusses. The reporter will be responsible for sharing the ideas of the small group with the larger group a little later.*" If there is only one person standing next to a quote, ask him or her to choose a group to join. He or she may take the quote chosen off the wall and bring it with him or her when joining the selected group. The group's task in this case will be to incorporate both quotes into their discussion. (3 minutes)

Processing Questions:

Ask students to process the questions together in their small groups according to the directions above in Step 3. Pass out pre-printed questions or direct attention to the board or slide. (approximately 10 to 25 minutes)

> Discuss together what you believe this quote means. Talk about why each of you chose it.
>   ✓ What about this quote resonates with you?
>   ✓ How does it fit with your personality?
>   ✓ How does it fit with the person you want to be?
>   ✓ How does it fit with the leader you want to be?

> Discuss the experiences you have had that influence your views about leadership.

- ✓ What leadership skills and behaviors have you seen in class and school that have been effective and reflect this style of leadership?
- ✓ What leadership skills and behaviors have you seen in other places in the community that have been effective and reflect this style of leadership?
- ✓ How do you think others see you as a leader? Is it similar to the quote you picked?
- ✓ What can you do to be more like the leader exemplified in the quote you picked?
- ➤ How do you think you can demonstrate effective leadership qualities in various environments such as:
  - • School
  - • Your community
  - • Personal relationships?

Final Processing Questions for Large Group:

- ✓ As you leave this group today, what is one thing that someone else said that impacted your views about leadership?
- ✓ As you leave this group today, what is one goal that you have to improve your leadership skills here at school, in your community, or in your personal life?

Cautions: School counselors should be sensitive to children who have difficulty standing or who may have difficulty with reading the quotes. It may be helpful for the group leader to read each quote out loud and/or have students raise their hands to choose a quote rather than walking around the room.

Adaptations: Depending on time and interest, the group leader could facilitate a discussion, using the processing questions, with all the students at once rather than using a "recorder/reporter" format in small groups.
Give a list of quotes to each student and instruct them to rank in order of importance such as their top 3 quotes. Students could then join groups based on the quote that they chose to be most important. The students could then also share their other top two quotes with the small group in

order to deepen the discussion and gain a greater understanding of others' viewpoints on leadership.

Credit/References

Kruse, K. (2012, October 16). 100 best quotes on leadership. Retrieved from http://www.forbes.com/sites/kevinkruse/2012/10/16/quotes-on-leadership/

Siebold, T. (2013, February 23). Stand by your quote. Retrieved from http://www.workshopexercises.com/Leadership.htm#L1

About the Contributors:

Bria Booker is a graduate of Indiana University- Purdue University, Fort Wayne, a licensed School Counselor, and a Student Assistant Specialist at Prince Chapman Academy.

Heather Reynolds is a Graduate Student at Indiana University- Purdue University, Fort Wayne and a School Counseling Intern.

Kerrie R. Fineran is an Assistant Professor and Coordinator of the School Counseling Program at Indiana University- Purdue University, Fort Wayne and a licensed School Counselor. Finerank@ipfw.edu

Family Drawings and Career Guidance: Lessons 1, 2, and 3

Submitted by Mary Gomez, Ph.D.

School Level: High.

Target Population: Grade 9.

Estimated Time: Three lessons of 30 to 45 minutes.

Materials: Blank paper, magic markers, crayons, or colored pencils, computer access to Internet for each student, registration guide, blank 4-year plans for each student.

Goal: 9th grade students will be able to create a 4-year high school coursework plan based on a career choice.

ASCA Standards:

Academics
Standard B: Students will complete school with the academic potential to choose from a wide range of substantial potential options, including college.
> A B2: Plan to achieve goals

Standard C: Students will understand the relationship of academics to the world of work and to life at home and in the community.
> C1: Relate School to Life Experience

Career Development
Standard A: Students will acquire the skills to investigate the world of work in relationship to knowledge of self and to make informed career decisions.
> A 1: Develop Career Awareness

Standard B: Students will employ strategies to achieve future career goals with success and satisfaction.
> B 1: Acquire Career Information
> B 2: Identify Career Goals

Standard C: Students will understand the relationship between personal qualities, education, training and the world of work.

Lesson 1

1. Begin with: *Students, today we are going to begin thinking about a career for ourselves. Raise your hand if you have already thought about what you would like to be doing for a career 10 years from now? (Go around and have students say what they would like to do.) Oftentimes, people pick their careers based on what occupations that their parents or brothers or sisters have. So, today, we are going to have some fun by drawing a picture.* (5 minutes)

2. Give each student a blank sheet of paper. Ask each of them to draw a picture of their family doing something. In the picture include a tree, house, and all family members doing something. Label each family member. (Be prepared for questions such as: "What if my dad or mom does not live with us? Or what if my brother/sister is in college?" Response is: "Put them anywhere you would like in your drawing." At this point, also tell them that after everyone is done with their family drawings they will share some or all of their drawing so they are not surprised when asked to later. (15 minutes)

3. As the students to turn the paper over, ask them to write on the back of the paper the following information:
   a. date of the drawing
   b. list the family members and their careers.

For example, one family member may be a doctor, fireman, construction worker, salesman, housewife/husband, etc. Other family members may be in college at (name) university, others may be in 1st 2nd, or 3rd grade. Emphasize that being in school is a job.

   c. Each student then puts his/her name on the list and the career he/she would like to have.

4. Students stand up and share what each family member is doing in the drawing and the career of each family member.

5. End with:
   ✓ What did you learn about your family choices of careers?
   ✓ Are they the same as yours? Why or why not?

6. Homework assignment: Ask your parents:
   • What courses were the most valuable to them in high school?
   • If they had it to do all over again, would they chose the same career?
   • What do they like the most about their career?
   • What do they least like about their job?

Lesson 2

1. Start by processing the information that the students found from their parents with questions such as:
   - ✓ What courses did you parents believe are important to take in high school?
   - ✓ What were your parents' responses to their career choices?
   - ✓ What did their parents like?
   - ✓ What did they dislike?
   - ✓ Would they do it all over again? (15 to 20 minutes)
2. Demonstrate in class the different sites available to the students to look at their particular career. Navigate the websites so that students can explore their own career choice. Some of the websites include: the College Board website; https://bigfuture.collegeboard.org/explore-careers/careers/exploring-careers-step-by-step, or the ACT website: http://www.actstudent.org/career/
   a. Include in the demonstration how students would find out about high school courses needed, post-graduate education needed, career outlook and salary,
3. Homework assignment: Think about the courses you will need to take while in high school.

Lesson 3

1. Begin with discussion about the career search. Ask:
   - ✓ What surprised you about your career choice?
   - ✓ What are some of the courses you will need to take in high school?
   - ✓ What are some of the courses you need to take in college?
   (15 to 20 minutes)
2. Begin the creation of the 4-year plan. Say: *The four year plan is your coursework outline to help you graduate from high school and help you in obtaining your career goal. Post graduate planning starts now. All of you coursework and your grades today will influence your career choices. The 4-year plans will be kept in your file in the counselor's*

office, so that at the end of each semester, you can look at it or modify it as your coursework or career interests change.

   a. Pass out the registration guide and pass out a blank 4 year plan (see sample coursework plan). (Another suggestion is to bring a sample of a filled out course work plan from a senior.)

   b. Ask students to write at the top of the paper: name, date, career choice, and education needed.

   c. Then make a list of courses you will take each year, by semester. Start with this semester and what you are taking. *Remember, this is a tentative coursework plan. You can change it as needed when you register for classes each year."*

   d. Answer any questions from the students.

   e. Give a due date for finishing the 4-year plans.

3. Encourage students to make an appointment with the counselor to go over the coursework plan before the due date. Tell them that counselors will return to the classroom at least one more time during the quarter to answer any questions about the 4-year plan and then again at the end of the quarter and collect 4-year plans.

About the Counselor:

Dr. Mary Gomez is a Psychologist and Consultant, University of Denver, Counseling Psychology. drmaryg@ecentral.com

Name: _____
Date: _____
Career Choice: _____
Post-Graduate Education needed: _____

4-Year Course Plan

Freshmen Year

Semester 1 Courses

English: _____
Social Studies: _____
Math: _____
Science: _____
Foreign Language: _____
Electives/Other: _____
Electives/Other: _____

Semester 2 Courses

English: _____
Social Studies: _____
Math: _____
Science: _____
Foreign Language: _____
Electives/Other: _____
Electives/Other: _____

Sophomore Year

Semester 1 Courses

English: _____
Social Studies: _____
Math: _____
Science: _____
Foreign Language: _____
Electives/Other: _____
Electives/Other: _____

Semester 2 Courses

English: _____
Social Studies: _____
Math: _____
Science: _____
Foreign Language: _____
Electives/Other: _____
Electives/Other: _____

Junior Year

Semester 1 Courses

English: _____
Social Studies: _____
Math: _____
Science: _____
Foreign Language: _____
Electives/Other: _____
Electives/Other: _____

Semester 2 Courses

English: _____
Social Studies: _____
Math: _____
Science: _____
Foreign Language: _____
Electives/Other: _____
Electives/Other: _____

Senior Year

Semester 1 Courses

English: _____
Social Studies: _____
Math: _____
Science: _____
Foreign Language: _____
Electives/Other: _____
Electives/Other: _____

Semester 2 Courses

English: _____
Social Studies: _____
Math: _____
Science: _____
Foreign Language: _____
Electives/Other: _____
Electives/Other: _____

NCAA Awareness and Prospective Student-Athletes

By Jaclyn Cavalluzzo

School Level: High.

Goals: Students will:
1. Learn about National Collegiate Athletic Association (NCAA) guidelines in terms of what NCAA entails, the differences between Divisions, and core course requirements for eligibility.
2. Understand what the NCAA Clearinghouse Eligibility Center is and what steps to take as a prospective student-athlete.

Target Population: Potential Student Athletes at beginning of 9th grade.

Possible Classes to Be Integrated: During the 1st week of PE class.

ASCA Standards:
C:A1 Develop Career Awareness
C:A1.3. Develop an awareness of personal abilities, skills, interests and motivations
C:A1.7. Understand the importance of planning
C:B2 Identify Career Goals
C:B2.1 Demonstrate awareness of the education and training needed to achieve career goals.

Estimated Time: 30 minutes.

Materials: NCAA Power point and printed versions for students. (download from asgw.org)

Special Directions:
Do an assessment of which students might be interested in collegiate athletics. This data can determine what year (freshman or sophomore) is appropriate to provide a lesson on NCAA.

Lesson

1. Counselor begins with: This presentation is to help you become aware of and reflect upon your personal athletic interest and the college planning associated with NCAA and Division I, II or III athletics. Refer to power point slide #2 for specific questions on how to increase interaction among group members. (3 minutes)

2. Provide an overview of what NCAA is and why it is important to high school and collegiate student-athletes (Power point slide #3). Also discuss the list of NCAA sponsored sports (Power point slide #4). Ask students what sports they are interested in and why they are interested in that particular sport. (4 minutes)

3. Discuss the differences between Divisions I, II and III sports in terms of athletic demand and scholarship information. Division I and II sports have specific academic and athletic demands while Division III holds less of an emphasis on these demands (Power point slide #5). Ask students how demanding they think it is to play a sport in college and how much college sport involvement they think they can handle. On average Division I is the most demanding level; however, this will vary depending on how competitive the school is. On average, Division I could practice 3 to 4 hours per day, Division II approximately 2.5 to 3 hours and Division III, 2 hours. Again, this range may differ depending upon the competitiveness of the school. Some Division II or III schools may practice more hours per week than a Division I school. Research and interaction with college coaches is critical to obtain this knowledge. Regarding traveling and game schedules this would also depend on the competitiveness of the school. When looking at season length, Division I schools may have a longer practice or travel season (four months) then Division II and III schools (two to three months) and Division II may have a longer season then Division III. However, this is not always true; again research on particular schools need to be carried out. Having students understand these demands from the beginning is critical for realistic goal setting toward collegiate athletic involvement. (5 minutes)

4. Ask students what they think a core course is for NCAA. Outline the exact definition of what a core course is (Power point slide #6). (1 minute)

5. Discuss differences in division I, II and III core course academic eligibility requirements (Power point slides 7 to 9). Have students discuss strategies to stay on top of their core course academic requirements (examples: keep a copy of their yearly courses; organize their own four year academic plan according to eligibility requirements from power point; have students discuss the importance of passing these core courses to remain academically eligible for when it is time to apply to college). (9 minutes)

6. Provide a brief overview of the NCAA eligibility sign up center for potential college bound student-athletes (Power point slide 10). Now that the session is coming to an end and a lot of information has been discussed, have students share if their thoughts have changed regarding collegiate sports. Do they think it will be more work then what they initially thought? Or has this session helped students understand the process and increase their interest in collegiate sports even more? (8 minutes)

7. Stress the importance of expressing their increased interest in collegiate sports to their school counselor ASAP so the student can then sign up with the eligibility center at the beginning of their sophomore school year and provide student-athletes with a checklist for their freshman and sophomore year (Refer to Power point slides #11 and #12 for this information).

Processing Questions:
✓ What information did this lesson provide you with that may be beneficial to you in the future?
✓ Now knowing the demands of a student athlete in relation to eligibility requirements, what do you want to continue to think about?
✓ What information might you look into to further your research of participation as a college-bound student-athlete?

Cautions: Exposure to what NCAA entails is important for all students to understand as athletic abilities may not be realized until junior or senior year.

Possible Follow-up Small Group or Individual Topics: Specific demands and differences between high school and college student-athletes, specifically between Division I, II or III universities; ACT/SAT information regarding codes sent to the NCAA Eligibility Center (junior year), formation of athletic cover letters and resumes (also junior year); enrollment statistics as a collegiate student-athlete, an overview of realistic expectations of collegiate athletics in terms of student portion of the commitment as a student-athlete.

Credit/References

NCAA Eligibility Center. (2013). *2013-14 Guide for the college-bound student-athlete.* Indianapolis, IN: NCAA Publications. Retrieved from http://www.ncaapublications.com/p-4236-2013-14-ncaa-guide-for-the-college-bound-student-athlete-sold-as-a-packages-of-25-due-summer-2013.aspx
https://web1.ncaa.org/hsportal/exec/links?linksSubmit=ShowActiveLinks

About the School Counselor:

Jaclyn M. Cavalluzzo is a School Counseling Student at the University at Buffalo, SUNY. jc428@buffalo.edu.   She is currently a School Counseling Intern at Lancaster High School outside of Buffalo, NY.

Interdependence Day
Submitted by Laura Walker and Rebekah Byrd

School Level: High.

Target Population: Grades 9 and 10.

Goals: Students will:
1. Be able to define interdependence.
2. Identify personal strengths for current career choice.
3. Find connections with classmates and their current career choices.
4. Have an understanding of how we can all work together despite different careers.

ASCA Standards:

A:B1.2   Learn and apply critical-thinking skills
C:A2.5   Learn to respect individual uniqueness in the workplace
C:B1.2   Identify personal skills, interests, and abilities and relate them to current career choice.

Estimated Time: 30 minutes.

Materials: White board and marker, paper (construction or copy), markers/crayons; each student needs a piece of scrap paper and a pen/pencil.

Lesson

1. Introduce today's lesson by asking students what *interdependence* means. The focus should be on connection and interaction with others. Record their ideas on the board. It may be necessary to break the word *interdependence* down into its root *depend* which means "to place reliance or trust" (Merriam-Webster). Next, discuss the prefix *inter-* and its meanings "between, among, together" or "reciprocal" (Merriam-Webster). Finally, discuss the word *interdependence* as a whole. Some responses are: -all things depend on one another, everything is balanced, or we all need others.

2. Explain the activity. Each student will choose either to draw a picture or write words, phrases, and/or a story on where they see themselves in 20 years. You can write on the board what year it will be and how old they will be. Ask them to focus on their career. What do they see themselves doing at this moment in their lives? They may also decide to incorporate personal goals as well (e.g., getting married and having a family). State that everyone will share their work after they are finished, and they may share as little or as much as they like

3. Hand out construction or copy paper and markers/crayons/pens. Give them 7 minutes to complete their work. After everyone is finished, have each student share their drawing or writing. As each student shares, the other students are to write down on their scrap sheet of paper how they will interact with each person <u>in a professional capacity</u> in 20 years. More specifically, ask them to think about how they will interact with others through his/her career.

Examples are: As a school counselor, I listen to a student share that they expect to be a physical therapist. I would write on my scrap paper that I may invite that student to speak for Career Day.

-The student who wants to be a physical therapist shares his/her desire with the class. Another student who plans to be a teacher would write on his/her scrap paper that s/he may work with the physical therapist at school.

-The student who wants to be a teacher shares with the class, and a student who wants to be a firefighter may write that s/he would visit the school to ensure safety for students and staff.

4. After every student shares, everyone should have a list of their classmates and how they will interact professionally in 20 years. From here, you can put students into small groups randomly or by career area (medical, education, etc.) to process or process as a class.

Processing Questions (15 minutes):

✓ How do you think interdependence will help you in your professional life?

✓ How do you think you will rely on others in your career? How will others rely on you?

✓ What was it like to predict your own career in 20 years?

✓ What are personal strengths that you used to help you decide which career to share with the class?

✓ What was it like to predict who you would interact with in your career?

✓ What factors helped you determine who you would interact with and how?
✓ Was it difficult to decide how you would interact with classmates through your careers in 20 years? Why or why not?
✓ How can you use your personal strengths to work with others who have different careers?

Cautions: If using this lesson to focus on careers, it may be beneficial to conduct a career interest inventory with students beforehand to allow for more thoughtful discussion. Students may be unsure what career they want to currently pursue; some students may be in between two or more careers. Encourage them to choose the career they feel best suits their personal strengths at this point in time though it is likely they will change their minds. Also, students may tend to state the same interaction with every student; encourage them to think outside the box.

Adaptations: This activity could be adapted to use with 8th grade students. You can also change the focus to academic or social issues that are being experienced in a particular grade level. However, students will have a more present-oriented focus as opposed to future-oriented. For example, if you wanted to focus on academics and taking responsibility for their own learning, you could ask students to envision how they depend on others during class time (i.e. others' behavior affects time spent on learning). Also, if you wanted to focus on social issues such as bullying, you could ask students to think about how they depend on their friends or acquaintances in social situations (i.e., looking out for them in case of threat or danger).

About the Counselors:

Laura M. Walker, MA, LPCA, NCC; is a School Counselor in Hendersonville, NC. walkerlm3@gmail.com

Rebekah Byrd, Ph.D., LPC, NCC, RPT; is an Assistant Professor of Counseling and School Counseling Program Coordinator at East Tennessee State University. byrdrj@etsu.edu or rebekah.byrd@gmail.com

Rearview Mirror

Submitted by Mark Newmeyer and Victor Tuazon

School Level: High.

Target Population: Grades 10 to 12.

Goals: Students will state specifically what they have learned about careers or themselves.

ASCA Standards:

A:A3.5 - Share knowledge
PS:A1.9 - Demonstrate cooperative behavior in groups
A:B1.2 - Learn and apply critical-thinking skills
PS:A2.6 - Use effective communications skills.

Estimated Time: 30 to 60 minutes.

Materials: Paper, pencils.

Lesson

1. Counselor states: "This activity is to help us understand and appreciate the impact this group/class has made to your growth and learning. Let's use the analog of a car. Say you are in a car driving away from the group/classroom experience you have just completed. All the other students are visible through the rearview mirror. What would you say to each student about what you have learned from them or from the class?"

2. Students are then asked to write down their thoughts on a piece of paper before sharing their responses to the class.

Processing Questions:

✓ How would you compare your responses today with what you might have said previous to this group/classroom experience?

✓ Let's continue the metaphor of the car. Think of a car. As we look in the rearview mirror we can see where we have been. When we look forward, through the windshield, we see where we are going. You've completed an activity about what has happened. Would it be possible to now look forward and share where you are going? How does where

you have been impact where you are going? What do you want to remember?"
- ✓ How would the future be different if this group/classroom experience did not happen?
- ✓ What have you learned from the activity?
- ✓ What would you change and leave the same if the activity were to be re-performed?"

Emphasize answers that involve personal growth (e.g., "Because of Melissa and Ben's help, I now know how to…" or "When we worked in a team to solve the problem it was much easier. "). Discourage negative talk about others (e.g., Monica's contributions in solving the problem didn't really help and I wish I would have never asked her to work with me.")

Cautions: A carefully constructed culture of trust and respect for each other is necessary.

Adaptations: This activity can be used after a particular group or classroom event or as a group/classroom termination activity. Student can each write down their answers and the school counselor can mail the envelopes at a later date as a reminder of what they have learned from their experience. Additionally, the metaphor of the car and looking both backwards and forwards can be emphasized to help students not only consolidate past learning and experiences, but to look ahead and forecast about the future of each student. High school seniors in particular can share what they have learned and how they have grown other the years.

Credit/References

Conyne, R.C., Crowell, J.L. & Newmeyer, M.D. (2008). *Group techniques: How to use them more purposefully.* Upper Saddle River, NJ: Pearson Merrill Prentice Hall.

About the Counselors:

Mark Newmeyer, Ed.D., is an Assistant Professor in the School of Psychology and Counseling at Regent University. mnewmeyer@regent.edu.
Victor Tuazon is a Masters Student and Graduate Assistant at Regent University where he is completing a dual-track master's degree in School Counseling and Mental Health Counseling. victtua@mail.regent.edu

A Day in the Life of a College Student

Submitted by Emily Herman and Jake J. Protivnak

School Level: High.

Population: Grades 11 and 12.

Goals: Students will learn information about the college experience.

ASCA Standards:

A:C1 Relate school to life experiences
A:C1.1 Demonstrate the ability to balance school, studies, extracurricular activities, leisure time and family life
A:C1.6 Understand how school success and academic achievement enhance future career and vocational opportunities
C:A1 Develop career awareness
C:A1.5 Learn to make decisions
C:A1.6 Learn how to set goals
C:A1.7 Understand the importance of planning.

Estimated Time: 3 hours.

Materials: Recent graduates who are current college students (at least 6).

Special Directions: Schedule this lesson so it coordinates with a time when college students are available to be invited back to the school to speak with current high school students (e.g., when college students are on break). Prior to the guidance lesson, meet with the college students and provide them with an overview and goal of the activity. Let them know where they will be stationed throughout the school (e.g., school counselor office, cafeteria, gym, etc.).

Lesson

1. Introduce the Activity: "Students are more successful in college if they are well prepared. The goal of this activity is to provide you with an opportunity to add to your preparation for college through discussion with recent graduates from your school. During this time you will have the opportunity to ask questions of graduates of this school who are

currently in college and find out what college life is like from their prospective. These college students were in your position (i.e., juniors and seniors from your high school) only a year or two ago and they can share their experiences in college and answer your questions. Although a school counselor has information regarding the college preparation process and issues related to transitioning from high school to college, it is additionally beneficial to hear the experience and advice from recent high school graduates who are currently living the college life.

2. Encourage students to determine what concerns them most about college (e.g., paying for college, making friends, living away from home, being academically successful, etc.). Ask them to take a moment to write down their top concerns and/or questions.

3. Divide the class into six groups (e.g., 3-4 students). Appoint a leader who will serve as a time-keeper. Charge the leader with the task of moving the group onto the next college student every 10 minutes. Provide each leader a set of clues for where the six college students will be located throughout the school.
   o At each spot along the hunt, the groups of students will find a college student who is a recent graduate of the school. They will have the opportunity to ask questions about the college experience to each college student, approximately 10 minutes with each.

4. Distribute the list of possible questions they may ask the college students.
   o Encourage the students to select questions to ask the college students that relate to their top concerns regarding attending college. Ask the leader to be sure that every student in the group is able to ask at least one question during the activity. Remind the students that they only have 10 minutes with each college student before they need to move on.

5. After 90 minutes (i.e., speaking with six different college students and time to move), ask students to return to initial meeting place.

6. Ask the students to share what they learned from their conversations with the college students. Processing Questions:
   ✓ What surprised you about your conversations with the college students?
   ✓ How were the answers to your questions similar or different among the different college students?
   ✓ How have your feelings about college changed?
   ✓ What was the most helpful thing you heard?

✓ What questions remain unanswered?

7. Encourage students to:
- continue gathering information about college (e.g., college visits, speaking with college students/reps., online college information searches),
- schedule an appointment with the school counselor to ask unanswered questions, and 3) consider ways that they can positively impact future college students by returning to their high school to discuss their college experience.

Questions College Students can Ask High School Students

The following are examples of questions that the college student can ask the high school students. Each college student will only have approx. 10 minutes with each group of students. Prior to beginning the activity, the school counselor can work with the college students to clarify any questions:

✓ Tell me three things that describe you and/or your interests.
✓ Describe your ideal career.
✓ What colleges would you like to apply to?
✓ How will you decide which college is the best fit for you?
✓ What, if any, goals do you need to set to increase your chances of getting into your college of choice?
✓ What are your biggest concerns regarding college applications?
✓ What are your concerns related to paying for college?
✓ What are you most excited about regarding starting college?
✓ What concerns or anxieties do you have about transitioning into college?
✓ What, if anything, do you need to change to increase your likelihood of being successful in college?
✓ What questions do you have for me about my college/university?

About the Counselors:

Emily Herman, MS.Ed., LSC, is the Director of College Counseling at John F. Kennedy Catholic High School in Warren, OH and an Adjunct Instructor in the Counseling Program at Youngstown State University. Eherman@warrenjfk.com.

Jake J. Protivnak, Ph.D., PCC-S, LSC is the Department Chair and Associate Professor in the Department of Counseling, Special Education, and School Psychology at Youngstown State University in Youngstown, OH. jjprotivnak@ysu.edu.

Resume Writing for High School Students

Submitted by Amanda Alger and Melissa Luke

School Level: High.

Target Population: Grades 11 and 12.

Goals: Students will:
1. Document academic and work experiences in resume format for prospective employers or colleges.
2. Obtain recommendation approval from three teachers, coaches, or other school staff.

ASCA Standards:

A: B1.4 Seek information and support faculty, staff, family and peers
A: B2.6 Understand the relationship between classroom performance and success in school
A: C1.3 Understand the relationship between learning and work
C: A1.3 Develop an awareness of personal abilities, skills, interests and motivations
C: A2.6 Learn how to write a resume.

Estimated Time: Two 40- minute lessons at least a day apart.

Materials: **Resume Writing** handout (Alger & Luke, 2014) paper, pen, computer, and printer.

Special Directions: The day or two before the lesson students should be asked to start thinking about work experience, volunteer work, school activities, honors/awards, academic courses or training that they could include on a resume for future job or college interviews and provided with any information school counselors have that is relevant (e.g., their academic, vocational, and avocational involvement throughout their educational career).

Lesson

1. Begin the lesson by inviting students to share and discuss reasons why they might need a resume. The School Counselor could use the

following sample statements/questions to initiate the conversation: "What is a resume?" "Why would a high school student need a resume?" "What is the purpose of a resume?" Possible answers may include when applying for a job, college interviews, or internships. The school counselor should suggest additional experiences that students may not realize when a resume would be useful, such as when asking for a letter of reference, applying for a summer or extracurricular opportunity (summer enrichment), or even to post/share on social media sites such as Linked In, Career Builder, or Facebook. (5 to10 minutes)

2. Ask students to complete an outline of their contact information, education, work experience, achievements, volunteer experience, interests/ activities, and specific skills or training. Provide sample templates and resumes for students to view while working on their outlines as a guide or reference. Listed below are a few links with free samples and templates for student resumes. (20 to 25 minutes)

http://guidance.spps.org/sites/53385aa7-d627-400a-9c42 d9ff23a9c96b/uploads/juniors_-_writing_a_resume.pdf
http://www.aie.org/finding-a-career/sample-resumes-and-templates/Resume-Sample-High-School-Student-Academic.cfm
http://jobsearch.about.com/od/resumesandcoverletters/l/blhighschool2.htm
http://jobsearch.about.com/od/sampleresume1/a/high-school-resume-examples.htm

3. After students have completed the outline, they may begin either handwriting or typing out a rough first draft of their resume. Students may choose to use Word resume templates if available. (15 minutes)

4. As students begin finishing their drafts, have them pair up with another student for peer editing. Students should look for the use of action words (organized, led, calculated, trained, tutored, inventoried, designed, etc.) and proper use of punctuation and spelling. The resume should be organized and have a uniformed look to it. Students may choose to have more than one peer review their resume before they complete a second draft. Suggest people who might be helpful to do the second edit such as teacher, coach, other school staff, employer, or family member. (10 to 15 minutes)

5. Students will use the feedback from the peer editing and their own creativity to create a second draft of their resume. It is important to mention to students that writing is a process and that their resumes

are a work in progress as they gain more experience and post-secondary education. (15 to 20 minutes)

6. For the reference section, have students list the names of three people they will contact/ have contacted for permission to use as a reference or to write a letter of recommendation for a job or college application. The school counselor may suggest students ask a current or past teacher, coach, club advisor, administrator, or employer for a reference. Remind students to ask permission from the person they would like to list as a reference. (5 minutes)

7. A "final draft" of the students' resumes should be kept in their career and/or college portfolios.

Processing Questions:

✓ What was it like for you to do the activity in class today?

✓ What is the purpose of a resume?

✓ What should be included on a resume?

✓ How did you proceed with the task? Where did you start? What was easy/hard? And most importantly, what might this tell you about your working style?

✓ How does a resume represent you as a person?

✓ How would you describe your moral character?

✓ While the match between skills, experience, and career choice is not always clear, what do you notice about these links? Related, what future career might be a predicted extension from your current resume?

✓ Why are honor and higher-level courses important?

✓ How would you describe your work ethic?

✓ Describe what you learned about yourself or something that was reconfirmed.

✓ Are there any themes that you notice or patterns that you have observed about your own career related development or that of others?

✓ What challenges do you anticipate related to this work? How might you respond if you do encounter these?

✓ What is the appropriate action to take when approaching a teacher, coach, or other school staff for a letter of recommendation or to use as a reference?

✓ How did you utilize career related skills when completing the 'homework' assigned? What other transferable skills might you not always recognize in yourself?

Adaptations: For students without a lot of work experience, they may need to rely on their academic courses and related skills as well as their avocational activities to display their abilities for future opportunities. School counselors should be prepared to prompt student thinking by asking about their community involvement, including religious and philanthropic organizations, as well as clubs and leadership service. For example, the school counselor can prompt students' thinking with the following:

1. Explain a course that you have excelled in and why. What courses have you most enjoyed and why?
2. Do you speak or read any second languages?
3. What physical competencies or athletic abilities do you possess?
4. Describe any volunteer experiences that may have had.
5. Tell me what you have done in the summer or over school breaks.
6. Describe some of the activities you have participated in through your church, synagogue, mosque, or community center.

This lesson can be adapted for younger students and by asking students to create a resume for a particular character in a book, television show, or movie. For example, students could discuss Quinn (or another character) in the television show *Glee*. In addition to academic, vocational, and avocational experiences, school counselors can develop supportive material that assists students in identifying the characters' skills and help them to frame these as potentially transferable to post graduate contexts.

As an alternative, the school counselor might prepare a short narrative that describes a person and ask that students all work from the same template. Students may benefit from working in small groups to share their ideas and observations. The school counselor can circulate the room, helping students identify similarities and differences in what they identified.

About the Counselors:

Amanda L. Alger, M.Ed., NBCT; is a Graduate Student and Instructor in Teaching and Leadership at Syracuse University. Previously, Amanda Alger taught middle and high school students Literacy Skills in various English and Writing courses. alalger@syr.edu.

Melissa Luke, Ph.D. is an Associate Professor, Interim Chair, and Coordinator of School Counseling at Syracuse University. Previously, Dr. Luke was a School Counselor and High School Teacher. She has recently developed an online school counseling class. mmluke@syr.edu.

Suggested Resume Outline (Alger & Luke, 2014)

Contact Information
> Full Name:
> Address:
> Phone #:
> Email Address:

Education
> High School:
> Address:
> Years attended:

Work Experience
> Job Title:
> Company:
> Responsibilities:
> Start and End Date:
> Reason for Leaving:

Volunteer Experience
> Company:
> Responsibilities:
> Start and End Date:

Achievements
> Honors or Awards (Academic or Athletic)
> Perfect Attendance

Interests/ Activities
> Sports:
> Hobbies:
> Clubs:

Specific Skills or Training
> Apprenticeships:
> Computer Skills:
> Intrapersonal Skills:
> Work Ethic:

References
> Teacher:
> Coach:
> Administrator:
> School Counselor:
> Employer:

Castles in the Sand: Using Sandtrays to Promote Career Awareness in Schools

Submitted by Karen Moore Townsend and Sandra Loew

School Level: High.

Goals: Students will:
1. Develop an awareness of personal abilities, skills, interests, and motivations.
2. Recognize that personal abilities, skills, interests, and motivations are related to career choice.
3. Enhance the understanding that work is an important and satisfying means of personal expression.
4. Make decisions and set goals related to career choice.

ASCA Standards:

C:A1.3 develop an awareness of personal abilities, skills, interests and motivations
C:A1.5 learn to make decisions
C:A1.6 learn how to set goals
C:B1.2 identify personal skills, interests and abilities and relate them to current career choice
C:C1.3 identify personal preferences and interests influencing career choice and success
C:C1.7 understand that work is an important and satisfying means of personal expression.

Estimated Time: 30 to 45 minutes.

Materials: Sandtrays, sand (or rice, aquarium gravel, rock, or other suitable substance), a variety of miniatures to be placed in the sand (e.g., toy tools, instruments, and other items representing various types of work; small dolls or figures, some of which suggest career choices such as toy soldiers, while others could be representative of the student or others in the student's life; tiny books or other objects that might be representative of educational choices; items that could represent the importance of family or leisure activities such as a tiny baby doll, a small house, a miniature beach ball, a toy boat; other miniatures that could be used metaphorically such as a small fence, a bridge, small blocks, stones, dice, miniature hats).

Lesson

1. The counselor provides each student with a tray filled with sand. A variety of numerous miniatures that may be arranged in the sand tray are arranged in a central location. Then the counselor directs the students to take a moment for each to think about his or her career journey and interests, including any past and/or present experiences, along with future aspirations. The counselor next encourages the students to let the miniature objects choose them. The counselor follows up by asking the students to place their chosen objects in the sandtray and arrange the objects in a way that depicts their career growth and vision. Each student thus creates a miniature representative world in the sand (Oaklander). Students are allowed to share their sand trays with the other students.

Processing Questions:

✓ Describe the scene you have created.
✓ Are you in the scene? If so, where?
✓ Tell me what is happening in your sand tray.
✓ Tell me what will occur in the future according to your sand tray.
✓ What was this experience like for you? (Oaklander)
✓ What does your sand tray tell you about your career path?
✓ How might your sand tray be different if....?

In addition, if sand trays are created in a group setting, the counselor may choose to link themes of several students.

Cautions: It is important for the counselor to have a stance of "not knowing" rather than "analyzing" the sand tray. This is an exploration for the student and an opportunity to generate a discussion of "what next?" or how to make dreams a reality. Due to involving small objects, caution should be used if very young children have access to miniature objects that might pose a risk of choking if objects were placed in mouth.

Adaptations: Processing of sandtrays could be done in dyads, small groups of students, or with the whole class. Also, sandtrays can be a useful means of expression for children who struggle with verbal or literacy skills.

Credit/References

Amundson, N. E., Borgen, W. A., Iaquinta, M., Butterfield, L. D., Koert, E. (2010). Career decisions from the decider's perspective. *The Career Development Quarterly, 58,* 336-351.

Oaklander, V. (1988). *Windows to our children: A Gestalt therapy approach to children and adolescents.* Gouldsboro, ME: The Gestalt Journal Press.

Sangganjanavavich, V. F. & Magnuson, S. (2011). Using sand trays and miniature figures to facilitate career decision making. *The Career Development Quarterly, 59,* 264-273.

Zimmerman, A. L. & Knotosh, L. G. (2007). A systems theory approach to career decision making. *Work, 29,* 287-293.

About the Counselors:

Karen Moore Townsend, Ph. D., NCC, is currently an Associate Professor in Counselor Education and Coordinator of the School Counseling Program at the University of North Alabama, Florence, AL. Previously, she was a School Counselor in a public K-12 school and a High School English, History, and Foreign Language Teacher. kmtownsend@una.edu.

Sandra Loew, Ph. D., LPC, NCC, is a Professor in Counselor Education and Coordinator of Field Experiences at the University of North Alabama, Florence, AL. saloew@una.edu.

Holland Dating Game and Body of Interests: Lessons 1, 2, and 3

Submitted by Rachel Landis

Target Population: High.

Goals: Students will:
1. Increase understanding of self.
2. Understand the influence of past experiences and decisions on the future.
3. Identify interests according to Holland.
4. Increase understanding of personal and career interests.

ASCA Standards:

PS: A1 Acquire Self-knowledge
PS:A1.2 Identify values, attitudes and beliefs
PS:A1.10 Identify personal strengths and assets
PS:A2 Acquire Interpersonal Skills
PS:A2.3 Recognize, accept, respect and appreciate individual differences
PS:A2.6 Use effective communications skills
PS:A2.7 Know that communication involves speaking, listening and nonverbal behavior
C:A1 Develop Career Awareness
C:A1.3. Develop an awareness of personal abilities, skills, interests and motivations
C:B1 Acquire Career Information
C:B1.2 Identify personal skills, interests and abilities and relate them to current career choice
C:C1 Acquire Knowledge to Achieve Career Goals
C:C1.3 Identify personal preferences and interests influencing career choice and Success.

Estimated Time: Lesson 1, 40 minutes; Lesson 2, 60 minutes; and Lesson 3: 40 minutes.

Materials:
Lesson 1: **Holland Dating Game** (IPFW Career Services, 2013), the "Singles Ads" included (or create your own with a fun photo/image of an individual that identifies with each Holland interest (e.g., an athlete for

Realistic). (A PowerPoint presentation with Googled images give students a visual.) (You can also adapt the names of the singles ads to cities within your state if you want, e.g. Inquisitive in Indiana).

Lesson 2: **RIASEC Worksheet** (IPFW Career Services, 2013) and online inventory. This lesson requires every student to have a computer/tablet connected to internet.

Lesson 3: **Body of Interests** (IPFW Career Services, 2013) which is an outline of a body (attached on last page) (printed on different colored paper for each student), **Career Exploration Recommended Worksheet** (Landis, 2013), tape.

Lesson 1: Holland Dating Game

1. Have the students move desks in the classroom to the sides so that you have a large open space in the middle of the room. (1 minute)

2. Have the students stand in a large group in the center of the open space in order to start in a neutral position. Tell the students, "We are going to do a Holland Dating Game to introduce you to different Holland career interest codes. I will show you different singles ads one at a time and read their description, and you will move to the right of the room if you are interested in this person, to the left of the room if you are not, or stay in the middle if you are not sure. Then we will discuss the reasons you chose your answer and move on to the next singles ad. It is okay to answer yes to more than one. Any questions?" (1 minute)

3. Read the singles ad for Holland's first interest (e.g., Conventional) and have the students move from the center to either the right or left side of the open space on how they fit the type of person being described in the ad (e.g., those answering yes would move to the right and those answering no would move to the left). (1 minute each ad)

4. Ask those answering yes the following questions: (5 minutes each ad):
   a. What about the description matched them and ask them for examples from their life to back it up (e.g., I liked the conventional ad because I clean my room for fun and enjoy being organized, so I think we would get along).
   b. What are the pros and cons of this interest? What would be challenging about this interest? (Highlight the skills from their examples that match the Holland interest singles ad such as curious/thorough/out of the box thinker/helper, give examples of different careers for this interest and see if they had held a job in that area or are interested in that area, point out themes from their

life you see that connect these things together such as they never do anything if it's not planned first).

    c. Who do you know in your family like this?

5. Do the same for the other 5 codes.

    a. Be sure to tell students it is okay for them to be able to answer more than one ad as Holland allows for multiple types. Tell students, "It is okay to choose more than one Holland singles ad. People can have up to three strong Holland interests."

6. Students should write down the top 3 Holland interests they chose during the Holland Dating Game activity. Invite students to share their "true" Holland code. You can say, "Who would like to share their top three Holland codes? What about those did you resonate with? Did you agree with everything in that code description for yourself? Does learning about these codes help you understand yourself better?"

7. Have students move desks back to their original places and let them know we will continue on this topic in the next guidance activity.

Holland Singles Ads (On PowerPoint if possible)

Conventional: I am desperately seeking a soul-mate. My ideal mate will be very detail oriented and enjoy well-structured activities. They will be persistent, patient, and well organized. They also must be very comfortable with the way things are and not try to change me as I have no intention of changing for anybody. If this is you, please reply to Curvy in Cleveland.

Enterprising: I am lost without my perfect companion. You must be able to lead down the road of love. My ideal companion will be sociable, assertive, persuasive, and enthusiastic. They must also enjoy performing in front of others and be able to set goals for our relationship and strive to reach them. Please, if you can be my leader, reply to Enthusiastic from Eastwood.

Social: Where o where is my love? I am looking for a person who loves to be connected with people. This person must enjoy helping others and be very friendly, outgoing, empathetic, and cooperative. They must also be patient with me and idealistic about the world. Does this fit you? If so, please respond to Sammy in Sandusky.

Artistic: Are you willing to go with the flow and take our relationship where it wants to go? I am a creative, independent, intuitive, and imaginative person. I am also a very complicated, emotional, open-minded, and impulsive person. I am seeking a like-minded person to create a masterpiece of a relationship with me. Is this you? If it is, Anna from Archbold would like to hear from you?

Investigative: I need someone to help me figure out the chemistry of love. Do you like to figure out how things work and discover the answers to problems? Are you inquisitive, independent, scholarly, and introspective? Do you enjoy working with numbers and science? If so please respond to Inquisitive in Indiana.

Realistic: I love hands on activities. I am very active and love being outdoors, but often enjoy quiet times by myself. I need someone who is just like me and is also stable, curious, persistent, practical, and independent. Please, if this is you, reply to Running Away in Rossford.

Lesson 2: Holland Codes and Online Inventory

1. Introduce the activity by telling the students, "Remember last time we had a guidance lesson we talked about the Holland Codes and you responded to Holland Singles Ads that you liked? The worksheet you will do today will continue to help you understand your own Holland Codes.

2. Pass out **RIASEC Worksheet** that provides a link (http://www.mynextmove.org/explore/ip) to take an online assessment to verify their Holland code and see if it differs from last guidance lesson in class, the true meanings of "RIASEC," and allow students to explore careers linked to the Holland code online. The handout also shows a visual of the Holland hexagon where they can circle their Holland code and learn more about careers with their Holland code online.

3. Tell students "First everyone needs to go to the website on your worksheet http://www.mynextmove.org/explore/ip and start the online assessment. Once you are at the site, hit the 'Next' button at the bottom to start. This should take approximately 30 minutes. Remember, just think about if you would *like or dislike* something, not if you have enough money or training to do it." Walk around the room to monitor students' progress and help with any questions.

4. Once students have completed the inventory, walk through the **RIASEC Worksheet** together. "Circle your Holland codes on the hexagon on your worksheet. Since you guys already are familiar with the six Holland codes from last guidance lesson, do you agree or disagree with the Holland codes this online inventory gave you? Why or why not? Are there other Holland codes you are still interested in?"

5. Instruct students to "Click on the O*Net Sites button at the bottom right side of the webpage, and click on O*Net OnLine. Then go to Advanced Search and select Interests from the picklist. Choose your Holland code combination and explore careers you are interested in. JobZone 1 may require a high school education, 2 usually requires a high school education, 3 most require training in vocational schools, related-on-the-job experience, or an associate's degree, 4 most require a 4 year bachelor's degree, and 5 most require graduate school. The sun means there's a bright outlook and the job is growing and the green leaf means it is environmentally friendly. Write the careers down on your worksheet you are interested in. Are there any careers you would rather have as a hobby and not as a career? Write these down on the worksheet. Are there any careers you are surprised by? What about excited about?" Complete the worksheet as a class.

6. Finish the lesson by telling students "You can continue exploring on O*Net's website and share this information with a parent/guardian at home. Part III of this guidance lesson will continue with Holland codes but you will be able to suggest careers for one another and hear from your classmates."

Lesson 3: Body of Interests

1. Introduce the activity by telling the students, "Remember last time we had a guidance lesson we talked about the Holland codes and you took an online assessment and explored careers with your Holland code? The worksheet you did will continue to help you understand today's activity but be able to hear from other students. First we are going to do a Body of Interests activity. I am going to give each of you a different colored piece of paper with an outline of a body on it. I want you to write your name on the back of the paper so it is anonymous. You are going to write inside the outline of the body, anywhere you want, your interests/activities. For example, this could include drawing, singing, horseback riding, cooking, sports, helping people, understanding how stuff works, etc.). When you are done and can't think of anymore, come up and get a piece of tape and hang the paper on a wall in the room and then sit back down. Once everyone has their body of interests hung, you will walk around the room and read all the body of interests and then write a suggested career or job for each person outside the outline of the body. Do not write on your own. I will give you 15 minutes and then you can get your body of interests and read what your classmates have suggested for you and we will discuss the activity. Any questions?" (1 minute)

2. Distribute the **Body of Interest** Handouts. Ask students to write their interests on it and then hang up each on the wall. (10 minutes).
3. Once all papers are hung, instruct students to walk around the room and suggest careers for their classmates based off the interests written (15 minutes depending on class size).
4. Once everyone has suggested careers on all the body of interests around the room, instruct the students to get their own body of interests and read what people have suggested for them (5 minutes).

Processing and Discussion Questions: (9 minutes)

As a group, reflect on the suggestions people wrote on their body of interests.

✓ Have you thought about that job/career before? Are there any that surprised you?
✓ How were they different/similar from the careers you found online with your homework worksheet?
✓ Do you have questions about what certain careers are from your Body of Interests or homework worksheet?
✓ What Holland codes are the careers suggested on your Body of Interests?
✓ Do they fit with your Holland code?
✓ What careers would you look into more?
✓ What careers would you prefer for leisure time only?
✓ What type of preparation would you need for this career?
✓ Do you think there would be any obstacles to following this career path?
✓ What did you learn about yourself? Your interests? Careers and jobs? What did you learn about others? What do you want to know more about?

Distribute **Career Exploration Recommended Worksheet** for students to continue their career exploration. Encourage students to make an appointment with the school counselor to follow up.

Cautions: Students may not want to share why they chose a specific singles ad during the Holland Dating Game, so be prepared to ask specific students why they stayed in the center, moved all the way to the wall, etc. For example, if you noticed a student immediately stand to one side of the room and they aren't participating in the discussion you could say, "John, I noticed you were very confident in your answer to this singles ad.

What about Inquisitive in Indiana do you feel strongly about?" If they still do not want to share, you can ask a different student.

Credit/References

Holland Theory Class Lesson (2013). EDUC X210 Career Planning Course. Fort Wayne, IN: IPFW Career Services.

Interests Class Lesson (2013). EDUC X210 Career Planning Course. Fort Wayne, IN: IPFW Career Services.

Holland, J. L. (1996). Exploring careers with a typology: What we have learned and some new directions. *American Psychologist, 51*(4), 397–406. doi:10.1037/0003-066X.51.4.397

About the Counselor:

Rachel Landis is a Graduate Student and School Counseling Intern at Indiana-University Purdue University, Fort Wayne. utesre01@ipfw.edu

Career Exploration Recommended Worksheet

Occupational Outlook Handbook
A-Z Index
www.bls.gov/oco/

Dictionary of Occupational Titles (DOT)
http://www.wave.net/upg/immigration/dot_index.html#menu

Occupational Outlook Quarterly
http://www.bls.gov/opub/ooq/ooqhome.htm

Act's World-of-Work Map
http://www.act.org/world/world.html

National Career Development Association
http://www.ncda.org

Job Shadowing
http://www.jobshadow.com/

Career One Stop
www.careeronestop.org

Major-related Information - IPFW Career Services
http://new.ipfw.edu/offices/career/students/exploring-majors-and-careers.html

What Can I do with this Major?
www.whatcanidowiththismajor.com/major/

O* Net Online
http://www.onetonline.org/

My Next Move Interest Profiler
http://www.mynextmove.org/explore/ip

Learn More Indiana
www.learnmoreindiana.org

RIASEC Worksheet

First, take the online interest profiler at: http://www.mynextmove.org/explore/ip

1. Learn more about each interest by clicking on it. Do you agree with your top 3 interests?

YES   **NO**

Explain what you like/dislike about your interests:

_____

_____

_____

2. Circle your top interests on the Holland Hexagon. Interests that are closer to each other are more common to be found in careers together. Interests that are farther away/opposite each other are less common to be found in careers together.

   Questions?

_____

_____

_____

_____

Realistic   Investigative

Conventional   Artistic

Enterprising   Social

3. After reviewing each of the remaining 4 interests, do you want to explore career options for any of the other general interests?   **YES**   **NO**

   If "YES," which one(s)?

_____

_____

_____

_____

4. Rank order your top 5 interests and what you would consider pursuing a career in.

   1) _____

   2) _____

   3) _____

   4) _____

   5) _____

5. Since different careers require different levels of preparation, which job zones are you interested in?

1-Little or no preparation
2-Some preparation
3-Medium preparation
4-Considerable preparation
5-Extensive preparation

6. Which related occupations(s), if any, would you rather keep as leisure activities and not pursue as a career?

_____

_____

Review the areas under each occupation you selected to pursue further. Write down What They Do, Knowledge, Skills, Abilities, Personality, Technology, Education, and Job Outlook *that are interesting to you* in the following areas.

WHAT THEY DO/ON THE JOB YOU WOULD_____

_____

_____

SKILLS_____

_____

_____

ABILITIES_____

_____

_____

EDUCATION_____

_____

_____

_____

... KNOWLEDGE

_____

_____

_____

TECHNOLOGY_____

_____

_____

PERSONALITY_____

_____

_____

JOB OUTLOOK_____

_____

_____

_____

Body of Interests Handout

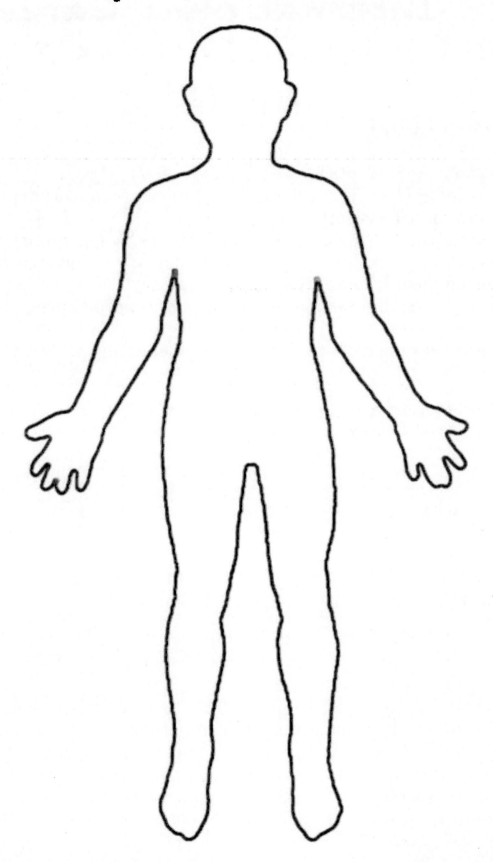

International Career Exploration: Lessons 1 and 2

Submitted by Angela D. Coker, Ph.D.

School Level: High.

Goals: Students will:
1. Broaden their career and vocational interests in working in international environments.
2. Explore vocational and career possibilities from a global perspective.
3. Discover and explore multicultural interests within a career development framework.
4. Increase their knowledge about career/vocational programs and opportunities.
5. Identify strategies for exploring and facilitating career interests globally.

ASCA Standards:

C: A1   Development Career Awareness
C: B1   Acquire Career Information
PS: A2.4 Recognizes, accepts and appreciates ethnic and cultural diversity.

Estimated Time: Two lessons of 35 to 40 minutes each, at least a week apart.

Materials: A world map via the Internet (if no internet access exists, a paper world map), paper, and pencils.

Lesson 1

1. The School Counselor begins with: "The employment landscape of the US economy has changed significantly requiring more and more Americans to be flexible and adaptable as they journey through their career development (Savickas, 2012). Similarly, the world has fast become a global village possessing many career and vocational opportunities. Students in the U.S. are encouraged in this activity to

expand their career interests and vocational landscape to include exploring career interests and possibilities beyond their country of birth. Further, not only could expanding one's vocational landscape broaden career opportunities, it can also expand an individual's cultural awareness, knowledge, and understanding of themselves and the world.   In this lesson, students are encouraged to explore their career interests and values as it relates to considering jobs globally. For this activity, I am going to divide the class into four randomly self-selected groups. No group should have more than five individuals. Try to work with classmates that you don't know very well. Remember, this is a good time to make new connections with each other. Have a pen and paper ready to take notes. You will have about 15 minutes to reflect your thoughts with each other. Discuss in your small groups the following questions:"

✓ What is the difference between having a job and having a career?

✓ When you hear the term career development what thoughts come to mind?

2. The School Counselor then explains that careers typically require specialized long-term training, whereas jobs are often vocational opportunities that do not require specialized advance academic training or skills (e.g., work as a server at McDonalds is typically considered a job vs. being an doctor or an accountant requires additional education beyond a high school diploma).

3. The School Counselor suggest to students that to understand career development is about understanding themselves, personal interests, skills, values, and talents. Career development also requires individuals to understand the world of work and being able to find a good match or fit (Niles & Harris-Bowlsbey, 2005) between their career interests and their personalities. To help enhance student interaction, the School Counselor may ask the following questions:

 "Think about your career interests, what skills or special knowledge will it require? How might your personal values influence you career choices?"

The School Counselor should encourage maximum student participation. As students share their responses, validate their reflections. For example, the School Counselor might say "that is a very good response, thank you for sharing your thoughts."

4. Next, have students remain in their individual small groups and consider the following set of questions about their cultural interests and knowledge (15 to 20 minutes).
   - ✓ What does it mean to live in a global village?
   - ✓ What countries do you have an interest in visiting? Why?
   - ✓ What cultures do you have knowledge of or find interesting? Why?
   - ✓ Think about your career interests. Have you ever considered exploring a career overseas?

The instructor should move around between small groups to monitor the discussion to keep the students focused and not allow students to engage in political debate about the pros and cons of serving in the military. In order to prevent this, the School Counselor may say the following: "Students remember that everyone is entitled to their own opinions about serving in the military. We are here today to discuss opportunities in career development, not political issues."

5. The School Counselor invites students to come back as a large group and have them highlight some of the conversations they had in their small groups. To process the activity, ask students to respond to the following questions:
   - ✓ What did you learn about yourself and your classmates regarding ideas about career development as a result of this discussion?
   - ✓ What did you learn about yourself and your classmates regarding ideas about cultural interests as a result of this discussion?
   - ✓ What new areas of career interests or options would you like to explore?

As a summary, the School Counselor highlight themes or skills such as some students might cite that they realize they may not have previously considered career planning to include international interests or involvement while others may have already had opportunities to participate in study abroad programs that expose them to other cultures and or opportunities.

6. At this point, the School Counselor can give students examples of different career options that have an international focus:

- The Peace Corp (an opportunity to combine cultural/international interests, with career development, and values of volunteering.)
- Teaching overseas (there are many teaching opportunities for young people who have an interest working overseas. Some of these opportunities include teaching in a specific content area like history, geography, or mathematics. Some teaching can also involve being an English as a second language instructor.
- Serving in the military (serving in our nation's armed forces such as the army, navy, marines, or air force is another way for individuals to combine civic values with career, cultural, and travel interests)

7. Lastly, the School Counselor will ask students to write answers to following questions before Lesson II on International Career Exploration. Also, encourage students to seek help and dialogue with family members as they reflect on each question.

Homework Activity:

✓ Develop a list of pros and cons of working overseas.
✓ Consider ways to gain work experience overseas (e.g., study abroad experiences, volunteer opportunities).
✓ Develop strategies for exploring a career overseas (e.g., internet searches, discussions with parents, other teachers, mentors, etc.

Lesson 2

1. The School Counselor begins with a summary of Lesson I focusing on career development, cultural interests, and values. To spark discussion, the School Counselor asks: "Who else would like to summarize their understanding of what we did in class regarding this topic?" "What new things did you learn about career development and planning?" Encourage students to share their continued reflections on the topic.
2. The School Counselor continues: "In this lesson, we will explore their career interests and values as it relates to considering jobs or careers globally.
3. Divide the class into four randomly self-selected groups and ask students to work with individuals they have not worked with in the past and have a pen and paper ready to take notes. Tell students that they will have about 15 to 20 minutes to share their answers and

thoughts with each other. Ask them to discuss the homework questions given to them during the previous activity.

4. Each small group will designate a spokesperson to report and highlight the main themes or ideas expressed in the small groups.

5. Ask students to reflect and make meaning regarding their responses in their small groups.

✓ What does the lists of pros and cons say about their understanding of working overseas?

✓ What might it say about their career values regarding work environments?

✓ Also, what are some of the common strategies cited?

✓ Which career exploration strategies have they not considered yet?

✓ What additional knowledge or resources do they need in order to learn more about career options internationally?

As a large group, ask the following process questions:

✓ How would you summarize what we did in activities involving Part I and in Part II?

✓ What new things did you learn about potential career options internationally?

✓ What did you learn about your career and multicultural interests?

✓ Did this activity increase your interest in international career exploration? Why or Why not?

As they discuss, the School Counselor should summarize and highlight that this is an exercise in career exploration. Encourage students who are interested in a career overseas to seek more information. Examples of where they might go to seek more information include a visit to a career counselor's office, visiting local libraries to obtain books about international careers, conducting specialized internet searches, discussions with individuals who have experience working overseas, etc. As a potential follow-up activity the School Counselor may even consider inviting a guest speaker to address the class and share their experiences working overseas. If there is sufficient class interest, another possible follow-up activity may include a field trip to an international organization or center that has a specific international focus (examples may include the organization Doctors without Borders, or an international children's agency).

Cautions: There may be some students who have extensive travel experiences and who may feel the need to share these experiences with other students who have not had similar travel opportunities. In order to prevent less economically privileged students from feeling intimidated or silenced, be sure to stress that this is not an activity that focuses on where students have already traveled to, but where their cultural and career interests may be. To safeguard against this the School Counselor should say something like this, "students please be mindful that we are here to explore and discuss international career exploration. While it might be tempting to share our international travels with others, please focus on what you learned from the experience and not what fun you had there. Also, if you have not travel extensively, reflect on what you have learned about other countries through your readings. Share what attracts you to that culture.

Credit/References

Corey, G. (2010). *Theory and practice of group counseling.* Belmont, CA: Thomson Brooks/Cole.

Niles, S. G, & Harris-Bowlsbey, J. (2005). *Career development interventions in the 21st century* (2nd Ed.). Upper Saddle River, NJ: Merrill/Prentice-Hall.

Savickas, M.L. (2012). Life design: A paradigm for career intervention in the 21st century. *Journal of Counseling & Development, 90,* 13-19.

About the Counselor:

Angela D. Coker, Ph.D., LPC, NCC, is an Associate Professor of Counseling and Family Therapy, at the University of Missouri - St. Louis. She is a Fulbright-Hays Scholar who has conducted multicultural research in Brazil. She has also served as a Sabbaticant at the University of Botswana, in addition to a Visiting Scholar at the University of the Western Cape in South Africa. Email: cokera@umsl.edu

Show Me the Money: Career Choice, Financial aid, and Information Systems: Lessons 1, 2, and 3

Submitted by José M. Álvarez

School Level: High.

Target Population: Grade 11.

Goals:

1. To encourage students to think critically about the practicality of career choice based on their personality and their family's circumstances.
2. To teach students research skills including reliable Internet sites.
3. To motivate students to effectively explore potential career paths.
4. To teach students to identify reliable financial aid opportunities.
5. To teach students to successfully apply to and secure funding opportunities.

ASCA Standards:

A:B1.2 Learn and apply critical-thinking skills
C:A1.1 Develop skills to locate, evaluate and interpret career information
C:A1.3 Develop an awareness of personal abilities, skills, interests and motivations
C:B1.2 Identify personal skills, interests and abilities and relate them to current career choice
C:B1.5 Use research and information resources to obtain career information
C:B1.6 Learn to use the Internet to access career-planning information
C:B1.7 Describe traditional and nontraditional career choices and how they relate to career choice.

Estimated Time: Three 45-minutes lessons.

Materials: Stationary computers and printer(s) with access to Internet, pencils or pens, and paper, copies of handout for all students (*Álvarez, 2014*).

Introduction: This activity encourages you to assess your areas of competence and deficiency in relation to career choice, college/university of choice, and financial aid. It is vital for you to consider how your cultural background and values inform your perceptions of occupational choice as well as your confidence and satisfaction in decision-making. I will be of immediate assistance to facilitate the learning and research processes by offering you alternative approaches/perspectives to career exploration. The activity may motivate you to visit my office more frequently to discuss academic, career exploration, and possibly other issues.

Access to the Internet is critical to your academic, career, personal and social success. You need to know how to access the right information online to determine whether specific websites are reliable when researching career paths and accessing financial aid. To this end, it is imperative that you access reputable financial aid websites in order to supplement your education, particularly if you are interested in "hot career fields".

Lesson 1

1. (7 minutes). Please complete the questionnaire I am handing out. provided you (Appendix I); be honest. When you are finished, raise your hand for me and I will collect them.
2. (8 minutes). On the computer, complete an assessment personality test based on Carl Jung's and Isabel Briggs Myers' typological approach at http://www.humanmetrics.com/cgi-win/JTypes2.asp. This online questionnaire (Human Metrics Test) will provide you with a four letter type formula (e.g., INFJ) suggestive of your strengths and preferences.
3. (8 minutes). View the interpretation and a functional analysis indicative of your personality type (click on "self-awareness and personal growth"). Also, click on "career choices" to view the career track you might want to pursue based on your personality type.
4. (5 minutes). Copy the personality type box (e.g., INFJ and description) and paste it onto a Word document. Include your name, today's date, and the time. Organize these labels above the personality type box. Copy and paste at least three favored career options, as suggested by the "career choices" window, below the personality type box – you will need this data in Session 3. Print and retrieve the document.

5. (5 minutes). Visit the CASVE Cycle at http://www.career.fsu.edu/documents/cognitive%20information%20processing/core%20concepts%20of%20a%20cognitive%20approach.htm#CASVECycle (Peterson, Sampson, Reardon, & Lenz Core, 2003) and read the model thoroughly. Consider the use of this model when carrying out Sessions 2 and 3. It might be useful in better understanding what is involved in career choice, which entails asking important questions, such as what are my interests, skills and values? How much do I know about specific disciplines or occupations? You may leave this window open for future reference.

6. (12 minutes): Processing Questions:
   ✓ Was your perception of your personality and career interests parallel the vocations (e.g., job placement) suggested by the Jung Typology Test?
   ✓ What steps will you consider in choosing a profession or program of study that will meet your needs?
   ✓ How will this exercise influence you to make important decisions?

7. By completing this section, you have gained enhanced awareness of yourself (i.e., your areas of competence and deficiency in relation to career choice), the costs and benefits involved in pursuing a specific occupation that will affect you and others, and how to take action to plan and achieve your goals. Ultimately, your career choice will influence your personal and social success at some level.

Lesson 2

1. (10 minutes). Say: Today, We will discuss vocational/technical and traditional education by explaining the differences among the various types of venues available (e.g., community college, military, and public and private [nonprofit as well as for-profit] education). This should be a basic overview of differences among the various colleges or universities available. Raise your hand if you are ready to research colleges or universities that interest you.

2. (Five minutes). Tell students: Access the school's respective Internet proxy (e.g., Mozilla Firefox) and log on to its homepage. Login to your student email account; if you have a personal device, turn it on and access your student email. Open Google Chrome, but do not search/type anything at this point.

3. (Three minutes). Then ask them to: Create the following folder format in your bookmarks: **Folder 1, Major** (bookmark the CASVE Cycle website here); **Folder 2, Military Ed**; **Folder 3, Private Ed**; **Folder 4, Traditional Ed**; and **Folder 5, Vocational/Technical.**

4. (10 minutes). Tell students: Use Google Chrome to research educational venues. Find one site per category (in previous step) and add the bookmark.

5. (7 minutes). Then, open a Word document. Type your name, time, date and title. Use it to create a list of the venues of your choice. Copy the URL of each site and paste onto the document. Print and retrieve the document.

6. (10 minutes). Processing Questions:
   ✓ What are the implications of a two-year vs. four-year education?
   ✓ What factors predict successful completion of degree?

7. End with: It is important you are satisfied with the institution of your choice as it is important to the post-secondary experience and graduation. It is important to consider whether and how financial aid opportunities, geographic location, major, demographic component, and cost of living will motivate you to consider a specific educational path. We will continue to talk about that next session,

Lesson 2

1. (10 minutes). Begin with: Today, we will research financial aid opportunities. I will explain the differences among the types of financial aid available (e.g., federal, state, public and private). This should be a basic overview of the typical financial aid available to students, but be sure to discuss merit-based versus need-based financial aid. Raise your hand if you are ready to research financial aid. Open Google Chrome and access The College Board's "pay for college" website (https://bigfuture.collegeboard.org/pay-for-college). Read the "3 steps to getting financial aid" page and raise your hand if you have questions. Examples of typical queries are listed below.
   ✓ Q: What is FAFSA?
     A: It is the Free Application for Federal Student Aid.
   ✓ Q: Will I get the same monetary award from FAFSA if I attend an in-state versus an out-of-state university?
     A: No. The award granted to a student will likely vary from university to university.

✓ My GPA is fairly good, but my SAT scores are not great. Should I not be concerned with researching merit-based financial aid and apply only to the FAFSA?

✓ No. Even when applying to merit-based awards, some institutions may still consider family income as part of the overall application package. It is worthwhile to also apply to merit-based awards.

2. (10 minutes). Read and learn about the different "Types of Aid" at http://studentaid.ed.gov including grants and scholarships, loans, work-study jobs and tax benefits. Raise your hand if you have questions.

✓ Q: Is it possible for a student to be awarded more than one grant? A: Yes. However, double-dipping is not permitted. For instance, if you are awarded a Federal Pell Grant and a Federal Opportunity Supplemental Educational Grant (FOSEG) concurrently, the latter will supersede the former. Thus, you will receive only the FOSEG.

✓ Q: Is it feasible that a student receive a grant and a scholarship? A: Yes. Actually, upon completing the FAFSA, I strongly encourage you to submit as many scholarship applications as possible! There are literally thousands of scholarship awards made available by schools, employers, private enterprises, non-profit organizations, religious groups, professional institutions and social organizations.

✓ Q: Are there scholarships specifically for Hispanics/Latinos or for community volunteerism during Election Day? A: Yes. There are scholarship opportunities for cultural affiliation, civic engagement and political membership. The Hispanic Scholarship Fund (http://www.hsf.net) is one venue available to you.

3. *(5 minutes).* Familiarize yourself with "Net Price Calculator" or NPC (http://studentnpc.collegeboard.org/what-is-a-net-price-calculator), a tool that you can use to estimate your cost to attend a particular college or university (i.e., the "net" price versus the "sticker" price or full cost). Do not open unreliable sites that advertise NPC; online "preparer" websites involve fees (e.g., www.studentaidservices.com). Click the "Participating Schools" tab and search for the institution(s) of your choice. Each site will ask provide an option for you to sign in as a student. Determining the net price of each site might require 15-20 minutes. This is where the registration process is relevant.

4. (5 minutes). Open a student account with The College Board at https://account.collegeboard.org/iamweb/smartRegister (optional); it is easy and free. By establishing the account, you are able to save your work and return at a later time to complete it. Determine the "net

price" of one institution selected in Session 2; follow instructions carefully. After using their NPC, pay close attention to the estimated amount of funds your family is expected to contribute to pay for the specific college/university selected. Does the amount seem feasible?

5. Is the institution of your choice not a participating school (http://studentnpc.collegeboard.org/participating-schools)? If it is not (e.g., California State Polytechnic University, Pomona), raise your hand and I will help you find the estimated cost of attendance based on the current academic year. For instance, for Cal Poly Pomona, see http://www.csupomona.edu/~financial-aid/costs/costs-odd.shtml.

6. (5 minutes). Access the following websites; they are examples of reliable financial aid search engines: www.fafsa.ed.gov, https://bigfuture.collegeboard.org, http://studentaid.ed.gov, and www.finaid.org (with few advertisements). Use the bookmark feature to create a **Folder 6 - Financial Aid** to bookmark these websites.

7. (5 minutes). Visit the financial aid homepage of the institution(s) you chose in Session 2. Explore whether the college/university provides athletic, need-based, merit-based, and resident-only scholarships. For instance, in partnership with Live the Solution, Arizona's three state universities are launching **AZ Earn to Learn**, a groundbreaking need-based financial aid program available to Arizona high school students (http://www.azearntolearn.org). Some colleges/universities provide financial aid based on a combination of factors, such as merit-based and residency status. Northern Arizona University's Resident Lumberjack Scholars Award underscores the aforementioned (http://nau.edu/FinAid/Scholarships/Incoming-Freshman).

8. **Processing Questions** (10 minutes):
   ✓ What is financial aid and do I need to apply?
   ✓ How does one apply for financial aid, what is the first step?
   ✓ Who can I speak to about career choice, post-secondary education and career planning for dependable advice?

9. Be mindful to be organized and patient during the research process. To this end, it is imperative that you speak to your parents as well as your school counselor about financial aid. Combined, their knowledge and expertise about financial aid can help you widen your research, manage the application deadline process, and prioritize opportunities.

Cautions: Be sure students do not bookmark and/or apply to online "preparer" websites, such as www.fafsa.com rather than www.fafsa.ed.gov. Caution students that although www.fastweb.com may be a useful venue, it contains numerous advertisements.

Adaptations: The activity may involve a facilitator and co-facilitator or two guidance/career counselors (e.g., counselor and counselor intern). Also, Appendix I may be used as both a pre-test and post-test to obtain hard data.

Suggestions on How to Integrate into Curriculum:

Could be integrated into courses such as *Economics, Personal Finance, Credit* and *Debt*, or conducted during an 11th grade core course.

Next Possible Lesson Plan Topics:

- The Ins and Outs of Living Off- and On-Campus
- How do Self-perceptions and Cultural Beliefs Influence Career Trajectories?
- Career and Personality Tests Put to the Test!
- Senior Year, First Semester Follow Up: Set Major, and Secured Financial Aid

About the Counselor:

Currently, *José M. Álvarez, MA,* is the Sophomore Class Counselor at Salpointe Catholic High School, Tucson, Arizona. José is a graduate of the Counseling and Mental Health program at The University of Arizona, Tucson. jma@email.arizona.edu. jalvarez@salpointe.org.

APPENDIX I: GROUP PARTICIPANT PRE-GROUP PERCEPTIONS
(Álvarez, 2014)

Instructions: Read each sentence. Put a circle around the number that best describes your situation right now. The scale is: Strongly Disagree=1, Disagree=2, Uncertain=3, Agree=4, Strongly Agree=5

1. I feel motivated to apply to a college or university   1   2   3   4   5

2. I feel excited about visiting colleges/universities   1   2   3   4   5

3. I need more data regarding the transfer process   1   2   3   4   5

4. I will navigate the transfer process "successfully"   1   2   3   4   5

5. I know which major is relevant to my interests   1   2   3   4   5

6. I what kind of education is relevant to my career   1   2   3   4   5

7. I am aware of all financial aid opportunities   1   2   3   4   5

8. I am confident applying to postsecondary venues   1   2   3   4   5

9. I can distinguish facts from personal perceptions   1   2   3   4   5

10. I am concerned about post-secondary studies   1   2   3   4   5

12. I know what FAFSA is and how to apply   1   2   3   4   5

13. I discussed the above with my parent/guardian   1   2   3   4   5

14. I have taken the initiative regarding my career

path or post-secondary options (explain below*)   1   2   3   4   5

*Additional comments you would like to share with me:

School Counselors Share Their Favorite Classroom Guidance Activities

PERSONAL/ SOCIAL SKILL BUILDING CLASSROOM GUIDANCE LESSONS

Friendship Trail Mix

Submitted by Sarah Kitchens and Amanda Evans

School Level: Elementary.

Target Population: Grades K to 2.

Goals: Students will:
1. Discuss the meaning of friendship.
2. Recognize the diversity in our classroom through comparing similarities and differences among classmates and learning we can all be friends.
3. Explore strengths and values of each other and in self.

ASCA Standards:

A:A1.5 Identify attitudes and behaviors that lead to successful learning
A:A3.1 Take responsibility for their actions
PS:A1.6 Distinguish between appropriate and inappropriate behavior
PS:A2.1 Recognize that everyone has rights and responsibilities.

Estimated Time: 45 minutes.

Materials: White board, markers, large bowl, large mixing spoon, small bowls or cups, animal crackers, popcorn, cereal, mini pretzels, raisins, chocolate candy, marshmallows; and one onion, apple, orange, banana.

Lesson

1. Counselor begins with: Today we are going to discuss friendship and create a friendship trail mix. This will be done as a class to incorporate the importance of working together as a class. Also, with this lesson we will be able to discuss how one individual may change the class if they make bad choices. Write the word **Friendship** on the board.
2. Discuss with the students what qualities we want in our friends and the kind of friends we want to be (honest, trustworthy, share, kind, etc.). (10 minutes)

3. Show the students the apple, orange, and banana. As a class, discuss what is the same and what is different about the fruit. (5 minutes) Emphasize in their answers that just like the fruit, we are all alike and different in some ways. We all come in different colors and have different features but we are all special and are an important part of the class.

4. Ask students to compare what is alike and different between classmates that helps us work together and be successful as a class. Remind them to use their manners when comparing their classmates and to use kind words. Example: We are all different sizes; some of us are small size, medium size, and large size. (5 minutes)

5. Once you have compared students in the classroom, tell students that the big bowl is like their elementary school and there are many important things the school needs – especially good friends and happy days at school.

6. Ask the students how we can have happy days at school and work together. Discuss each suggestion and elaborate on their ideas. For each idea, add one item for the trail mix. (10 to 15 minutes)

- Example: "These are for the hard workers in our school... they always work hard to get their work done and try their best."
- Other suggestions to emphasize:
  - Well behaved students who use their manners: "Please," "Thank you," "Excuse me," etc.
  - Happiness when we spend time with our friends and learn.
  - Take Turns
  - Listen Well
  - Play well with others

7. Once you finish adding each item talk about how awesome the trail mix is, just like our school. Discuss how this makes everyone in the school feel (our friends, the teachers, counselor, principal, etc.). Discuss how colorful and diverse the trail mix is and remind them how the trail mix is similar to the fruit we discussed at the beginning of the lesson. Everyone in the school helps bring about an important aspect of our school. When everyone works together it makes for bright and happy days. (5 to10 minutes)

8. Pick up the onion and begin to peel it. Tell the students the onion is for the students in our school who call others names, don't share, and act like bullies.

9. The students may yell "NO" or "STOP"… be sure to ask them if they would like to vote if the onion should be added to the friendship trail mix.

10. Discuss with the students why they do not want the onion in their friendship trail mix. Make the connection on the importance of being nice to each other, showing respect, and caring for our friends.

11. Agree that you will not put the onion in the trail mix if the students agree not to be an onion.

12. Discuss with the students what would happen if you add the onion to the trail mix. (If we add the onion to the trail mix, it will ruin the taste of the tasty trail mix.) Then, make the connection to the classroom/ school. Just like adding the onion to the trail mix will ruin the taste of the trail mix, when our classmates make bad choices, they become like an onion (calling our friends names, not doing our classwork or homework, etc.). We all want to be like the tasty pieces of our friendship trail mix and help make our school a happy and bright place. (5 to10 minutes)

Processing Questions:

✓ What makes a good friend? (using good manners, sharing, caring)

✓ What makes a happy school? (students who use good manners, complete their classwork/homework, get along with each other, etc.)

✓ How is our classroom like our trail mix? (We are all different and unique, yet we can all help make up a happy room just like the yummy treat!)

✓ How is our classroom different than our trail mix? (We aren't food, we sometimes don't do what we're supposed to)

✓ How can we be a good friend and help add to the uniqueness of our classroom? (Use our manners, share with our friends, help each other out, be kind to others, etc.).

Cautions:

• Be careful with food allergies. NO PEANUTS!

• Be sure to sit the students in a circle where they can see what you are doing.

• Hygiene- Be sure everyone has CLEAN hands.

Adaptations: Send a letter home with the students before you plan to complete this activity. Have students bring in one item each needed for the friendship trail mix (animal crackers, cereal, raisins, marshmallows, small bowls/cups, etc.).

You can use this same activity to build a fruit salad with canned or fresh fruit, marshmallows, etc. Instead of the onion you can use a rotten banana.

- Extension: Write/ Draw on how to NOT be an onion or a rotten banana.

About the School Counselors:

Sarah Kitchens is currently completing her Ph.D. and is a GTA in Counselor Education at Auburn University. Previously, she was an Elementary Teacher and a K to 12 School Counselor.
Seo0003@auburn.edu

Amanda M. Evans, Ph.D., LPC, NCC is a Counselor Educator at Auburn University. Amt0004@auburn.edu

Fur-sonalities: Animals and Friendship Skills

*Submitted by Alaina Conner, LPC, NCC and
Jolie Ziomek-Daigle, Ph.D., LPC*

School Level: Elementary.

Target Population: Grades 1 to 3.

Goals:
1. To help students learn appropriate friendship skills.
2. To teach students how to be good friends by understanding the different types of personalities people may have.
3. To engage students in fun ways on how to be to a good friend.

ASCA Standards:
PS:A1.6 Distinguish between appropriate and inappropriate behavior
PS:A2.6 Use effective communications skills
PS:A1.10 Identify personal strengths and assets
PS:A1.11 Identify and discuss changing personal and social roles
PS:A2.2 Respect alternative points of view
PS:A2.3 Recognize, accept, respect and appreciate individual differences
PS:A2.6 Use effective communications skills
PS:A2.8 Learn how to make and keep friends.

Estimated Time: 30 to 40 minutes.

Materials: Pictures, stuffed animals and/or puppets of the following: monkey, shark, turtle, snake, lamb, and teddy bear, and the book **Hunter's Best Friend at School** (Elliot, 2005).

Introduction: Explain to students that there are many different types of friends, and it is important to know how different types of friends make us feel. State that you will using animals to help students understand this and to understand friendship skills. Our personalities that we show to others can be related to the personalities of animals, our "fur-sonalities"!

Lesson

1. Describe to students each of the following animal personalities below and explain that our personalities are similar to the types of friends that we are to others. Fur-sonalities! Say: We can be teddy bear friends, snake friends, shark friends, lamb friends, turtle friends, monkey friends, and many others types of friends. The type of friend we are will attract the same type, for example, if we are a snake friend, we will probably have many snake friends. It is important to understand our own fur-sonality and how it affects our friendships. (2 to 3 minutes).

2. Show students the puppet/picture/stuffed animal of the lion. Say: Lions try to be kings of the jungle. They roar loudly and intimidate or power over others. Lion friends yell at others and try to show that they have power over other friends. They sometimes bully others. Do you think you would like to be or have a Lion friend? (Emphasize that Lion friends may try to boss you around, get you to tease or make fun of someone with them, laugh at you when you do something embarrassing, etc.) (2 to 3 minutes)

3. Show students the puppet/picture/stuffed animal of the snake. Say: Snakes are really hard to trust. Sometimes they like you and sometimes they don't. Snakes sometimes lie to you or to adults. Snake friends may gossip or talk bad about you to others. Snake friends seem to be fun to be around sometimes, but they may bite or snap at you at other times. Do you think you would like to be or have a Snake friend? (Emphasize that a Snake may seem nice some days, but may be sneaky on other days, or that Snake friends may talk bad about you and lie and say they did not talk bad about you). (2 to 3 minutes)

4. Show students the puppet/picture/stuffed animal of the shark. Say: Sharks attack others, they can be very hurtful. Shark friends don't really care about how you feel, they do and say things that are hurtful. They always like to be better than you, even if it is hurtful to you. Shark friends are hard to be around. Do you think you would like to be or have a Shark friend? (Emphasize that Shark friends may act this way when they are angry, or may do or say mean things and not even realize that they are being mean). (2 to 3 minutes)

5. Show students the puppet/picture/stuffed animal of the turtle. Say: Turtles are very shy, and are often scared. They like to stay inside their shells, because they are afraid to come out and show you who they really are. They may be nice, but you can't get to know them very well because they never talk to you or anyone else. They keep to themselves and don't know how to play well with others. Do you think you would like to be or have a Turtle friend? (Emphasize to students that Turtle friends can be very, very nice, but they may never share anything about themselves or never ask you to play with them because they are too shy.) 2-3 minutes)

6. Show students the puppet/picture/stuffed animal of the monkey. Say: Monkeys are very silly, they do not know that there are times to be serious and times to be silly. They do not know how to take things seriously. While they may sometimes be funny, they can also sometimes be annoying. Sometimes they get in trouble in school because they are always goofing off. Do you think you would like to be a Monkey friend? (Emphasize that Monkey friends can often by so hyper that they get into trouble a lot, and sometimes get you into trouble by pulling you into their silly behavior.) (2 to 3 minutes)

7. Show students the puppet/picture/stuffed animal of the lamb. Say: Lambs are followers, not leaders! They don't know how to think for themselves, they just follow others and do what everyone else wants them to do. They may make fun of someone just because someone else tells them to. They just follow along with anyone who comes along. They may choose to not be your friend because someone tells them to not be your friend. They may bully others because one friend may be bullying someone. They just follow what others are doing. Do you think you would like to be or have a Lamb friend? (Emphasize that Lamb friends may follow someone into something dangerous because they just follow other people. See "Cautions" explanation below). (2 to 3 minutes)

8. Show students the puppet/picture/stuffed animal of the teddy bear. Say: Teddy Bears are very good friends! They are there for you whenever you need them by listening to you and comforting you. They keep your secrets, help you when you need help, and keep you company. They always let you play with them. If they see someone being bullied, they take up for the person being bullied. We like to be around Teddy Bear friends. (Emphasize that Teddy Bear friends may not always be *perfect* friends, but they try to be the best friends they can be.) Ask students for ways that they have seen someone be a Teddy Bear friend. (2 to 3 minutes)

9. If we want to have good friends, we must FIRST be a good friend! We should always try to be a Teddy Bear friend so that other Teddy Bear friends will be *OUR* friends!

10. Read the book **Hunter's Best Friend at School**. Discuss periodically throughout the book the type of "fur-sonality" or friend that Hunter and his best friend are being. (Example: On the first few pages, have students discuss what types of friends Hunter and Stripe are to each other, good friends/teddy bear friends or Lamb friends when they are doing the exact same things and following each other. Later in the story, when Stripe is cutting up his frog, discuss with students how Stripe is acting like a Monkey friend. When Strip is acting up during circle time, and Hunter disapproves and ignores his friend, what kind of friends are each of them being?) (10 to 15 minutes)

11. If time permits, discuss additional processing questions below.

Processing Questions: (5 to 10 minutes)

✓ What kind of friend do you think you are? (Ask students to describe their "fur-sonality" to you.)

✓ Do you sometimes act like a monkey friend? What kinds of things do you do when you act like a monkey friend? (suggest answers if necessary, such as running in the hallway, bumping into others for fun in line, making silly noises during class time)

✓ Do you sometimes act like a shark friend? What kinds of things do you do when you act like a shark friend? (suggestions for answers include not letting someone play with you, doing or saying things when you are angry that could hurt someone's feelings, taking somebody's belongings without asking)

✓ Do you sometimes act like a turtle friend? What kinds of things do you do when you act like a monkey friend? (suggestions for answers include being too shy to meet new people, not wanting to play with other people sometimes, wanting to be alone all the time, having a hard time deciding what to play)

✓ What do Teddy Bear friends do for each other? What can we do to be Teddy Bear friends? How do Teddy Bear friends respond to shark/monkey/turtle friends?

✓ Are there times when you might *feel* like a teddy bear and other times when you *feel* like a monkey? (Allow time for response). We may not always act out these fursonalities, but sometimes we may feel this way.

For example, on some days I may feel like a turtle, if I am sad or having a bad day, I may need some alone time. On other days I may feel like a teddy bear, in a good mood and wanting to play with everyone. What do you do when you don't feel like a teddy bear all the time?

Cautions: Students may attempt to say that they like Lamb friends when you are explaining this fursonality. Be very concrete and specific about how dangerous Lamb friends can be, such as explaining how Lamb friends may follow so much that they follow into something dangerous. For example, Lamb friends may follow others and make bad choices when others make bad choices (e.g., breaking school rules, bullying others, smoking/doing drugs).

Adaptations: Add or adapt any of the above animals to fit the "fursonalities" you are trying to emphasize or teach. For example, use a monster to teach about angry friends, a dog to teach about loyalty, or a chameleon to teach about camouflaging or hiding our true selves or our feelings. Use of any other friendship book is appropriate, such as **Stand Tall, Molly Lou Melon** (Lovell, 2002, Putnam Juvenile), **Enemy Pie** (Munson, 2000, Chronicle Books), or **Scaredy Squirrel** (Watt, 2008, Kids Can Press, Ltd.).

Credit/References

Adapted from **Puzzle Pieces: Classroom Guidance Connection** (Senn & Sitsch, 2001). Youthlight, Inc.

About the Counselors:

Alaina Conner, LPC, NCC; is a Ph.D. Student at the University of Georgia. Previously, she was an Elementary School Counselor. Alaina@uga.edu

Jolie Daigle, Ph.D., LPC; is an Associate Professor at the University of Georgia. jdaigle@uga.edu

Bully Brains and Basketball Games

Submitted by Alaina Conner, LPC, NCC
and Jolie Ziomek-Daigle, Ph.D., LPC

School Level: Elementary.

Target Population: Grades 1 to 3.

Goals:

1. To help students learn the definition of bullying and to identify specific bullying behaviors.
2. To teach students how to respond to bullying behavior through use of questioning and role-playing.
3. To engage students in a fun way to learn about bullying behaviors, ways to respond, and ways to transfer learned behaviors to the "real world".

ASCA Standards:

PS:A1.6 Distinguish between appropriate and inappropriate behavior
PS:A2.6 Use effective communications skills
PS:C1.4 Demonstrate the ability to set boundaries, rights and personal privacy
PS:C1.5 Differentiate between situations requiring peer support and situations requiring adult professional help
PS:C1.7 Apply effective problem-solving and decision-making skills to make safe and healthy choices.

Estimated Time: 30 to 35 minutes.

Materials: Bucket (large enough to throw a ball into for basketball game), Small ball (tennis ball size), Role play questions, **Simon's Hook: A Story About Teases and Putdowns** by Karen Gedig Burnett (2000).

Introduction: Today we will be working on ways you can learn to get along with others, and we will be learning about bullying behaviors, how to respond to bullying, and practicing ways to respond to others when you are confronted with bullying. Raise your hand if you have ever seen someone being bullied? Does anyone want to share a time when you saw someone being bullied? (2 minutes)

Lesson

1. Begin by asking students for their definition of bullying. Have them give examples. Explain to students that bullying is REPEATED (it happens more than once and sometimes over and over again), INTENTIONAL (it is on purpose, the person is trying to bully), and POWER-BASED (a person is trying to gain power over another person) and explain all three concepts. (5 minutes)
2. Discuss with students the five ways of responding to bullying behaviors. (5 minutes)

    IGNORE   *If that doesn't work...*
    (Ask students: What does this look like? Wait for responses.
    If needed explain- It is pretending that the person isn't there or
    isn't bothering you)
    MOVE AWAY   *If that doesn't work...*
    (What does this look like? Moving seats or walking away
    from the person, maybe even standing near an adult).
    TALK FRIENDLY   *If that doesn't work...*
    (What does this sound like? "Please stop! You are really
    bothering me, you need to stop."
    TALK FIRMLY   *If that doesn't work...*
    (What does this sound like? "I asked you nicely to stop, and now
    I am telling you, leave me alone.")
    GET ADULT HELP
    (What does this mean? Walking to an adult and telling the
    adult that you are being bothered and you would like for it to
    stop.)

3. Read the book **Simon's Hook** by Burnett (2000).

4. Ask the processing questions below regarding the story. (5 minutes)

✓ What is a tease or a put down? Give some examples from the book. (Examples: if someone makes fun of you for wearing glasses, or if someone laughs at you when you fall down).

✓ Have you ever been teased or put down? (Remind students not to give names of other students to ensure emotional safety of other class members).

✓ Ask students to discuss ways that they could respond to these bullying behaviors using the five steps.

School Counselors Share Their Favorite Classroom Guidance Activities

Play a game of *Bully Basketball* (Senn & Sitsch, 2001), using the bucket and ball. Separate the class into two groups (you may decide to have students count one and two to assign the groups, or separate the students based on where they are sitting).

5. Have each team take turns responding to the following bullying situations (below). You may assign the questions to students as you deem appropriate, or have them draw questions from a hat. Explain to students the following rules: If the team member answering the question responds with a "correct" answer, one team member gets the opportunity to make a "basket" and score one point. Points may be taken away for any team not following rules such as screaming, yelling, or un-sportsmanlike behaviors during the basketball game.

Questions for Basketball Game:
- Another student rolls his or her eyes at you every time you say something, how should you respond?
- You see a student in your class get pushed down by another student, and you think it was on purpose. What do you do?
- Kids on the playground are leaving you out and saying they won't allow you in their "club". What do you do?
- Another student tells you that you smell bad. This student has told you this more than once. What do you do?
- You overhear another student saying dirty jokes to your friend, and your friend seems to not like what is being said. How should you respond?
- A kid in your class always kicks your feet when you are walking in line. You are getting really angry because it keeps happening. What do you do?
- What do you do if you see a friend of yours bullying another student on the playground?
- How do you respond if someone makes fun of you on the school bus every day?

6. After all the questions have been answered and the game is over, discuss the following processing questions below (5 minutes)
✓ How do you think you will use these role plays to respond in a real situation?
✓ What will you do if you see another student being bullied?
✓ Do you have a responsibility to help that student? How do you help them?
✓ What should you do if you don't know how to help yourself or someone else you know is being bullied?

Cautions: Time management will need to be considered, you may want to break into separate lessons.

Adaptations: Can use any other definitions of bullying and ways to respond to bullying. Playing the game and reading the book can be reversed in order.

Credit/References

Adapted from **Puzzle Pieces: Classroom Guidance Connection** (Senn & Sitsch, 2001). Youthlight, Inc.

Burnett, K.G. (2000). **Simon's Hook: A Story About Teases and Putdown**s. Felton, CA: GR Publishing.

About the Counselors:

Alaina Conner, LPC, NCC; is a Ph.D. Student at the University of Georgia. Previously, she was an Elementary School Counselor in Georgia and Illinois. Alaina@uga.edu

Jolie Ziomek-Daigle, Ph.D., LPC; is an Associate Professor at the University of Georgia. jdaigle@uga.edu

Say Something
Submitted by Mary Beth McCormac

School Level: Elementary.

Target Population: Grades 2 or 3.

Goals: Students will demonstrate:
1. Saying something to the child being bullied.
2. Saying something to the child bullying.
3. Telling an adult about bullying.

ASCA Standards:

P/S: B1.3 Identify alternative solutions to a problem
P/S: B1.4 Develop effective coping skills for dealing with problems
P/S: B1.8 Know when peer pressure is influencing a decision

Estimated Time: 30 to 40 minutes.

Materials:

Moss, P. (2004). **Say Something**. Gardiner, ME: Tilbury House Publishers.

Special Directions: Before beginning have everyone point at their partner to make sure everyone has a shoulder partner (person sitting close by). Move a student if necessary (may need one group of 3 if odd number).

Lesson

1. Begin with: What does it mean to *include* everyone? What are some things second graders do to *exclude* others? (Even saying, "I want to sit with my best friend" can make others feel excluded at school.) Review key vocabulary:
   * *Bullying* (3 part definition: one-sided; repeated; on purpose)
   * *Bystander* (sees or knows bullying is happening but does nothing to stop it).

2. (3 minutes) Introduce book with: This book is about bystanders. Why do you think the author called the book **Say Something?**
3. (7 minutes) Read book. Stop a few times and ask questions.
   a. Why do you think this boy gets teased? (p. 8)
   b. Children who are different than their peer group in some way are often bothered by teasing and sometimes bullying. Why did the girl narrating the story not say something? (p. 14)
   c. Most students remain quiet because they don't think it is their responsibility or they don't want to be picked on themselves. What would you have thought if the girl laughed here? Laughing and providing an audience is joining the bullying; sometimes we call them hurtful bystanders. Do you agree with her brother? (p. 26) Vote with thumbs: Agree, unsure, disagree and discuss.
   d. By not saying anything the students in the cafeteria allowed the girl to be bullied. What could the children at the other table, the bystanders, have done to help? Why did the girl telling the story decide to sit with the African American girl on the bus the next day? (p. 28) She now knows how it feels to be excluded and teased. She had empathy for the other girl and wanted to make her feel better.
4. (5 minutes) Review key points:
   a. Bystanders are generally safe if the bullying is not physical and there is an adult is close by. They can help the person being bullied by refusing to stand by. If there is only one student doing the bullying and you are with friends that will support you, usually it is safe to refuse the bullying and say something to the child who is bullying.
   • Ask: Is it easy to tell a child who is bullying to stop, or hard? Why? (It's hard because I might get teased, too. I don't want to be a goody-goody. I'm scared, I might get hurt. I don't think they mean anything by it.)
5. (10 minutes) Practice with a partner. Counselor divides group into shoulder partners and have partners stand should to shoulder and observe a model role play done by the counselor and teacher, or

counselor and a student.

    a. If the students are not familiar with using "I messages" model both types of responses: a) Stop it, that's bullying; and b) I feel mad when people make fun of my name I need you to call me by my real name. Introduce each role-play one at a time. The roleplays are not acting out bullying; they are practicing responding in a helpful way to bullying behavior.

Assign which student (i.e., based on who is closest to the window/door side of the room or odd number if divided by numbers) who will be getting teased, and which student will stand up and say something to the person who is getting teased. *Give the groups a chance to switch roles if time.*

    b. The partner who did not have a chance to "say something" will speak up to the other who is doing the verbal bullying.

    c. Assign which partner will be a teacher and who will report bullying to the "adult."

    d. After each brief practice session have one pair stand up and act out their response. Give feedback.

6. (5 minutes) Wrap-up using processing questions.

Processing Questions:

✓ Who should the bystander say something to in the cafeteria? (lunch room monitor) On the bus? (patrol or driver)

✓ What could you say to a student doing the bullying? (That's not cool! Stop it, that's bullying!)

✓ What about to the student being bullied? (Come play with us. I don't agree with what was said.)

✓ What if you are being bullied? (Please stop, I haven't done anything to you. An "I" message could also be used like, "I feel left out when there is no place for me to sit at the lunch table with the group.")

✓ What about when reporting to an adult? (I think ___ is bullying ___ because ____.)

Cautions: If students have had previous experiences with being bullied, it might bring up feelings and experiences they have not resolved.

About the School Counselor:

Mary Beth McCormac is an Elementary Counselor in Arlington County, Virginia. mary.mccormac@apsva.us

Don't Say Ain't: Addressing Linguistic and Cultural Differences Between Home and School Cultures

Submitted by Dr. Emily Goodman-Scott

School Level: Elementary.

Target Population: Grades 2 to 5.

Goals: Students will:
1. Have an increased understanding that their home and school can have different cultures.
2. Gain awareness of peers' linguistic and cultural traditions.
3. Gain an increased sense of normalcy regarding their home linguistic and cultural traditions.

ASCA Standards:

PS:A1.1 Develop positive attitudes toward self as a unique and worthy person
PS:A1.2 Identify values, attitudes and beliefs
PS:A1.5 Identify and express feelings
PS:A2.3 Recognize, accept, respect and appreciate individual differences
PS:A2.4 Recognize, accept and appreciate ethnic and cultural diversity
PS:A2.5 Recognize and respect differences in various family configurations

Estimated Time: 30 minutes.

Materials: Book **Don't Say Ain't** by Irene Smalls (2004), whiteboard and markers.

Lesson

1. The School Counselor begins by asking students to describe ways in which different people are unique, while the school counselor lists these traits on the whiteboard. Emphasize cultural and demographic characteristics such as language, race, family traditions, etc.

2. Reflecting on the students' answers to the previous question, the school counselor will discuss the age-appropriate meaning of the word *culture* (e.g., clothing, language, holidays, etc.) and discuss that (a) students' cultures can be unique from each other, and (b) home cultures can be different from the school culture (e.g., food served at home may be different from the type of food served in the school cafeteria).

3. Read the book **Don't Say Ain't** by Irene Smalls. This book describes a girl, Dana in the 1950s who lives in an inner-city African American community and is given the opportunity to go to a special school for gifted students. Dana struggles with the many differences between her neighborhood and her new school, such as different language/speech, different clothing, and different games/interests. Dana finds herself caught between two worlds and not fully a part of either one. This story ends in Dana realizing that the cultures at home and school are different, and that she can appreciate and be a part of both.

4. After reading the book, the school counselor can facilitate a discussion relating this story to the students' experiences encountering differences between home and school cultures; students can share their experiences adjusting to school culture. Emphasize cultural aspects such as language, food, traditions, etc.

5. The school counselor can ask students to list differences between school and home cultures while writing a list on the whiteboard (the most common items listed by students were food, clothing, traditions, language, and celebrations).

6. At the end of the lesson, the school counselor can summarize and reflect on students' responses, what they learned, and ask students to apply this knowledge to their future thoughts and actions.

Processing Questions:

✓ Early in the story, how did Dana feel going back and forth between her neighborhood and her new school?

✓ Have you ever had feelings like Dana's (e.g., if your home culture has been different from the school culture)?

✓ What did Dana do about the struggle between home and school culture (e.g., what changed for Dana?)?

✓ How can students in our school adjust to the differences between home and school cultures?

Cautions: It is suggested that school counselors take caution in facilitating this lesson if there are few students of diversity in a class, which could lead to these students feeling isolated or singled-out.

Adaptations: The definition of culture and the depth of the conversation can vary according to students' developmental levels. This lesson is especially helpful after a school's International Festival or other activities discussing school/student diversity/differences.

About the Counselor:

As a School Counselor, *Dr. Emily Goodman-Scott* opened a new elementary school in a diverse Washington DC suburb. After being a School Counselor for several years, Emily completed a Ph.D. in Counselor Education from Virginia Tech and now aspires to be a Counselor Educator. egscott.vt@gmail.com; www.emilygoodmanscott.com

It's Ok to Be Me

*Submitted by Lorraine J. Guth, Claire J. Dandeneau,
and Katie L. Lukehart*

School Level: Elementary.

Target Population: Grades 2 to 6.

Goals: Students will:
1. Celebrate the uniqueness of self and others.
2. Acquire self-knowledge regarding their special qualities.
3. Learn more about the special qualities of peers in the group.
4. Enhance communication skills.

ASCA Standards:

PS:A1.1 Develop positive attitudes towards self as a unique and worthy person.
PS:A1.10 Identify personal strengths and assets.
PS:A2.2 Respect alternative points of view.
PS:A2.3 Recognize, accept, respect, and appreciate individual differences.
PS:A2.4 Recognize, accept, and appreciate ethnic and cultural diversity.
PS:A2.6 Use effective communication skills.

Estimated Time: 40 minutes.

Materials: The book **It's Okay to Be Different** (Parr, 2001), three different colored plastic pails approximately 8 inches in diameter, three sheets of paper for each student (size of paper should be about 8.5" X 5.5"), three 5"X 8"index cards or pieces of paper, tape, and pencils/markers for each student.

Special Directions Before Activity:
1. The recommended class size is about 21 students and students will be divided into three small groups. Before the activity begins, the space should be arranged where there is a separate station (or place in the

room) for each small group to gather. At these stations, students could sit on the floor or on chairs/desks depending on the classroom configuration.

2. One bucket should be placed at each station. Using the marker, one index card, should be labeled **"Family/Heritage"**; one index card should be labeled **"Talents/Abilities"**; and one index card should be labeled **"Personal Qualities/Characteristics."** Each index card gets taped on one bucket.

3. At each station, there should be enough sheets of paper for each student in the class. Each sheet of paper for the Family/Heritage station should have "Something special about my family or heritage is..." typed at the top; each sheet of paper for the Talents/Abilities station should have "A special talent or ability I have is..." typed at the top; and each sheet of paper for the Personal Qualities/Characteristics station should have "A unique personal quality or characteristic I have is..." typed at the top.

4. Markers or pencils for each student in the small group should be placed at each station.

Introduction: The School Counselor should go over group norms. The school counselor could say: "It is important that we create an environment where all students feel respected and safe to share during classroom guidance activities. As a group, please share some important guiding behaviors that we can agree to follow such as respecting what others share in this group." The school counselor can elicit or suggest other norms such as maintaining confidentiality, taking turns, listening to others, etc. These norms could be written down for future lessons as well.

Lesson

1. **Reading Book (9 minutes).** The School Counselor explains, "We will start this lesson by reading a book titled *It's Okay to Be Different* written by Todd Parr." This book contains pictures with captions that celebrate the uniqueness of people.

[Note: The school counselor should read the book out loud and make sure all can see illustrations. The concluding part of the book states "It's okay to be different. You are special and important just because of being who you are" (Parr, 2001, last page).]

2. **Form Small Groups (2 minutes).** The school counselor states: "I invite all of you to participate in an activity today that celebrates the special qualities that you all possess. I will divide you into three small groups.

[Note: The school counselor could create the small groups by having members count off 1, 2, or 3; or the groups can be divided using words such as apple, peaches, or pumpkin pie.]

3. **Move to Stations (1 minute).** After the groups are formed, the school counselor states: "Each group will go to the designated place in the classroom where there is a colored bucket, paper, and pencils/markers. Group 1 should move to the **Family/Heritage** station; Group 2 should move to the **Talents/Abilities** station; and Group 3 should move to the **Personal Qualities/Characteristics** station. Each group will sit around their designated bucket."

4. **Participate in First Station (7 minutes).** After students move to the stations, the school counselor states, "Next to the bucket will be sheets of paper with a prompt for you to answer. Please write your name on the paper and complete the prompt on the paper using words or drawings. After everybody is done, you are invited to share your response with the other students in your small group. When done, please place your completed sheet in the bucket."

[Note: The school counselor can mention that the sharing of responses is voluntary. Students are invited to share at a level that they feel comfortable. Again, the prompts for each group are: Group 1 - Something special about my family or heritage is...; Group 2 - A special talent or ability I have is...; and Group 3 - A unique personal quality or characteristic I have is...]

5. **Rotate to Next Station (7 minutes).** After the first station is complete, the school counselor states, "Students, please move to the next station in a clockwise manner and complete the prompt for the new station. Please write your name on the paper and complete the prompt on the paper using words or drawings. After everybody is done, you are invited to share your response with the other students in your small group. When done, please place your completed sheet in the bucket."

6. **Rotate to Next Station (7 minutes).** After the first station is complete, the school counselor states, "Students, please move to the next station in a clockwise manner and complete the prompt for the new station. Please write your name on the paper and complete the prompt on the paper using words or drawings. After everybody is done, you are invited to share your response with the other students in your small group. When done, please place your completed sheet in the bucket."

7. **Processing the Experience (7 minutes).** After the activity is over, the school counselor can ask the following processing questions. In addition, the school counselor could comment on how the buckets are full of unique qualities that make the class special. The school counselor could also have the students create a collage or poster that displays all of the unique qualities that were shared. This creation could be displayed in the classroom or school.

Processing Questions:

✓ What thoughts or feelings did you have while you were writing your responses for each bucket?
✓ What was it like to share more about yourself with other members of your class?
✓ How can your special qualities contribute to the class/school?
✓ What did you learn about others in the class?
✓ What are some things you and your classmates have in common?
✓ How can the common special traits contribute to the class/school?
✓ How can we continue to create a classroom/school environment that celebrates the uniqueness of everyone?

Cautions: Students should be instructed to share at a level in which they feel comfortable. The school counselor can circulate around the classroom during the activity to ensure students are adhering to the group norms that were previously established and to also provide help if needed.

Adaptations: This activity can be shortened in length if needed by eliminating one (or more) of the station rotations [e.g., removing Step 6]. Needed accommodations should also be made for students with disabilities, such as physical or learning disabilities. For example, the individual accommodations needed should be determined in advance of the lesson so that all students may participate.

Credit/References

Parr, T. (2001). **It's Okay To Be Different**. New York: Little Brown and Company.

About the Counselors:

Lorraine J. Guth is a Professor in the Department of Counseling at Indiana University of Pennsylvania. She has international school counseling experience, and most recently helped to establish the school counseling profession in the country of Bhutan. lguth@iup.edu

Claire J. Dandeneau is a Professor and Department Chairperson in the Department of Counseling at Indiana University of Pennsylvania. She has extensive group work experience including being a therapeutic wilderness counselor. cdanden@iup.edu

Katie L. Lukehart is a Rehabilitative Therapist at Johns Hopkins Bayview Medical Center and recently graduated with her Master's degree in Clinical Mental Health Counseling from Indiana University of Pennsylvania. klukeha1@jhmi.edu

Who is on Your Team? Lessons 1, 2, and 3

Submitted by Jennifer Rogers

School Level: Elementary.

Target Population: Grades 3 to 6.

Goals: Students will:
1. Understand what a support team is, what a role model is, and characteristics of people who are not on their team.
2. Identify people who are supportive of them.
3. Create a visual representation of those people who support them and keep it for future reference.

ASCA Standards:

7.3 Personal/Social Development:
f. Students will identify resource people in the school and community and know how to seek their help
g. Students will apply effective problem-solving and decision-making skills to make safe and healthy choices.

Estimated Time: Three 30-minute lessons.

Materials: Chalk board/white board/large piece of paper as demonstration in front of whole group, colored pencils or crayons, pens or pencils for each student, large piece of paper (at least legal size) for each student.

Lesson 1

1. Counselor begins with: "Good Morning. For those of you who don't know me, I am your school counselor. Can anyone share what you think I do for the students in this school?" Students share their ideas. Emphasize meeting with students to talk about problems they are having at school, working with teachers and parents to help students, come in to classrooms to talk about things like bullying or career day in the students comments. (2 minutes)
2. Counselor continues: "Along with some of the things that we just talked about, a school counselor is also here to help you develop good

School Counselors Share Their Favorite Classroom Guidance Activities

decision-making skills. Can anyone tell me what you think decision making skills are?" Student share their ideas.

Emphasize using a thoughtful process to solve problems, and picking the best option available in student comments. (3 minutes)

3. Counselor says: "For the next three times we are together as a group, we are here to work on how to make good decisions about what kind of people are good supporters of you. I like to call them your team mates. Have any of you been on a team before? What does a team do?" Student share their ideas.

Emphasize helping each other, working together to improve, and having common goals in student comments. (5 minutes)

4. Counselor continues: "It sounds like we have a variety of experiences with team membership. And most times those teams are ones that we don't choose. But the great thing about this is that your team is that they are people who support and help you. The purpose of this lesson is to help identify what a good support team looks like. We will talk about what a supportive friend does and does not do. Together we will work on building your skills to find people who support you. We will call them the people who are on your team. Before we begin, I would like to ask that we respect our group members and allow them to share without talking over them and allow them to have their own opinions that may differ from yours."

5. Counselor continues: "To get to know each other, I am going to ask you to sit next to someone with the same color shirt that you are wearing. Then introduce yourself to that new person and ask each other: If you were given a superpower, what would it be and how would you use it to help people?"

(Write questions on board so students can refer to it while discussing).
(5 minutes)

6. Counselor asks partners to introduce each other to the rest of the group. (5 minutes)

7. Counselor says: "Now that we are getting to know each other, we can begin our discussion about what a support team is. Members of your support team are those who have your best interests at heart. People who are there for you in good times and bad times. This can be a friend, family member, neighbor, teacher, counselor, church leader, team coach, or someone else. Does anyone have an example that they'd like to share of someone that might be a good support team member?" Students share their examples to check for understanding among the whole group.

Emphasize examples where student is being supported, such as the friend who helped you when you were having a hard time understanding a math assignment or your Aunt who really listened to you when you were upset about your missing dog.

8. Counselor continues with: "Great examples. Let's create a picture of those people. I'd like you to draw 5 people that you believe would be great members of your support team. Underneath each person, write who they are to you (friend, family member, etc.) and what they do to support you."

Counselor hands out paper, crayons, pencils, markers, etc.

Counselor writes directions on the board and create an example of own support team for the group to see. (10 minutes)

9. Counselor says: "Would anyone like to share with the group their drawing of support team members?" Allow for a few students to share with the group the details of their drawings. If no one shares, the counselor can talk about their own support group and check in again to see if anyone would like to share.

Emphasize the details. For example, in my picture, my Dad is holding a fishing pole because when we go fishing I talk to him about my life.

10. Counselor ends with : "Thank you for sharing. I am going to collect your drawings and we will use them again the next time we meet. Until then, I'd like you to keep a look out for those qualities of people who support you and those who don't. We will be discussing this next time."

Lesson 2

1. Counselor hands back drawings. Counselor says: "As you may remember, last time we met we were talking about your support group. Your support group is your team. People you can go to when you are having a hard time. On these sheets you drew some people who you can count on as members of your team. And your team may look different than everyone else's. Not everyone will have the same type of people. Let's look at your drawings. Some of you drew friends as members of your support group. Are friends important? How do people select friends? Who would like to talk about how they selected their friends?" (5 minutes)

2. Students volunteer to share how they select friends.

Emphasize how they became friends. For example, we ride the same bus, my mom and her mom are best friends, they are in my class, I met them playing basketball. Then emphasize why they chose that person to be their friend: we have a lot in common, they make me laugh, etc.

School Counselors Share Their Favorite Classroom Guidance Activities

Emphasize the importance of friends: someone to talk to outside your family, someone who shares interests with you, someone who can be honest with, etc.

3. Counselor continues: "Those are some great thoughts. Let's write them down. On the back of your paper draw a line down the middle of the paper. I want you to think about some of the friends you have had in your life. On one side write the positive qualities of a friend and on the other side write the negative qualities you have experienced with your friends." (10 minutes)

4. Counselor says: "Okay let's share our ideas with the group. Who can tell me some positive qualities of friends?" Write them down somewhere all students can see. "What about some negative qualities?" Write them down as well.

Suggestions for positive qualities: Friends are…kind, loyal, trustworthy, share things in common, laugh, respectful, fun, understanding, etc. Suggestions for negative qualities: Friends don't name call, put you down, intimidate or scare you in to doing something you know is wrong, make you feel bad about yourself, or overload you with their problems without caring about yours, etc. (10 minutes)

5. Counselor: "Now that we have created a list of positive and negative qualities and a drawing representing who is on your team, how do you think you might use this to help you in the future?" Allow students to tell you how it can be used.

Suggestions for use: Refer back to it if having difficulty understanding if the person is behaving like a good friend, Refer back to it to remember who is on your team, Remember who supports you and how they support you. (5 minutes)

6. Counselor ends with: "I am going to collect your work again. When we meet next week we are all going to add one more person to our team. Your assignment before we meet again is to think about role models. Do you have any role models? Don't answer yet, I want you to think about this and we will work on it together next time."

Lesson 3

1. Counselor hands back drawings. Counselor begins with: "Last time we met we worked on what a qualities a good friend has. We also looked at qualities of people who we don't want on our team. Today, I'd like to add one more person to your team. A role model. Would anyone like to share what they think a role model is?" Students discuss of the title role model. (5 minutes)

2. Counselor continues: "Great ideas. The definition of role model that we want to use is someone who you admire and think you may want to be like. It isn't trying to copy them because you are still uniquely you. But it is adopting some trait that the role model has that you would like to have too. For example, your role model may be a hard worker, or get good grades, or be a sports star, or sing really well, or have a lot of patience, or not get their feelings hurt easily. You may already have someone on your team who is one or you may have to think of someone else. Let me give you some time to think about it."

3. Walk around and ask students if they need help thinking of someone. Brainstorm with individual kids based on their goals and interests. (5 minutes)

4. Counselor says: "Ok, it looks like everyone has chosen someone. What I would like you to do is now draw your role model. If your role model is already represented by a person on your team, I'd like you to draw the characteristic that you'd like to imitate. For instance, if your brother is on your team and you'd like to be a better student like him, you can draw books or a report card." Hand out pens/pencils/markers. (5 minutes)

5. While students are working, write on visible surface: My role model is _____ because _____. I want to be able to _____. I will work toward that goal by _____.

Counselor can write own example to help kids think about this. <u>My role model</u> is my teacher <u>because</u> she is very patient and kind to all the students. <u>I want to be able to</u> have patience and not get mad at kids in my class. <u>I will work toward that goal by</u> counting to 10 in my head before getting mad to stop from yelling at them.

6. Counselor continues: "Ok, now please look at what I have written on the board. It is what I'd like to you write down and fill in the blank parts with what you'd like from your own role model. I will give you a few minutes to complete this and if there is time we can hear from some people who'd like to share about their role models." (10 minutes)

7. Counselor says: "Would anyone like to share what they've written about their role model? Who is your role model? Is it someone from your team or someone completely different? Let's share some ideas about the strength/skill/talent that you want to have in your life. How would you go about working toward that goal?" (2 minutes)

8. Allow a few students to read their responses or talk about their role models.

9. Counselor: "Thank you for sharing. Did anyone get stumped thinking about how to accomplish your goals? If so, does anyone else have ideas about how this student might accomplish their goals. Let's brainstorm." (5 minutes)

10. Student share: If time allows, discuss one student's goal and have the rest of the group help them come up with ideas about how to attain their goal.

11. Counselor: "We have done good work together. On your paper, you should have people who are on your team and a role model. Those people all have your best interests at heart and support you. These are the people that you can count on for help. Now that you have a tangible picture of those people who are on your team that you can take home, what do think you'll do with it?" (Student share. Emphasize that they can use it in the future to help determine who is on their team. (3 minutes)

12. Counselor ends with: "If you ever have difficulties or are having a hard time, these are the people who will support you. Thank you for being such a great group."

Cautions: There may be students in the group who are unable to identify anyone who is on their team or supports them. If this happens, the counselor may want to say, "If you are having difficulty choosing anyone in your life who supports you, go ahead and just draw people that you know. We can meet later to determine if there are any ways that they can support you." Before the next group meeting, you will need to meet with this student to determine if this activity is appropriate for them. During the individual meeting the counselor and the student can review all of the people in the student's life to find out more about her/his support system. At the very least, their counselor is on their team.

About the Counselor:

Jennifer Rogers is currently a Doctoral student at the University of New Mexico. Previously, she was a School Counselor in Reno, Nevada. jmrogers@unm.edu

Animals All Around
Submitted by Rebekah Byrd, Laura Walker,
and Kelly Emelianchik-Key

School Level: Elementary.

Goals: Students will:
1. Be able to define values (defined as something one believes to be important.
2. Discuss and define acceptance of differences.
3. Have an understanding of what it means to accept differences.
4. Understand how values relate to acceptance of differences.

ASCA Standards:

A:A3.2 Demonstrate the ability to work independently, as well as the ability to work cooperatively with other students
A:A3.5 Share knowledge
A:B1.2 Learn and apply critical-thinking skills
PS:A1.1 Develop positive attitudes toward self as a unique and worthy person
PS:A1.2 Identify values, attitudes and beliefs
PS:A2.1 Recognize that everyone has rights and responsibilities
PS:A2.2 Respect alternative points of view
PS:A2.3 Recognize, accept, respect and appreciate individual differences.

Estimated Time: 35 minutes.

Materials: Prepared index cards (created beforehand and based on the number of students in class) with one animal name on each (dog, cat, bird, mouse), dry erase or chalk board, and a timer. Even (or close to even) group distribution is recommended.

Introduction: (10 minutes): Welcome students and start lesson by asking the class, "How do you define the word "values"? Ask for volunteers to raise their hands if they can give examples, then list them on the board. Some examples include (these can be suggested to assist students in coming up with their own examples, or can be added to the list after they come up with examples on their own.)

 a) something a person believes in,
 b) something someone believes to be true,
 c) an idea shared by a family, social group, community, culture, religion,
 d) belief perspective,
 e) an idea about what is good or bad,
 f) a rule,
 g) a principle,
 h) a guideline for someone's behavior, and/or
 i) a standard or quality considered worthwhile or desirable.

For younger grades, specific examples of values may be more developmentally appropriate to discuss. For example, sharing, caring, telling the truth, respect, (etc.).

2. Ask the class to give examples of how you can accept differences of others. Let students give examples. Examples can be adapted for specific age groups as noted below. Some examples include:

 a) understanding that everyone is different (This is key to your discussion with K to Grade 3 students),
 b) differences are what makes us unique and interesting (Discuss with K to Grade 3 students how the world would be if we were the same.),
 c) understanding that people have different family ideas, communities, cultures, backgrounds, preferences, abilities, belief perspectives, religions, family incomes, etc. (This discussion will be more in-depth for upper elementary grades. You can discuss each topic, citing examples they have experienced in their own lives.),
 d) respecting those that are different from us (Discuss how to show respect to others who are different.) and/or
 e) acknowledge, understand, and accept other's ideas, beliefs, and perspectives (For upper elementary grades, you may note how to respect others despite disagreeing with others' choices.).

*Note: Emphasize the importance of withholding from judging whether a difference is right or wrong and how this is a part of acceptance and understanding for others.

Lesson (10 minutes)

1. Tell the students that they are going to do an activity that requires *no talking* and that they must keep the noise level to a minimum.
2. Hand each student an index card with an animal on it (dog, cat, bird, mouse). They are not to tell anyone what animal is on their card. Next, by acting and sounding as their specific animal, they are to find others like them until everyone has found all members of their group. After all of the group members are found, they are to sit with their group, be quiet, and wait until the other groups are finished. They have 3 minutes to complete this portion of the activity (set timer).
3. While students are seated quietly in their groups, discuss the following (give them about 3 minutes)
    a) How did you find each other?
    b) How did you know how to act?
    c) How did you know how to sound?

(Focus on themes such as how they observed one another, how they knew how to act, how others may have acted differently (acceptance of differences), and how they responded)

4. Next, ask students to move around the room *reacting* (quietly) to the other animal groups as these animals might act if they were all together (e.g., cats may run from dogs; mice may run from all three; dogs may want to play with others while not understanding why the other animals are scared). Allow students to take on group characteristics and react to each other for about 2 to 3 minutes. Let students know they will stop when the timer sounds.
5. Have students return to their seats, and move into debriefing/processing questions as a class.

Processing Questions: (15 minutes)

Let students share by discussing how each group found all of its members. (3 to 5 minutes)

o What was finding your members like?
o What were some feelings associated with being in a group?
o What about labels attached to being in a group? (Explore labels attached to different animal groups (dogs chase cats) and if these labels are always correct (my dog and cat are best friends, etc.).
o How does this concept relate to you as school? (Connect activity to student groups and labels- student will bring up stereotypes). Give definition and examples of stereotypes and discuss if these are always

true- related information to previous discussion on values and differences.

o What does this activity have to do with 'values' and 'acceptance of differences'?
o Tell why it is important to you to accept others differences and honor diversity.

(Focus on themes such as differences people have, how to accept these differences, why differences and acceptance of them is important.)

Adapted Processing Questions for K to Grade 3:

o Tell how you found other members in your group? How did you know they were in your same group?
o How did you like being a part of your group?
o How did you all act (this will be based on the animal they were acting like)? (Explore labels attached to different animal groups (dogs chase cats) and if these labels are always correct (my dog and cat are best friends, etc).
o Discuss how sometimes people act differently than we think they will and how everyone is different.
o How did this activity help us understand acceptance of differences?
o Why do you think it is important to respect others' values?

Cautions: Most of the time allotment in this lesson is dedicated to processing because in the author's personal experiences, students have much to say on this topic and tend to bring up stereotypes on their own. Knowing your students, the specific class, and the age group should allow you to proceed with this caution in mind, while tying the lesson back to the initial processing of 'values' and 'acceptance of differences'. Unsolicited feedback from students has revealed that this particular lesson has been a consistent favorite among classroom guidance activities. ☺

Adaptations: Other processing questions that could be added based on what school counselor observes in activity and/or based on age/grade level of students include:

o If you could not find others in your group, why not?

o How did you think your animal would act that may have been different from how others acted as the same animal?

o Why do you think others may not have done the same thing?

o What did you like about their interpretation?

o If you had to re-do your animal action, what would you do different this time?

School counselors could also include a conversation about perception. Process how each person thought their animal would sound and act a different way and how the way we perceive things can be different for everyone- just because we perceive things differently, does not mean we are wrong.

Credit/References

Adapted from: Byrd, R. (2010). *Act like an animal.* CARE NOW Program Manual. Unpublished.

About the Counselors:

Rebekah Byrd, Ph.D., LPC, NCC, RPT; is an Assistant Professor of Counseling and School Counseling Program Coordinator in the Department of Counseling and Human Services at East Tennessee State University. byrdrj@etsu.edu; rebekah.byrd@gmail.com

Laura M. Walker, MA, LPCA, NCC; is a School Counselor in Hendersonville, NC. walkerlm3@gmail.com

Kelly Emelianchik-Key, Ph.D., LPC, NCC; is an Assistant Professor in the Counseling Department at Argosy University in Atlanta. kemelianchik-key@argosy.edu

Behavior Lemonade

Submitted by Megan Beeching and Kerrie R. Fineran

School Level: Elementary.

Goals: Students will gain increased insight about positive and negative choices and discuss how choices affect their life.

ASCA Standards:

PS:A1.6 Distinguish between appropriate and inappropriate behavior
PS:A1.10 Identify personal strengths and assets
PS:B1.2 Understand consequences of decisions and choices

Estimated Time: 30 minutes.

Materials: 1 cup lemon juice concentrate, ¾ cup sugar, 2 quarts water, pitcher, measuring cups, plastic cups, napkins, spoons. (Begin with a pitcher full of 2 quarts of water.)

Lesson

1. Begin by asking the class: "Who has made lemonade before? What are the ingredients? We are going to talk about how our life is like lemonade. It has ingredients called choices or behaviors. Some choices, like not following directions are sour like lemon juice. Some choices, like cleaning our room when we're told are sweet like sugar."

2. Have students volunteer examples of negative behaviors. Invite each student that volunteers to pour some lemon juice into the pitcher of water. When students produce 5 or more sound examples, all of the lemon juice should be mixed in the water.

3. At that time pour a VERY SMALL amount of the sour lemon water for students. Ask students who would like to try the SOUR drink and describe their experiences. Explain that negative behaviors are like lemon juice in that they make life sour.

4. Next, have students volunteer positive behavior examples. Invite volunteers to pour some sugar into the pitcher. When students provide at least 5 examples of positive behaviors all of the sugar should be in the lemonade. Explain that positive behaviors are like sugar in that they make life sweet. Pour some finished lemonade for them to enjoy while process questions are facilitated.

Processing Questions:

✓ What are some "sugar choices" we want to make more of as a group? How will we do this?

✓ What are some "lemon choices" we want to make less of as a group? How will we do this?

✓ How can we make more "sugar choices" than "lemon choices" in our individual lives?

✓ How do your choices affect your time at school? At home?

✓ How do your choices affect your relationship with family? Friends? Teachers?

✓ What did you learn about your choices/behaviors in class today?

Cautions: Students may need many examples and modeling. Students lacking fine-motor skills may need help pouring lemon juice or sugar into the pitcher. Be aware of any health conditions that may preclude students from drinking the juices used in the activity.

Adaptations: To promote more group interaction, students could work together in the large group to identify 5 negative behaviors and 5 positive behaviors. When the group offers the 5 negative behaviors, make one pitcher with "sour drink." When the group offers the 5 positive behaviors, make a separate pitcher with "sweet drink." Give each student two cups and have them try them one right after the other.

Another adaptation would be to give half the group the sour drink, the other half of the group the sweet drink and have them compare their experiences. The original lesson was done to facilitate exploration of negative feelings toward parents' divorce but also questions could be geared toward decisions affecting academic success or failure.

Credit/References

Idea for using lemonade as an analogy was taken from Amanda Zimmerman from the website http:// schoolcounselingfroma-z.blogspot.com/ title "A Bitter Sweet Lesson".

About the Counselors: *Megan Beeching* is a graduate and Lab Mentor of the school counseling program at Indiana University- Purdue University, Fort Wayne. megan.beeching@gmail.com

Kerrie Fineran is an Assistant Professor and School Counseling Coordinator at IPFW, and a licensed School Counselor.

Diversity Rocks

Submitted by Katie L. Lukehart and Lorraine J. Guth

School Level: Elementary/Middle.

Target Population: Grades 3 to 8.

Goals: Students will:

1. Learn more about diversity and its meaning.
2. Acquire self-knowledge regarding their unique qualities and values.
3. Increase their awareness of others' diverse qualities within the group.

ASCA Standards:

PS:A1.1   Develop a positive attitude towards self as a unique and worthy person.
PS:A1:9   Demonstrate cooperative behavior in groups.
PS:A1.10 Identify personal strengths and assets.
PS:A2.2   Respect alternative points of view.
PS:A2.3   Recognize, accept, respect, and appreciate individual differences, including ethnic and cultural diversity.
PS:A2.6 Use effective communication skills.

Estimated Time: 40 minutes.

Materials: Small rocks varying in shapes and colors that could be purchased from a craft store or found in nature. Make sure there are enough extra rocks for each student to have a selection (double the number of rocks per students is suggested).

Special Directions: This activity can be conducted with a full class of approximately 20 students. Depending on the class size, students can be split into small groups, and then brought together for discussion after the completion of the activity. So if the class size was 20 students, it is recommended that there be two small groups of 10 students.

Before the activity begins, arrange desks or chairs in a circle around the room for each group of students. Students may also sit in a circle on the floor depending on the classroom configuration. The rocks should be spread out on the floor or on a table situated in the middle of the circle.

Lesson

1. **Ground Rules** (5 Minutes). The School Counselor and students should work together to establish ground rules at the beginning of the activity to ensure the safety of students when using the rocks in this activity. Group norms such as respect for others, taking turns, and confidentiality should also be discussed. For example, the school counselor could state, "Before we begin our activity, we are going to discuss some norms for our classroom lesson. First, students should work together and take turns choosing a rock. If two students would like the same rock, please quietly communicate with each other to find a compromise/solution. Second, the materials of this activity should be used in a safe manner. Third, each student must show respect for his or her classmates. This includes being quiet while another is talking, listening, and giving everyone time to participate. Lastly, anything that is said or done during this activity must be kept confidential. This means that no one should discuss this activity with other people outside of this classroom. What other norms should we include?" The school counselor can approach this norm discussion in a collaborative, interactive process so students feel part of creating a safe and respectful group atmosphere.

2. **Introduction of Activity (1 minute).** The school counselor explains, "You will be participating in a 'Diversity Rocks!' activity designed to get to know yourself and others in the group better. Carefully study the rocks that are in the center of the circle, paying attention to the shapes, sizes, and colors. When ready, you will each carefully select a rock that best represents you in some way. "

3. **Student selection of rocks (2 minutes).** After the activity is introduced, students should select their rocks. Students are allowed to look for a rock at the same time in an orderly fashion to ensure that everyone has a fair selection.

4. **Student study of rocks (2 minutes).** After students select their rocks, they should be given some time to really study its uniqueness.

5. **Group Discussion of Uniqueness (10 minutes).** Have each student describe to the others in the small group why his or her rock was chosen to represent his or her unique qualities. Then, have students discuss the unique qualities and themes that emerge from the discussion. Possible questions to encourage discussions include:
   ✓ What kind of common themes did you notice members of your group sharing?
   ✓ What did you have in common with some of the other students in your group?
   ✓ What did you notice that was unique about yourself or others in your group?"

6. **Group Discussion of Common Features (10 minutes).** After the discussion of uniqueness, ask students in the small group to volunteer to share the common features of all of the rocks in their group. The school counselor could have students link this to commonalities that they share as a group. For example, the rocks may be made up of similar materials inside. This could be related to how students have similar feelings inside. All rocks also vary in shape and size but in the end they are still rocks. This can be related to how all the students are human beings and classmates with common connections.

7. **Processing the Experience (10 minutes).** After the activity has concluded, the school counselor can ask the following processing questions to all students in the class. The school counselor could also take this time to share his or her observations or feelings about the completion of the activity.

Processing Questions:
   ✓ What thoughts or feelings did you have while you were picking your rock?
   ✓ What was it like to share more about yourself with other members in your class?
   ✓ How can your unique qualities contribute to the class/school?
   ✓ What did you learn about others in the class? Was there anything that surprised you?
   ✓ How can the common qualities contribute to the class/school?
   ✓ How were you able to connect to what other class members shared?
   ✓ What are some things your classmates have in common?
   ✓ How can we as a group work to embrace the individual differences and similarities of everyone in the school?

Cautions: The school counselor should pay special attention to the adherence of group norms throughout the activity. Establishing the norm of safety at the beginning of this activity is essential to help ensure that students use these rocks in a safe manner.

Adaptations: This activity can be broken into two lessons if more time is needed. For example the first lesson could involve steps 1-4 and the second lesson could focus on steps 5-6. Special consideration would need to be taken to adapt to the developmental level of participants. For students with behavioral difficulties, softer materials could be substituted for rocks. For example, oranges, leaves, or flowers could be used. Needed accommodations should also be made for students with both physical and learning disabilities. Accommodations should be determined in advance of the activity so that all students may participate.

About the Counselors:

Katie L. Lukehart is a Rehabilitative Therapist at Johns Hopkins Bayview Medical Center and recently graduated with her master's degree in Clinical Mental Health Counseling from Indiana University of Pennsylvania. klukeha1@jhmi.edu

Lorraine J. Guth is a Professor in the Department of Counseling, Indiana University of Pennsylvania. She teaches in the School and Clinical Mental Health Counseling programs. She has international school counseling experience, and most recently helped to establish the school counseling profession in the country of Bhutanlguth@iup.edu

Connecting Students to the Civil Rights Movement Through Music:

Submitted by Barb Wilson, Ph.D. and Jolie Ziomek-Daigle, Ph.D.

School Level: Elementary.

Target Population: Grades 5 and 6.

Possible Classes to Be Integrated: Social Studies curriculum or during **Black History Month.**

Goals: Students will:

1. Be able to briefly explain the Civil Rights Movement.
2. Understand how expression in music and writing can be tied to historical events.
3. Identify at least one song related to the Civil Rights Movement.
4. Understand social injustices that occurred prior to and during the Civil Rights Movement and provide examples of current day social injustices.
5. Relate lesson on civil rights and music to current day.

ASCA Standards:

PS:A1.1 Develop positive attitudes toward self as a unique and worthy person
PS:A1.4 Understand change is a part of growth
PS:A2.4 Recognize, accept and appreciate ethnic and cultural diversity
PS:B1.7 Demonstrate a respect and appreciation for individual and cultural differences
PS:C1.2 Learn about the relationship between rules, laws, safety and the protection of rights of the individual.

Estimated Time: 45 to 60 minutes (may be divided into two lessons).

Materials: Audio/visual equipment to play songs, song lyrics (www.azlyrics.com, www.metrolyrics.com) for each student, **Music of the Civil Rights Movement** (Wilson, 2011) worksheet for each student.

Lesson

1. **Introduction.** School Counselor says: "The Civil Rights Movement was a time of transformation in American history. The movement was deeply rooted in expression and music as methods of coping and sharing information. This activity explores songs related to the Civil Rights Movement and as an expression for discussing social justice. Social injustices of current day will also be explored. By the end of this activity, you will be able to identify at least one (1) song from the civil rights movement and will understand how music played a role during this time in history. (1 minute)

2. Talk about expression and music. Tell the students that words can become a song when put to music. Through words and music people are able to express feelings, emotions, and share information about events. Think about songs that make you feel happy (i.e. upbeat dance music). Think about songs that celebrate life (i.e. The "Happy Birthday" song). Songs can also mark moments of sadness and struggle. Sometimes the act of writing a song can be healing in addition to listening to the song itself. (3 minutes)

3. Ask students to identify at least three (3) current popular songs. Write the names of the songs on a board or large paper if possible. Prompt students by asking them what artist they like or what song they downloaded recently. Ask students to share why they like the songs and/or what feeling the songs give them. You may want to write keywords as the students discuss the songs. Emphasize songs about social acceptance (i.e., image, LGBTQ) and highlight the emotional reasons why the students may like particular songs (not just because the artist is attractive or it has a good beat). (3 to 5 minutes)

4. Discuss any overlapping themes or words between the songs, such as acceptance, differences, society, hope, and change. (3 to 5 minutes)

5. Briefly discuss the Civil Rights Movement. Say: "The Civil Rights movement was a time in American history focused mainly on achieving and protecting equal rights for all people. Minorities, such as African-Americans and women, had historically been treated with less equality than their White and/or male peers. The movement was marked by protests and changes in laws. Music played a major role in the Movement." For example, radio stations used music to relay coded messages about the historical march in May, 1953. Later known as the Children's Crusade, hundreds of children marched in downtown Birmingham, Alabama to talk to the mayor about discrimination.

Through music, children learned when and where this event would take place. (2 to 3 minutes)

6. Give each student a copy of the worksheet **Music of the Civil Rights Movement** (Wilson, 2011). Explain to the students that one song, *This Little Light of Mine* is a gospel song and can commonly be heard in Christian churches. However, the purpose of listening to this song is in no way the promotion of Christianity. These songs are about accepting yourself and others. *This Little Light of Mine* celebrates our individuality and our importance. *A Change is Gonna Come* is about having hope during times of discrimination. And *Pride* celebrates Martin Luther King, Jr., and his work with social justice advocacy. (2 minutes)

7. Three songs are listed on the worksheet: *This Little Light of Mine, A Change is Gonna Come*, and *Pride.* Play each song and allow students to read the lyrics as each song is playing. After every song has played, briefly discuss the lyrics and emotional responses (i.e. sadness, hope).
   ✓ Ask the students to think about the feelings they felt as they listened to the songs.
   ✓ Ask them to think about what message the song writer was trying to relay through the song.
   Try to get the students to understand and empathize with the oppressed people of the Civil Rights era. (10 to 15 minutes)

8. Have students complete the worksheet as they listen to the songs. (10 minutes)

9. Allow time for additional sharing of thoughts, song titles, and questions from the students. Allow students to volunteer to share the answers they have written. Walk through each question and prompt when needed. Prompts may include emotion words or sharing examples of groups in current society who might identify with the songs (i.e., LGBTQ community, teenagers).
   ✓ What were the social injustices of the Civil Rights Movement (racism, discrimination, segregation, others)? What were the outcomes of the Civil Rights Movement? Why does this matter today?
   ✓ What are the social injustices of today? At our school? In our communities? In our country?
   The emphasis is on helping the students process the songs they heard and bring it to current trends in society and in their own lives. (10 minutes)

10. Wrap up. Ask students identify one "take away." The take-away should be related to equality, accepting others, or the use of music to evoke emotion. (5 to 7 minutes)
   ✓ How was music used during the Civil Rights Movement?
   ✓ How did you identify with any songs discussed?
   ✓ What can you do to change the injustices? Can you identify one person who is creating positive change?

Next Possible Lessons or Topics: "The Mighty Times: The Children's March" movie and lesson outlined by Teaching Tolerance (www.teachingtolerance.org).

About the Counselors:

Barb Wilson, Ph.D., NCC, LPC is a School Counselor at West Hall Middle School, Oakwood, Georgia. drwilson@yahoo.com

Jolie Ziomek-Daigle, Ph.D., LPC, is an Associate Professor and School Counseling Program Coordinator at University of Georgia. jdaigle@uga.edu

Music of the Civil Rights Movement (Wilson, 2011)

Possible songs:
- "This Little Light of Mine" by Harry Dixon Loes
- "A Change is Gonna Come" by Sam Cooke
- "Pride" by U2

After we listen to the songs, take a few minutes to answer the following questions:

1. Which song(s) really stood out to you? Why?

2. Have you heard any of these songs before? Which one(s)?

3. Did any of these songs make you uncomfortable? Why?

4. Thinking of society today, what are some examples of social injustices?

EXTRA (if time is allotted): If you could write a song about your own life, your family's history, where you live, etc:

1. What would be the title of your song?

2. Use the space below to write lyrics, lines, or words you would definitely want to include in the song.

Managing the Uncontrollable
Submitted by Jennifer L. Marshall

School Level: Middle.

Goals: Students will be able to:
1. Recognize through a concrete visual medium what their uncontrolled stressors are in their life at the time of the group.
2. Identify their stressors in a safe environment, both those that are within their control and those that are out of their control.
3. Discuss different coping skills to be used with the stressors they can control.

ASCA Standards:
7.1.1. Standard 1: Students will acquire the attitudes, knowledge and skills that contribute to effective learning in school and across the life span
e. Students will identify attitudes and behaviors that lead to successful learning.
n. Students will share knowledge

Estimated Time: 50 minutes.

Materials: Paper, pens, pencils, and/or markers/crayons.

Specific Directions:
1. **Introduction:** The School Counselor begins with: "Uncontrolled stress is something everyone deals with in their life. This stress can stem from school, friends, and family. A stressor in your life can be when you get into an argument with your parents because you were supposed to clean your room over the weekend and you forgot. Some stress can be controlled (when you clean your room). Other stress is out of our control (your parent's reaction to you not cleaning your room)." This activity will help students to identify some of their stressors, begin to understand the stressors that can and can't be controlled, discuss coping skills to deal with their stressors, and also set some goals and interventions to work toward dealing with these stressors. (1 minute)
2. The School Counselor relates the following, "I had car trouble the other day and was late for work. I was very frustrated and angry. As you can see from my picture, my stick person has her hands up to her head and she is frowning right next to the car." After the School Counselor

gives a personal example, then they ask each student to take out their paper and pens and say, "I am going to give you 2 to 3 minutes to draw whatever comes to mind when I say, 'uncontrollable stress'. You don't need to have a drawing background and you may draw stick figures if you like. You will be asked to volunteer to share your picture. You will then be asked to describe what you have drawn and how it represents uncontrollable stress. If you are not comfortable sharing your picture you may describe it to the group and discuss how it represents uncontrollable stress." (2 to 3 minutes)

3. After all students have drawn their pictures, the leader asks for volunteers who are comfortable to show their drawing and explain how their picture represents uncontrolled stress to them. (18 minutes)

4. Then the School Counselor asks students what commonalities they are aware of in the picture. Emphasize patterns and themes within the student's pictures which then can be related to the discussion on control and stress later. (5 minutes)

5. The School Counselor leads a brief discussion on uncontrolled stress and how this stress might affect an individual physically, mentally, and socially. The School Counselor might say: "Uncontrolled stress is something that is out of a person's grasp to change. This can be very frustrating, anger provoking and make individuals feel helpless at times. These types of emotions can affect our physical, mental and social well being." Process using these questions:
   ✓ How do you define uncontrolled stress?
   ✓ What in your picture represents uncontrolled stress to you?
   ✓ What commonalities do you see in your picture when compared to others in the group? (10 minutes)

6. Next the Counselor asks students to turn their papers over and list the factors that they can control in their picture and the factors they can't control in their picture. The School Counselor might relate to their earlier drawing of the broken down car and being late to work. "In my drawing that I showed you earlier, I could (not control) my car being broken down, but I (could control) calling into work and letting them know I was going to be late." (5 minutes)

7. Use the following process questions to help students think about and discuss coping skills that can be used for their stressors:
   ✓ How does stress affect you physically? Mentally? and Socially?
   ✓ How do you handle general stress?
   ✓ Are your coping skills for general stress the same that you would use for uncontrollable stress?

School Counselors Share Their Favorite Classroom Guidance Activities

✓ Describe the coping skills you use or might use for controllable stress.

✓ How can you use these coping skills when controllable stress occurs at school? Home? Friends?

✓ Describe the coping skills you use or might use for uncontrollable stress.

✓ How can you use these coping skills when uncontrollable stress occurs at school? Home? Friends? (10 minutes)

8. Finally, the Counselor asks students to look at the stressors they can control and set at least 2 goals with interventions that they are willing to work on this week to decrease some of that stress. The students can then write these in a notebook or the School Counselor can provide paper. Then the School Counselor can ask the students to keep their goals in a safe place where they can access it again in a week when asked. The School Counselor then should follow up with students a week later to see if they are working on their goals. (5 minutes)

Example: A 7th grade female student drew a picture of 6 stick figures, 3 figures on one side and a squiggle line dividing the other 3 stick figures. Three stick figures were close and holding hands on one side and on the other side the 3 stick figures were next to each other, but not close. The student described the situation as such: All the figures represented her and her friends. In describing the friends she related that the three holding hands included her and two close friends. The other three figures opposite the squiggle line were also her friends at one time, but had lately become argumentative and mean to her and her other two close friends who were represented by holding hands in the picture. She related that the uncontrolled stress came from these three antagonistic friends particularly because they were assigned to work together in a school function and the female student did not know how to handle their mean remarks and rude behavior during the function, particularly because her 2 other close friends would not be present. It was also apparent in the drawing that the student represented herself as smaller than the other figures who appeared to be holding her up by the hand. This point in the drawing was discussed in group and the student related that she felt very reliant on her two close friends, especially since the conflict with the other girls. She also related that she felt caught in the middle (she also drew herself closest to the squiggly line) between the 5 girls and wanted desperately for everyone to get along like they did earlier in the relationship.

The student was then asked to list the factors she could control and not control in her picture. She listed that she could control her reactions and thoughts toward the argumentative friends. The factors out of her control were the three argumentative friend's attitudes, thoughts, and behaviors.

The students listed the following as a goal and intervention she would try:

Goal: I will decrease my anxiety while at the school function with the 3 friends by 20% as evidenced by walking away from any situation in which I feel I am being provoked by the other girls.

   Intervention: I will walk away from any situation in which I feel I am being antagonized by these three individuals.

   Intervention: I will also count to 10 and use breathing exercises if I become angry with these individuals.

   Intervention: I will try getting all six of us together in one room to discuss our relationship as well as discuss what we want from the relationship.

Cautions: Some students may not want to draw or are embarrassed to show there drawing. With these individuals you might have them just describe their drawing instead of showing it. It is also helpful if you draw something as the group leader and share your uncontrollable stress.

Adaptations: You could also have them just use words or magazine pictures, instead of drawing a picture to describe their uncontrollable stress.

Resources

Biegel, G. (2010). *The stress reduction workbook for teens: Mindfulness skills to help you deal with stress.* Oakland, CA: New Harbinger.

Davis, M., Eshelman, E. R., & McKay, M. (2008). *The relaxation and stress reduction workbook.* Oakland, CA: New Harbinger.

Shapiro, L., Sprague, R., & McKay, M. (2009). *The relaxation and stress reduction workbook for kids: Help for children to cope with stress, anxiety, and transitions.* Oakland, CA: New Harbinger.

About the Counselor: *Jennifer L. Marshall* is an Associate Professor at Troy University in Panama City, Fl. jmarshall90113@troy.edu

Not Just for Playing Charades: The Role of Non-Verbal Communication

Submitted by Dr. Melissa Luke, Ph.D. and Allison M. Hrovat, MS

School Level: Middle.

Goals:
1. To observe the impact of non-verbal communication gestures.
2. To actively engage in a process of demonstrating and responding to paralanguage/ non-verbal communication gestures.
3. To demonstrate increased awareness of the role of paralanguage in interpersonal communication.
4. To explore each participant's experience of the activity, and the meaning attributed to non-verbal communication.
5. To reflect on what is communicated by non-verbal behaviors, and how students can more effectively read the non-verbal behaviors of others as well as be aware of what he/she is communicating through their own use of paralanguage.

ASCA Standards:
PS:A2.3 Recognize, accept, respect and appreciate individual differences
PS:A2.6 Use effective communications skills
PS:A2.7 Know that communication involves speaking, listening and nonverbal behavior

Estimated Time: 40 minutes.

Materials: Index cards with directives (explained below).

Introduction: Nonverbal behaviors and gestures are an important mode of communication and are estimated to influence 60%-80% of communication (Sue & Sue, 2003). It has long been thought that emotions can be interpreted from facial expressions (e.g. Fields, 1953), and that physical gestures imply meaning particularly when understood within a cultural context. Because children and adolescents often struggle with the language needed to express how they are feeling, and with reading the tone, gestures, and expressions of others, social skills can be enhanced by offering students an opportunity to actively engage in a reflective process focused on attending to non-verbal communication.

Lesson

1. Students are placed into groups of 2 or 3 and are told:
   Have a 2 to 3 minute conversation on any of the following:
   - The last time I went to a restaurant...
   - My favorite memory from last year was...
   - If I could be have a super power it would be...

   The School Counselor asks for volunteer students to share what they observed and experienced. The school counselor uses linking to help students identify similarities in their experiences, despite the prompt chosen. (6 to 8 minutes)

2. The school counselor randomly hands out an index card to one person in each group. The index cards have been previously printed with the following further directives: (3 to 5 minutes)
   ✓ One person sits; the other stands
   ✓ Continually walk towards your partner as you two talk
   ✓ Periodically, take a step back from your partner when you talk
   ✓ Insert "um" and "like" frequently when you speak
   ✓ Tilt your head frequently as you and your partner talk
   ✓ Be sure to speak louder than your partner
   ✓ Frequently lower your voice during your discussion
   ✓ Touch your partner on the hand or shoulder as you talk
   ✓ Talk as quickly as you can when it is your turn to speak
   ✓ Use inflection at the end of each of your statements
   ✓ Pause for a few seconds periodically as you speak.

3. The school counselor then instructs the student groups to select a different prompt and have another 2 to 3 minute conversation. This time however, the person with the index card needs to follow the directions during the conversation. (6 to 7 minutes)
   - The last time I went to a restaurant...
   - My favorite memory from last year was...
   - If I could be have a super power it would be...

4. Processing Questions: (12 to 15 minutes)
   - ✓ What did you notice during this activity?
   - ✓ What are you thinking and feeling about all of this?
   - ✓ What did it feel like when your partner ____ (insert directive from card)?
   - ✓ What did it mean when your partner _____ (insert directive from card)?
   - ✓ What are some ways you can politely interact with someone who...(insert specific communication style difference, i.e.: likes to stand very close, speaks very loudly or very softly, etc.).
   - ✓ What might you do differently as a result of this activity?

The school counselor should emphasize the connections between the content of the conversation and the nonverbal behavior taking place as the student answer these questions.

5. The school counselor is advised to summarize a quick review that includes observations of what took place in order to crystallize the learning that occurred. To accomplish this, the school counselor will want to be able to generalize observations across participants. For example, the school counselor may begin by saying "In doing this activity, we noticed that people communicate in many different ways. People might communicate, or we might interpret, certain types of messages based on tone of voice, physical proximity, (etc.). Those elements of communication can impact our feelings about the interaction, the meaning we make from the interaction, and our ways of responding." From this introduction, the school counselor can then point to specific examples that occurred during the experience, and can ask for student input as appropriate to effectively summarize the experience. (3 to 5 minutes)

Cautions: In processing this activity, the counselor should be prepared to appropriately process the different interpretations of non-verbal behaviors that are possible, especially as related to culture. The school counselor may wish to discuss how the same behavior, like looking a person in the eye, can be interpreted by some people as a sign of respect or honesty, and by others this could be seen as interpersonally threatening or pushy, possibly even disrespectful. Counselors should additionally be reflective about how ability and developmental stage impact non-verbal forms of communication, and to provide some more explicit instruction about non-verbal communication when needed.

Adaptations: This activity can be easily adapted for use in the schools with elementary, middle, and high school students needing support in developing social skills and recognizing social cues. For example with elementary students, the school counselor can ask all students to sit in a circle and ask for volunteers to come into the center of the circle for the 'experiment' conversations, using directives that are age appropriate and/ or suited to the needs of the student(s) (i.e., asking one student to back away while the other is talking to them). With middle school students, the school counselor can provide fewer directives and process these one interaction at a time (i.e., What might it signal when another person is backing away from a conversation with you? What might you be communicating if you back away from another person who is speaking?), the activity can be simplified for a younger audience. In doing so, the school counselor can unpack the commonly inferred interpretations of nonverbal behaviors, as well as highlight some idiosyncratic or less common impressions. It is important to highlight that our intended message may not always match others' experience of our nonverbal behavior (e.g., I use my hands a lot when I get excited or interested, but to some people it is interpreted as dominant or imposing).

About the Counselors:

Dr. Melissa Luke, Ph.D is an Associate Professor and Coordinator of School Counseling in the Counseling and Human Services Department at Syracuse University. Previously she was a high school teacher and counselor. mmluke@syr.edu

Allison M. Hrovat, MS is a Doctoral Candidate in Counseling and Counselor Education in the Counseling and Human Services Department at Syracuse University. amhrovat@syr.edu

There's Power in Being a Bystander... Use it or Lose it!

Submitted by Caroline J. Lopez and Christine Suniti Bhat

School Level: Middle.

Goals: Students will:
1. Understand the important role bystanders can play in reducing harm in cyberbullying situations.
2. Explore their own attitudes and beliefs on the role bystanders can play in cyberbullying.
3. Acquire the skills to respond appropriately to cyberbullying situations.

ASCA Standards:

PS: A1.2 Identify values, attitudes and beliefs
PS: B1.4 Develop effective coping skills for dealing with problems
PS. B1.5 Demonstrate when where and how to seek help for solving problems and making decisions.

Time Length: 45 minutes.

Materials: http://www.youtube.com/watch?v=iDBiqUWRtMo (Note: feel free to use any other media clip that highlights the pain and suffering experienced by targets of bullying and cyberbullying); *Cyberbullying Scenarios* (Lopez & Bhat, 2014)

Preparation: School counselor may choose to create role-play scenarios or may have students create their own scenario. If the scenarios are generated by the leader, they should be created prior to the session.

Lesson

1. Introduce the topic to students: "Today, we are going to learn about the role bystanders can play in cyberbullying situations. Before we begin our discussion I would first like to introduce to you the story 13 year old Ryan Halligan. As you watch the video clip, I would like you to think about how you might respond if you saw what happened to Ryan occurring here at your school." (5 minutes)
2. Play the video. (5 minutes)

3. Lead a discussion with the processing questions below. (10 minutes)

4. Divide students into groups of 5 or 6 and provide each group with one of the *Cyberbullying Scenarios* (Lopez & Bhat, 2014). Have group members identify the key roles (cyberbully, victim, bystanders) in each one. Groups will role play the scenarios and role play one of the responses that they have written on the chart. (20 minutes)

5. Closing: "Today we learned about the role bystanders can play in cyberbullying situations. Some of the strategies bystanders can use include (read from the student generated chart.) Although it can be easy to do nothing, you should remember that as a bystander you have tremendous power to stop cyberbullying. On a piece of paper I would like you to finish these sentences:
   - Today I learned....
   - If I witness cyberbullying, one strategy I will use is.....
   (5 minutes)

Processing Questions:

✓ What are some examples of ways someone can be a bystander to cyberbullying?

✓ What are some reasons that students may hesitate to become involved?

✓ How can not getting involved add or contribute to the problem?

✓ What actions could you take if you were a bystander to cyberbullying? (in your responses think about how you might respond to the victim, the cyberbully or cyberbullies, or adults you could turn to). Write these on a chart.

Points to Emphasize: Bystanders have tremendous power to stop the spread of cyberbullying. By doing nothing, we become complicit in the victimizations that is happening in front of us.

Bystanders who do not intervene, may experience:
   ✓ Pressure to participate in the bullying
   ✓ Anxiety about speaking to anyone about the bullying
   ✓ Vulnerability to becoming victimized
   ✓ Guilt for not having defended the victim

Group leaders may also discuss the pros and cons of taking action as a bystander vs. doing nothing.

Not Taking Action:
   • Pros: cyberbully won't bother you.

- Cons: cyberbullying may continue and get worse victim may feel increasingly worse over time, cyberbully may pressure you into participating.

Taking Action:
- Pros: you help stop the cyberbullying, the victim may feel better.
- Cons: you may feel anxious or scared, cyberbully may retaliate or start picking on you.

About the Counselors:

Dr. Caroline J. Lopez is currently an Assistant Professor in the Counseling and School Psychology program at Chapman University in Orange, California. Previously, she was a Middle School Counselor. clopez@chapman.edu

Dr. Christine Suniti Bhat is an Associate Professor in Counselor Education at Ohio University. Previously, Christine was a *Safe and Drug Free Schools* Coordinator and Teacher. bhatc@ohio.edu

Cyberbullying Scenarios
Caroline J. Lopez and Christine Suniti Bhat (2014)

1. Julia and Samantha are both 7th graders who attend the same school. They were best friends until they had an argument. They have not been friends since then. Julia was so upset with Samantha that she decided to post a picture of Samantha on her Instagram account. On the picture Julia wrote the words "loser" and "slut" over Samantha's face. She also wrote, "Samantha is sad and pathetic, she needs to kill herself already!!" Julia asks several students in class to follow her Instagram page which is now dedicated to mean pictures of Samantha.

2. Alicia is an 8th grader at ABC Middle School. Alicia has a crush on a boy in her class named Andrew. In a text message, Alicia decides to send Andrew a "sexy" picture of herself. After receiving the picture, Andrew decides to forward the picture to a bunch of his friends with the words "Alicia looks like a cow, forward this picture if you agree!" While hanging out after school with Andrew and a few other friends, Andrew tells you he is going to forward the picture to the rest of your friends.

3. Angel is a 6ᵗʰ grader who would one day like to become a professional dancer. He practices at home and will video tape his dance choreography and post it on YouTube. Eric is a 7ᵗʰ grader who is known at school for picking on younger students. After viewing Angel's YouTube video, he decides to write several comments on Angel's YouTube post:
Eric's comments on YouTube are below:
Monday 3pm: "Wow! Angel is so gay, everyone stay out of the locker room he might want to be your boyfriend!"
Monday 7pm: "What a loser, gay boy can't even dance"
Tuesday 5pm: Hey, I know you heard me today at school calling you by your new name, ANGELA! I am going to call you that from now on, gayboy. You might as well be a girl.
Tuesday 8pm: "Gayboy sucks. If really want to see him dance, trip him at school when you see him."
Wednesday 4pm: Hey everyone click the "dislike" button. He needs to know this video sucks!
Thursday: "Hey, gay boy, why didn't you show up to school today? No one wants to see your ugly face dancing on TV, go drown in a pool.
You and a group of your friends notice the comments on YouTube.

4. After school, while with her friends Becky decides to text message Jonathan, a boy in her class who likes her. She sends him text messages saying that she likes him. She does this to trick him into sharing his personal feelings. He shares with her his feelings toward her. She laughs and shares with the rest of the group.

5. Hugo and Mariah have been dating for a while. After a messy breakup Hugo decides to make a fake Facebook account using Mariah's name and photos. He sends messages posing as Mariah to the school. His friends post rude comments and tell you to add the fake profile.

6. Marcus has his own blog on Tumblr. He talks about his family problems and other issues about his life. Eric has found the page and has shared Marcus's personal posts to all the kids in class. He also sends anonymous hate messages to Marcus. He shares the page link to his group of friends.

7. Mary loves taking pictures. While snapping photos, her friend Amber slipped and fell. In the picture Amber's dress flew up and her underwear is showing. Amber asks Mary to delete the photo, but Mary thinks it's funny. Mary decides to post it on Facebook anyway.

8. Sophia and Monica like the same boy. Sophia decides to pull a prank on Monica after school. She asks someone in her group of friends to record it and she posts it on YouTube, Instagram and Vine. Everyone in your class including you can now see it.

Communication Box

Submitted by Stephanie Hammond and Christopher P. Roseman

School Level: Middle.

Goals:
1. Learn and explore effective communication strategies between individuals and in groups.
2. Improve communication skills to foster new ideas, work collaboratively, and navigate/resolve conflict.

ASCA Standards:
ASCA Personal/Social Standard A: Students will acquire the knowledge, attitudes, and interpersonal skills to help them understand and respect self and others.

Estimated Time: 30 to 45 minutes.

Materials: Paper boxes, medium in size, should be solid on the bottom and all four sides, top is made of two flaps that fold together. Other supplies include craft paint, brushes, stickers, markers. Friendship rocks (one for each student) should be small in size with a smooth surface to be able to write one word on them using paint, stickers, or markers.

Set Up: There should be three separate tables; one with the paper boxes, one with the creative instruments (paint, markers, stickers, etc.), and the last one with rocks. Each group will select only one box; each student will select one rock of their own.

Lesson

1. The School Counselor begins with: "This activity is entitled Communication Box which is designed to have you engage with one another in a collaborative manner without use of any social media or electronic devices. This activity allows for each of you participate using both non-verbal and verbal communication to work together toward a common goal. The Communication Box will teach each of you how to use appropriate communication skills to develop an end-result that the group is pleased with.
2. Counselor randomly assigns participants to groups of six students and instructs them to sit together in silence for 3 minutes at their empty

designated table. The silence is used to teach the students that communication still occurs when no words can be spoken.

3. The Counselor instructs each group (order can be determined by facilitator) to select their paper box and creative instruments but no rocks. The group will be advised that they can decorate the box in any manner they wish to as long as there are no inappropriate words, drawings, or symbols. They may verbally communicate during this process on how to design the box and each student is encouraged to engage in decorating the box. (15 minutes)

After the box is chosen, group members will share the art materials. Group members will implement interpersonal skills to ask for needed materials (e.g., "Can you please hand me the stickers?", "Can I use the blue paint when you are done?"

4. The Counselor will call on one group at a time and each member will choose 3 rocks of their own

5. Students will then be instructed to add words to their rocks using the markers, paint, and stickers that represent what is most important in friendship (e.g.. humor, kindness, share). (5 minutes)

6. Students of every group are asked place their rocks in the box and close the lid.

7. The Counselor then opens each box and reads the words on each rock.

Processing Questions:

✓ What was it like to have to share the materials?

✓ Why did you choose the rocks that you did?

✓ What does the finished box with the rocks represent for them?

✓ After each box has been opened and each group has processed; allow the entire group to process what the box and rocks mean as a group symbol?

✓ What do you like about other group members boxes and why?

✓ What did you learn about communication on an individual basis? Within a group?

About the Counselors: *Stephanie Hammond* is a School Counselor with Bio-Med Science Academy.
shammond@biomedscienceacademy.org
Christopher P. Roseman, Ph.D., PC-CR, NCC is an Assistant Professor in Counselor Education Program at the University of Toledo.
Christopher.Roseman@utoledo.edu

Identity Auction
Submitted by Melissa Luke

School Level: Middle.

Goals: Students will:
1. Be able to prioritize the salient aspects of their identity.
2. Be able to explain the connections between these identity factors and more tangible reflections of such (auctioned items).
3. Have increased awareness about how their identity (and potentially aspects previously unarticulated) can impact their decision making in the classroom context.
4. Discuss their experiences (thoughts, feelings, and behaviors) during the activity and hypothesize about the potential relevance in other group contexts.

ASCA Standards:

PS:A1.2 Identify values, attitudes and beliefs
PS:A2.3 Recognize, accept, respect and appreciate individual differences
PS:A2.4 Recognize, accept and appreciate ethnic and cultural diversity
PS:B1.2 Understand consequences of decisions and choices
PS:B1.3 Identify alternative solutions to a problem
PS:B1.8 Know when peer pressure is influencing a decision
C:A1.3. Develop an awareness of personal abilities, skills, interests and motivations
C:A1.5 Learn to make decisions

Estimated Time: 40 to 45 minutes.

Materials: 5 x7 " index cards (enough for all students, plus one); play money (handout provided to make) and 2 or 3 'credit cards' (I've use those mailed as advertisements and use an indelible marker to denote the simulated credit 'limit'); objects for auction/distribution (enough for each student in class, plus one), these can be as simple as pictures from a magazine, found items from a junk drawer, purchases from a dollar store, or otherwise donated things; and gavel and fake microphone (not needed adds to the playfulness).

Special Directions: Prior to students entering the room, the school counselor needs to arrange the objects that will be auctioned so that students have an opportunity to 'preview' these items.

Lesson

1. Counselor says: Today, we are going to identify and examine what aspects of your *identity* are important to you and how these identity factors may be reflected in what you value, as well as what you do. Because we are obviously not alone, and instead we are a classroom of individuals whose identities may intersect, overlap, or differ, we will also have a chance to experiment with how individual identities can impact what happens in a group setting (said another way, how we influence each other, perhaps even without knowing). (1 to 2-minutes)

2. The school counselor begins by soliciting examples of identity. S/he develops a broad range of examples, including visible and invisible identity factors. Emphasize the similarities and differences across the identified examples as the students discuss. (2 to 3 minutes)

3. The school counselor then offers a few formal definitions of identity such as what makes a person identifiable or recognizable or the parts of a person that make them unique. (1 to 2 minutes)

4. The school counselor delivers brief instruction about the ways in which identity can be reflected in and influence what we as individuals value, what we want, how we make decisions, as well as other examples of things we do. For example, the school counselor could say "Our individual identity can be shown or expressed in a lot of ways. As a mom, my value of family togetherness might be expressed wanting to eat dinner together with my family or even a desire to cook for them. Another example might be like Mr. So and so (band teacher) who is a musician. His identity can be seen in his membership in a band, frequently listening to music, and even wearing T-shirts with his favorite musicians on them." (3 to 4 minutes)

5. The school counselor invites students to have an 'in vivo' experiment to test this out. The school counselor distributes one 5x7" index card to each student, and asks that s/he fold the card length wise. (1 to 2 minutes)

6. Students are then asked to identify their own personal top 3 identity factors of salience, recording just one on the card. The school counselor might say "for some of you, your age, gender, race/ethnicity, or religion might be very important in your identity, for others you

School Counselors Share Their Favorite Classroom Guidance Activities

may pay more attention to your family role or skills and abilities."
(1 to 2 minutes)

7. The school counselor discusses how aspects of identity can be manifested in or reflected in things. S/he provides some examples, like a person who self identifies as an 'Environmentalist' might reflect this in reusable cups or utensils. (1to 2 minutes)

8. Students are then called up in small groups (e.g. by table or location seated in the room) and asked to place their identity card on any item on display that represents some aspect of their values. (5 to 6 minutes)

9. The school counselor asks for a few volunteers to explain the connection between their identity factor, and the item itself. The school counselor can look for opportunities to assist students' awareness by using reframing, paraphrasing, summarizing as the students speak. For example, if a student says that s/he put their 'teenager' identity card on a matchbox car and says this is because I am learning to drive on my own, the school counselor can say and it seems like you're looking forward to some increased independence. (3 to 4 minutes)

10. The school counselor randomly distributes the play money and credit cards. (I use envelopes to do this so on the surface, everyone 'gets' the same thing, but inside there are varied amounts of money.) (2 to 3 minutes)

11. The school counselor then informs students that each identity factor/object will be auctioned off. Students can 'bid' using the money they have been given and though they will return the fake money, they can keep the objects. At this point, the school counselor invites a student to explain how an auction works and adds to or clarifies as necessary. It is important for the students to understand that process of turn taking during bidding. (3 to 4 minutes).

12. The counselor proceeds with 'auctioning' each item/identity factor, taking bids from the various students, and moving at a fairly quick pace. (10 to 12 minutes)

13. As the auction proceeds, the school counselor makes process observations about the decision making taking place, including group dynamics that unfold. Sometimes this includes students' strategizing with one another, students recognizing that not everyone was given the same amount or type of money, and sometimes even students not following the implicit rules or others' expectations.

12. Once all students have 'purchased' an object/identity factor, the school counselor summarizes this section of the activity by noting that

some students ended up with an identity factor that they had already determined as salient, while others may not have. S/he asks what might account for this and discusses the activity, using the following processing questions: (8 to 10 minutes)

✓ Let's start by discussing what you noticed about yourself in this activity?

✓ How did your thoughts, feelings, or behavior surprise you?

✓ In what ways did your behavior within the activity match / not match the identity you identified as salient?

✓ What did you notice happening in the group during the activity?

✓ How do you understand what you observed?

✓ What questions still remain and might you direct these to individuals within the group right now?

✓ What additional 'identities' did you become aware of through this activity? What helped raise your attention to the salience of this/these?

✓ What group norms or dynamics did you see emerging? How did you or others/ respond to these?

✓ In what ways were you tempted to behave during the activity? What stopped you from doing this?

✓ When else have you thought, felt, or acted similarly as you found yourself during this activity?

✓ What did you learn about how you (or other individuals) impact the group?

✓ How can your 'new learnings' be applied to a future situation? Explain.

Cautions: Because the activity has the potential to raise previously unacknowledged group norms and dynamics, the school counselor needs to be prepared to respond to this appropriately, such as inequality or 'favoritism', particularly with some student bravely noting jealousy, annoyance, fear, or guilt about who received the credit card with a high limit. If the school counselor observes this occurring, s/he can assist students' in labeling and normalizing this as a potential occurrence. Further, the school counselor might remind students that the assignment of envelopes what random and then acknowledge how powerful feelings can be evoked, asking for students to reflect on other times when this may have occurred.

Adaptations: This activity can be accomplished without any objects, with the auction itself consisting of only the identity factors. In such cases, the process is faster because it excludes the steps related to connecting identity factors to tangible reflection or expression.

About the Counselor:

Melissa Luke, Ph.D. is an Associate Professor in the Counseling & Human Services Department at Syracuse University. mmluke@syr.edu

Handout: School counselors can print as many of these as needed, and packaging in some fashion for students to use in the Identity Auction activity.

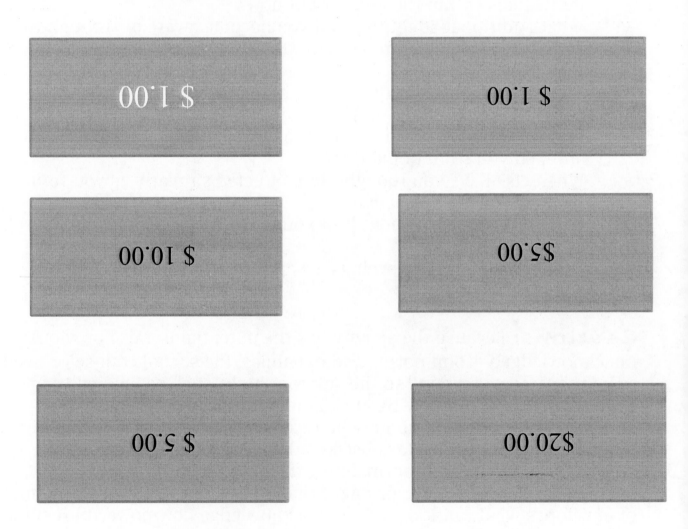

Happy is as Happy Does
Submitted by Karen McGibbon

School Level: Middle.

Goals: Students will:
1. Increase awareness about happiness.
2. Identify sources of personal happiness.
3. Learn a new happiness increasing activity.

ASCA Standards:

PS:A1.1   Develop positive attitudes toward self as a unique and
worthy person
PS:A1.2   Identify values, attitudes and beliefs
PS:A1.5   Identify and express feelings
PS:A1.9   Demonstrate cooperative behavior in groups
PS:A1.10 Identify personal strengths and assets
PS:A2.2   Respect alternative points of view
PS:A2.3   Recognize, accept, respect and appreciate individual
differences
PS:A2.4   Recognize, accept and appreciate ethnic and cultural
diversity

Estimated Time: 1 hour.

Materials: Blank paper, pen or pencil, **How Am I Feeling Today**
Chart (source: http://busyteacher.org/4605-how-are-you-feeling-today.html),
Positive Views Worksheet

Lesson

1. The Counselor begins with: Happiness can be defined in many
   different ways. Each of us will have our own unique definition, such as
   "happiness is having fun with my family". Sometimes we forget to
   think about how we feel and what we can do to improve the way we
   feel. Today we will not only identify how we feel, but we will also do
   something about feeling even better!
2. The Counselor explains that the faces on the **How Am I Feeling Today**
   Chart show some of the different ways people's faces look when they
   are feeling certain ways or showing certain emotions.

School Counselors Share Their Favorite Classroom Guidance Activities

3. Ask students raise their hands and take turns identifying the face and feeling that is closest to how they are feeling right now. The Counselor allows each student to speak and then summarizes by stating that "we all feel many different ways from time to time and today we are going to be talking about one particular feeling - happiness". (10 minutes)

4. The Counselor writes "Things that make me happy" on the board, then writes a list of five things that make her/him happy and explains to students why each thing makes her/him happy. Students will be asked to comment on this list. (5 minutes)

5. Students will then be asked to take out a blank sheet of paper and write a list of five things that make her/him happy. After the lists are completed, each student will read as many of their happy things as they are comfortable with to the class. (10 minutes)

6. The Counselor thanks the students for sharing their lists and ask the class if they noticed any similarities in the lists. *(5 minutes)*

7. The Counselor comments that everybody has something good about them or their life that they can choose to focus on even though people often focus more on the negative things in their life.

8. Students will then be asked to find a partner. They will each write, on the worksheet provided, five positive things about themselves, their classmates or friends, and what they think their life will be like in the next twenty years, and share it with their partner.
(10 minutes)

9. The group will then reconvene and each person will now share one of each type of positive thing from their partner's list with the whole group until everyone has shared. (10 minutes)

Processing Questions: (10 minutes)
 ✓ What was it like to identify positive things about yourself? Easy or hard? Why?
 ✓ Positive things about others?
 ✓ Say the positive things?
 ✓ What was it like to hear other's positive things?
 ✓ Do you see any connection between the things that you think about every day and your feelings? Explain more.
 ✓ What can you do to increase your happiness level every day based on what you wrote on the first list? Can you tie the people and positive things in there somehow too?

Cautions: Students should be encouraged to share only positive and wholesome things that make them happy with the group. If students share that they are unhappy when they use the feelings chart, explain that some days they may feel sad or angry but today we want to focus on the positives and to help turn those bad days around.

How to Integrate into Core Curriculum: Coordinate
with English Teachers and ask students to write essay " What I do to live a happy life".

Credit/References: *How Am I Feeling Today* chart. Retrieved
from http://busyteacher.org/4605-how-are-you-feeling-today.html

About the School Counselor: *Karen McGibbon*, MA, CCL is
the CEO/Founder 'Live Free' Coaching and Counseling Services, an Adjunct Lecturer at The Mico University College, and a PhD Student in Counselor Education and Supervision at Regent University, Kingston, Jamaica. karemcg@mail.regent.edu

Positive Views Worksheet

Myself	My Friends	My Future

334

How are you feeling today?

What You Have Always Wanted to Know But Were Afraid to Ask

Submitted by Sandra Terneus

School Level: Middle/High.

Goals: Students will:

1. Practice respect for different points of view, attitudes, and beliefs.
2. Practice better communication skills in regards to understanding what is said, what is heard, and what is assumed.
3. Have knowledge of individual differences as well as a sense of self-validation of values and boundaries within changing personal and social roles.

ASCA Standards:

PS:A1 Acquire Self Knowledge
PS:A1.1 Develop positive attitudes towards self as a unique and worthy person
PS:A1.2 Identify values, attitudes and beliefs
PS:A1.5 Identify and express feelings
PS:A1.7 Recognize personal boundaries, rights and privacy needs
PS:A1.11 Identify and discuss changing personal and social roles
PS:A2 Acquire Interpersonal Skills
PS:A2.1 Recognize that everyone has rights and responsibilities
PS:A2.2 Respect alternative points of view
PS:A2.3 Recognize, accept, respect, and appreciate individual differences
PS:A2.6 Use effective communication skills
PS:A2.7 Know that communication involves speaking, listening, and nonverbal behavior
PS:A2.8 Learn how to make and keep friends.

Estimated Time: 40 to 60 minutes.

Materials: paper, pens, and a whiteboard.

Lesson

1. School counselor begins with: Miscommunications can occur in all relationships such as not listening, not being attentive, feeling too shy or too worried to say what you really think and feel, etc. When young people do not feel confident, they may be shy and unsure as to what to say or how to say what they want to say. Sometimes, this approach to talking with another young person can lead to misinterpretation. For example, sometimes it is easier to simply say, "I'm fine," or "Sure," when you really don't quite know what the other person is asking of you or you don't feel like saying how you are really feeling and thinking. And sometimes, people may become angry or sad because of what they think the person says or because the person simply has a different point of view that's different from their own. Therefore, the goals of this activity are to 1) practice listening skills, 2) practice speaking skills, and 3) feel ok that another person may not have the same opinion that you have, and you are ok that they are different from you. This activity is for students to clearly define the role and appropriate behavior of a friend, the dynamics of the reciprocal nature of being a friend, and the benefits of being and maintaining good friendships throughout the lifespan (5 minutes)

2. It is helpful that before starting this activity that students understand and repeat the rules of respect back to the school counselor. The school counselor can also lead a discussion about possible pitfalls such as that even though we want to do our best, we are human and make mistakes, i.e., what should happen if someone in here makes a mistake and is disrespectful? The school counselor should write these consequences on the board, such as explain the rules again in case the student forgot, ask the student to listen only, or ask the student to leave the room and go to the library to study. The school counselor can ask the class as a whole for suggestions. Lastly, the school counselor can ask the students if they trust each other to keep the rules of respect; students can turn to each other and respond verbatim that they do trust each other. If any student has any misgivings or is uncomfortable, they may be excused.

3. Define **"Friend or Frenemy."** Allow the students to divide themselves into at least two groups of six to eight members; this allows students to feel a sense of comfort. The school counselor instructs all groups to discuss, "How do you know when someone is a friend?" "What does a person do or say which leads you to believe that this person is a friend?" "On the other hand, maybe you have had people in your life who is a frenemy – someone who is sometimes a friend and sometimes is not a friend. What does a person do or say which leads you to believe that this person is a frenemy?" The school counselor writes the responses on the whiteboard so students may compare and contrast responses. (5 minutes)

4. The school counselor asks members of the groups to share their thoughts about their definitions. The school counselor can further process learning by examining commonalities and uniqueness in answers in defining the characteristics of "friendship" and for "love." The school counselor may also extract characteristics of the parents' friendships and love as well as emphasizing positive personal boundaries. (5 minutes)

5. The school counselor then asks the individual groups to provide a definition and evidence of the term, **"Friendship."**
   ✓ What is the definition you will use?
   ✓ What is the difference between the behaviors of a friend and the behaviors or an acquaintance?
(For example, a friend is someone whom you may play games with, and an acquaintance may be someone whom you say hello. I would like to play dolls with my friend, Ann, but I would not like to play dolls with the mailman whose name is Alan.)
   ✓ What things would you feel comfortable telling a friend that you would not feel comfortable telling an acquaintance?
   ✓ Based on a continuum, what descriptors indicate an acquaintance, a casual friend, and a good friend?
The reason for asking these questions allow segue to the next part of the activity. Emphasize as the students answer: acquaintances are people whom I know their name but not know well; casual friends are people I know better and I will play and talk to them; good friends are people I know even better because I know more about them and we play together, and I like talking and playing with them a lot. (5 minutes)

6. Give each group of students a piece of paper and pen with the instructions to work together in developing at least 5 questions regarding "friendship" and how your peers relate. These questions are based on concerns they have wondered about and now have the opportunity to ask and get answer. Hence, what they have always wanted to know but were afraid to ask.

(In addition, the questions often lead to discussions in which students learn how one's behavior and/or perspectives influence another, and then how that person's reaction can influence the other.)Typical questions may include but not limited to, "Do you believe it is okay to hit or be hit by a friend?", "Is it a good thing to have one to three friends or is it better to be friends with everyone?", "How do I get someone to stop doing something that don't want them to do?", "If someone wants a true friendship, how does that develop?" (15 minutes)

7. A representative from each group will read one question from the list to the other group. As the opposite group answers the question, the school counselor facilitates communication in regards to clarity and specificity between the groups. For example, to explore the meaning of a vague response, the school counselor can respond with, "I don't think I understood what you meant. I had heard you say ____, and to me, that means _____. Do I understand you correctly?"

After each group verbally acknowledges comprehending the different perspectives and assumptions incurred by the question, having awareness of the intention behind the question, and having an answer which resolves the question (as well as any spin-offs questions), the next question from the group list is asked and processed until all questions from both groups' lists are addressed.

However, if the group thinks the proposed question is targeting a peer and/or not respectful, the group does not have to answer the question, but must explain why the question is interpreted as disrespectful. For example, one proposed question from the boys' group may be "Why do girls pout or give me the cold shoulder if I don't want her anymore as a girlfriend?" Although this question may be phrased innocently, the former girlfriend may actually be sitting in the girl's group and her peers may have knowledge that this question could be pertaining to her and feel uncomfortable with the potential intention. Therefore, the girls' group may decide not to answer the question directly and explain their reason. If the question was not directed at the former girlfriend, the boy's group has a chance to explain the true intention of the question, thus, increasing further understanding between the genders.

It is helpful for the school counselor to write the presenting question and steps in how it was resolved on the whiteboard. Summarizing and writing the responses on the whiteboard not only allows for learning but also allows the school counselor to call upon and engage the more quiet students.

8.As a conclusion, it is also helpful and hopeful to ask the students what the processing experience was like...to go from an unknown (their questions), create meaning from it (explore perspectives, assumptions, inhibitions, values), and then resolve (a concrete answer). An assignment of a reflection paper can also document learning.

Processing Questions:
✓ What was it like to does this? Easy or hard? Some parts easy? Some hard? Which ones and why?
✓ What did you learn from your peers? What assumptions did you make about your peers?
✓ Did you find yourself tuning out rather than listening while someone else was speaking? What would have happened if you had chosen not to take the steps to clearly understand the other's intentions?
✓ Was there a time in which you felt uncomfortable? How did you deal with it? Was it resolved? Are you satisfied with your answer? What would you do differently?
✓ Can a friend tell another friend "no," and still be considered a good friend? Can you feel okay about yourself if you say "no" to a friend? Are you able to say "no" and not feel lousy or regret it? What are your boundaries...when is it okay to say "no" and when is it not okay to say no? What would a friend say or do which would make you think this person is really not a friend?
✓ What do you do when a friend treats you in a way that you do not want to be treated and vice versa? Is there a behavior (statement or action) which is beyond forgiveness, and if so, what should be the consequence?
✓ What have you learned from people you know (not media) outside of school about friendship?

✓ What have you learned about yourself from this activity? What else do you need to learn? What would do or who would you consult if similar situations occur in the future? What would happen a year from now if a conflict develops in a friendship?

✓ In which situations (values/boundaries) would you stand firm, and which situations would you accept that people are evolving throughout their lives and have the right to change? Imagine yourself after graduating from high school…in what ways have you evolved…what do you need to focus upon in order to become that person?

✓ Where do we go from here…design our next activity.

Cautions: Due to the potential for violent retaliation by bullies, it is recommended that both bullies and puppeteers be excused from this activity. Collaboration and recommendations by the school teacher should be considered. Even with these precautions, it may be necessary for the counselor and/or school teacher to interrupt the activity, instruct the student about how he/she is being disrespectful, extend apologies, and excuse a student from the activity.

Adaptations: This activity may be enhanced and revised to fit any area in the personal and social domain (see below). The purpose is to help youth to be aware that making assumptions or being a placater is not necessarily the best answer. This activity allows students the opportunity to learn how to approach open communication and actively seek answers directly from peers. The practice of open communication allows students to also confirm other peers perspective as well as self validation.

"Do You Really Love Me?" Because literature has indicated that youth rely on media for dating guidelines, this same format as above can be used with a few adjustments. The class may be divided into two groups according to gender or physical attraction. The school counselor may introduce the five-minute get-started activity by instructing all groups to discuss, "How do you know when someone loves you?", "How do you know when someone really has genuine feelings for you or they just want to be your friend?", "Describe the difference in the relationships you have with a friend and with a date, and describe what you offer in relationships with a friend and with a date." These questions allow segue to the next part of the activity.

Continue the format as listed above; groups typically ask questions such as, "Why do girls cry all the time?", "Why do boys want to date every girl in the class?", "Do you know what girls feel like when you ignore them and won't talk to them?", "How do I know when a girl wants me to kiss her?", "How do I get someone to stop doing something that I don't want them to do?", "If someone wants a real relationship, how does that happen?", "Is it ok to text a person when you want to break up?", "How would you want someone to break up with you?"

Possible Future Lesson Plan Topics: Understanding the consequences of decisions and its reciprocal nature, and awareness of influence of peer pressure and steps to conflict resolution.

Credit/References

Huston, A. C., & Ripke, M. N. (2006). Middle childhood: Contexts of development: In A. C. Huston, & M. N. Ripke (Eds.), *Developmental Contexts in middle childhood: Bridges to adolescence and adulthood* (pp. 1-22). [Electronic version]. New York: Cambridge University,

Richard, J. F., & Schneider, B. H. (2005). Assessing friendship motivation during preadolescence and early adolescence, *Journal of Early Adolescence, 25,* 367-385. doi: 10.1177/0265407510373259.

Terneus, S. K., & Martin, H. D. (2005). Suggested interventions for relationship issues of adolescents and young adults. *Guidance and Counselling, 20, (3/4) 117-127.*

About the Counselor:

Sandra Terneus is a Professor in the Department of Counseling and Psychology, Tennessee Tech University, Cookeville, TN. sterneus@tntech.edu

Right Here, Write Now: Mindfulness in the Classroom

Submitted by Carla Giambrone

School Level: Elementary/Middle/High.

Goals: Students will:

1. Develop an awareness of personal feeling states, and make mind-body connections increasing student's locus of control.
2. Recognize that feelings are bodily sensations that are impermanent and do not define who they are.
3. Understand that feeling states come and go and no action needs to be taken; thereby, increasing the ability to think first and to make decisions based on self-knowledge and an understanding of choice.

ASCA Standards:

PS:A1.1   Develop positive attitudes toward self as a unique and worthy person
PS:A1   Acquire Self Knowledge
PS:A1.5   Identify and express feelings
PS:A2.3   Recognize, accept, respect and appreciate individual differences

Estimated Time: 15 to 20 minutes.

Materials: Emotions chart – such as the Emotions Vocabulary Chart available at: http://www.ami-tx.com/Portals/3/EmotionsFlyer.pdf, journal, pencil.

Lesson

1. The counselor reviews the emotional states on the Emotion Vocabulary Chart. The counselor models naming his/her current emotional state by saying, My name is _____, and right now I feel_____. Each student then takes a turn making the same statement without

comment or discussion. Next, the counselor directs the students to write the date and time in their journal, and to document the emotional state they named. The students then write one or two sentences that detail WHY they think they feel the way they do. The journal entries are not shared or discussed specifically.

Processing Questions:
✓ How does it feel to name your emotional state, right now?
✓ How long do you think this feeling will last?
✓ Where do you feel/experience this feeling in your body?
✓ What was this experience like for you?
✓ What does naming your current feeling tell you about feelings in general and what they are?
✓ What strategies do you have to learn and be attentive despite this emotional state? How can you work with it and around it?

Cautions:
It is important for the counselor not to problem solve or to analyze the students' statements. The counselor must also take some time to train the students not to comment, gesture, or respond to each other's statements. This is an opportunity for students to learn that feeling states are transitory, and to honor them without responding or reacting.

Adaptations:
Teachers can be coached to use this process, and to do a daily check-in. It can be similar to an academic probe that can serve to alert teachers and counselors of on-going issues with individual students that they can follow-up with privately.

About the Counselor:

Carla Giambrone, M.S. e-RYT, is currently a Ph.D. Student in School and Counseling Psychology at the University at Buffalo, SUNY. Carla is a vinyasa yoga teacher and has taught college writing, Reading and high school English. She writes and develops life path programs, and created a 40-day mindfulness and yoga program that focuses on mind-body integration that she teaches to groups around the world. She incorporates writing and mindfulness into her teaching and psychology research. carlagia@buffalo.edu.

Using Romeo and Juliet to Teach Suicide Prevention: Lessons 1 and 2

By Karen Moore Townsend

School Level: Middle/High.

Goals: Students will:
1. Understand that suicide is an irreversible choice.
2. Will gain factual understanding about suicide.
3. Be able to detect common warning signs of suicide.
4. Be able to identify suicidal warning signs and recognize the need to solicit help of a trusted adult.

Classes to Be Integrated: Any class that is reading *Romeo and Juliet.*

ASCA Standards:

PS:B1.1 understand consequences of decisions and choices
PS:B1.3 identify alternative solutions to a problem
PS:B1.4 develop effective coping skills for dealing with problems
PS:B1.5 demonstrate when, where and how to seek help for solving problems and making decisions
PS:C1.5 differentiate between situations requiring peer support and situations requiring adult professional help
PS:C1.6 identify resource people in the school and community and know how to seek help
PS:C1.7 apply effective problem-solving and decision-making skills to make safe and healthy choices.

Estimated Time: 45 minutes.

Materials: Several rolls of clear tape, pieces of construction paper/poster board spaced around the room for the following categories: **Basic Facts, Warning Signs, Verbal Indicators, Risk Factors** and **How to Help,** and notecards with each card containing one of the info (see end of activity), 10 sheets of notebook paper, pens or pencils.

Lesson 1

Introduction: Invite students to give an overview of the storyline of *Romeo and Juliet* by saying, "I'm aware that you have been reading *Romeo and Juliet* in class. Let's talk about what happens in *Romeo and Juliet*. How does the story begin? (Paraphrase responses.) What happens next? Then what? How does it end?" (Key elements from student responses may include the following:

Romeo believes he is in love with Rosaline who rejects his love. Romeo goes to a party where he meets Juliet and falls in love with her. He realizes that Juliet's family is a rival to his own family. Romeo and Juliet are secretly married by Friar Lawrence. As the rivalry continues, Romeo kills Juliet's cousin and Romeo is banished. Juliet's parents plan for her to marry someone else. Juliet fakes her own death by drinking a sleeping potion. Romeo finds Juliet and, believing her to be dead, takes his own life. Juliet wakes to find Romeo dead and kills herself.

Then tell students that "Although Shakespeare wrote *Romeo and Juliet* in the 1500s, many of the topics we see Romeo and Juliet struggle with are still pretty relevant today. Juliet is 'almost fourteen' and Romeo is not much older. They have strained communication and complicated relationships with their parents. They feel that they don't live up to adult expectations. They experience the competitiveness of rivaling peer groups. They are excited about being young and in love. At times they feel hopeless. Finally, they attempt to solve their problems through suicide. And today, teenage suicide continues to be a concern. Today we'll be talking about teen suicide and also ways to assist other teenagers who may need help." (4 minutes)

1. Divide the class into groups of 3. (3 minutes)

2. Give each group a roll of clear tape. (1 minutes)

3. Shuffle the notecards on which are written the bulleted items (see above). (1 minutes)

4. Turn the cards face down and let each group take a turn drawing a card from the pile until all cards are gone. (5 minutes)

5. Direct students' attention to the five categories written on construction paper/poster board which have been placed around the room (**Basic Facts, Warning Signs, Verbal Indicators, Risk Factors, How to Help**). (1 minute)

6. Groups should read their cards, decide which category each of their notecards belongs under, get up, and tape the notecard under the proper category. (5 minutes)

7. When all groups are finished, review the categories. Invite students to read the notecards aloud. Discuss the placement of each notecard. Students may place a notecard in a different category from the one suggested above. This is permissible, especially if students are allowed to openly process their selection. (10 minutes)

8. Encourage comments and discussion. (For example, say to students, "Note that under Basic Facts we see that suicide is preventable. Also, notice that girls are more likely to attempt a suicide but boys are more likely to complete a suicide. What might be a reason for this?" [Boys are more likely to use more lethal means.] Ask students, "Under Warning Signs, what might be some examples of risky behaviors that someone considering suicide might engage in?" Tell students, "Realize that changes in eating and sleeping could mean an increase or they could mean a decrease in these activities." Ask "Which notecard under Warning Signs could relate to the notecard under Verbal Indicator that reads 'I won't be needing these items anymore'?" [Throws away, gives away, or promises favorite belongings.] Ask students "What might be the effect when a person experiences more than one of the risk factors in a close range of time?" [His or her risk could increase.] (5 minutes)

9. Process the following questions regarding Romeo and Juliet:
   ➢ Which of the categories and notecards might have been applicable for Romeo and for Juliet?
   ➢ What choices might Romeo or Juliet have made differently that could have resulted in a more hopeful ending?
   ➢ What could others in the play have done differently that might have helped Romeo or Juliet?
   ➢ Who could Romeo or Juliet have turned to for help? (8 minutes)

10. Tell students, "If you are ever concerned that someone you know may be considering suicide, you can help by telling a trusted adult. Think of some trusted adults that you could tell. Consider adults in your family, your school, and your community. Know that I am here for you to talk to if you have concerns." (2 minutes)

Lesson 2

Introduction: Say "In our last meeting we discussed that some of Romeo and Juliet's problems were not that different from some that young people face today. They have strained communication and complicated relationships with their parents. They feel that they don't live up to adult expectations. They experience the competitiveness of rivaling peer groups. They are excited about being young and in love. At times they feel hopeless. Finally, they attempt to solve their problems through suicide. And today, teenage suicide continues to be a concern. Today we'll be talk more about teen suicide and also ways to assist other teenagers who may need help." (3 minutes)

1. Tell students, "If you are ever concerned that someone you know may be considering suicide, you can help by telling a trusted adult. Think of some trusted adults that you could tell. Consider adults in your family, your school, and your community. Know that I am here for you to talk to if you have concerns." (2 minutes)

2. Ask students, "What types of individuals might be examples of trusted adults?" Write their responses on the chalkboard/marker board. Examples might include school counselors, teachers, administrators, parents, ministers, community leaders. (10 minutes)

3. Divide students into groups of 3. (3 minutes)

4. Next, distribute paper and writing utensils to each group. (2 minutes)

5. Tell the class, "Each group should construct and write a different, more hopeful, alternate ending to *Romeo and Juliet*. You may wish to consider the following: What choices might Romeo have made that could have changed the ending of the play? What choices might Juliet have made that might have led to a better ending? Who else could

School Counselors Share Their Favorite Classroom Guidance Activities

have made different choices that might have impacted the outcome of the play?" (15 minutes)

6. Invite students to share their endings. (5 minutes)

7. Process the following questions with the class:
   ➤ What could you do if you have a friend you are concerned about?
   ➤ What can you do when you need help?
   ➤ Who would be examples of caring, helpful adults that you could turn to if you had a problem or if you knew of a friend who needed help? (5 minutes)

Cautions: It is important to note for counselors that talking about suicide has not been shown to increase suicidal ideation or attempts; instead, such discussion can diffuse suicidal thought and help individuals who are considering suicide. Counselors may wish to inform administrators and staff of the topic of this classroom guidance lesson so that they may better understand if someone reports a concern that while reporting may increase after discussion of this topic, actual incidences do not. Similarly, counselors may wish to send a note with this information home to parents of students who will be participating in the lesson to help them be better prepared should their child address the topic of suicide with them.

Adaptation: Students could act out a scene from their alternate ending. The writing or acting of the alternate ending could be assigned as a project in the English/literature/ language arts classroom.

Credit/References: Teen suicide. (n.d.) Retrieved from www.teensuicide.us
Shakespeare, W. (1998). *Romeo and Juliet.* New York: Penguin Putnam.
Suicide prevention. (n.d.) In *In the mix: Educators.* Retrieved from www.pbs.org/inthemix/educators/lessons/depression2/index.html

About the Counselor:
Karen Moore Townsend, Ph.D., NCC, is currently an Associate Professor in Counselor Education and Coordinator of the School Counseling Program at The University of North Alabama, Florence, AL. Previously, she was a School Counselor in a public K-12 school and taught High School English. kmtownsend@una.edu

Note Cards with 1 fact on each card
Basic Facts

- Suicide is the 3rd leading cause of death for teenagers
- Girls are more likely than boys to attempt suicide
- Boys are more likely than girls to complete a suicide
- Suicides can be prevented
- People who are thinking about committing suicide can receive help

Warning Signs

- Lack of interest in extracurricular activities
- Problems at or lack of interest in job
- Substance abuse (alcohol, legal or illegal drugs)
- Problems with behavior
- Withdrawal from family and friends
- Changes in sleep
- Changes in eating
- Neglecting hygiene or personal appearance
- Emotional distress that causes physical complaints (aches, fatigues, migraines)
- Difficulty concentrating
- Grades at school declining
- Lack of interest in schoolwork
- Risky behaviors
- Complains of boredom
- Does not respond to praise in same way as before
- Throws away, gives away, or promises favorite belongings
- Writes suicide notes
- Shows signs of extreme cheerfulness following periods of depression.

Verbal Indicators

- "I'm thinking about committing suicide"
- "I want to kill myself"
- "I wish I could die"
- "I want you to know something, in case something happens to me"
- "I won't be bothering you anymore"
- "I won't be needing these items anymore"

Risk Factors

- Substance abuse
- Depression
- Aggressive behavior
- Disruptive behavior
- Presence of firearms
- Abuse
- Family history

How to Help

- Offer support
- Take warning signs and verbal indicators seriously
- Get help from a trusted, caring adult

School Counselors Share Their Favorite Classroom Guidance Activities

Cross Over

Submitted by Judy Baumgartner and Maureen Brett

School Level: Middle/High.

Goals:

1. Learn that not everyone has the same opportunities in life.
2. Learn that having certain circumstances in life can affect how others view you.
3. Gain an understanding of privileges and opportunities.

ASCA Standards:

PS:A1.1 Develop positive attitudes toward self as a unique and worthy person
PS:A1.2 Identify values, attitudes and beliefs
PS:A2.3 Recognize, accept, respect and appreciate individual differences
PS:A2.4 Recognize, accept and appreciate ethnic and cultural diversity

Estimated Time: 20 to 30 minutes.

Lesson

1. School Counselor begins with "Today we are going to do an activity about opportunity and privilege. I'm going to make some statements that may or may not be true for you and your family. Please answer them honestly."
2. The Counselor gives the guidelines for the activity.
   - The activity is done in silence, no talking.
   - Listen to the statements carefully and answer them for yourself.
   - Always remember how you are feeling.
3. Ask students to create one straight line on one side of the room and hold hands.
4. The Counselor instructs students to take a step forward any time the statement is true for them individually. Students should try to remain holding hands for as long as they can. At the end of all questions, students should observe how far ahead/behind they are in relation to others.
5. Counselor states: *Take a Step Forward if:*
   - You have only one parent/guardian living with you at home.
   - You live in a community with people of different racial backgrounds.

- You have 50 or more books in your home.
- You have been the only person of your race/ethnicity in a social situation.
- You have a physical or mental disability.
- You are a person of color.
- You are or have a friend or family member who is gay, lesbian, bi-sexual or trans-gendered.
- Your parents encouraged you to learn about and embrace people different from you.
- You feel that it is your responsibility to speak up for people who feel isolated or alone.
- You think that you can make a difference in your school and community.

Processing Questions:

✓ How did it feel to participate in this activity? To be on a different line than others?
✓ What statements were challenging for you to respond to? Why?
✓ What did it feel like to let go of the person next to you? What did that tell you?
✓ What does your place in line tell you about the opportunities you have had in life?
✓ What does this tell you about our schools and community?

Cautions:
May elicit an emotional response. You can explore those reactions, and discuss ways to cope with differences in societal privilege. Assess participants' emotional state, and make a referral for individual counseling for follow up if necessary.

Adaptations:
Each time a student answers "yes", instead of stepping forward, they can cross to the other side of the room and face those who answered no; then return to the original line for next question.

Credit/References:
Adapted from an activity from **The National Federation for Just Communities.**

About the Counselors:
Judy Baumgartner is a Social Worker at Alden High School, Alden, NY. Jbaumgartner@aldenschools.org
Maureen Brett is a School Counselor at Lancaster Middle School, Lancaster, NY. mbrett@lacaster.wnyric.org

Anxious Adolescents: Lessons 1, 2, 3, and 4

Submitted by Stephanie Hammond and Christopher P. Roseman

School Level: High.

Target Population: Grades 11 and 12.

Goals: Students will learn:
1. Positives and negatives of anxiety.
2. How to assess their anxiety.
3. Skills to manage their anxiety.

ASCA Standards:

ASCA Personal/Social Standard A: Students will acquire the knowledge, attitudes, and interpersonal skills to help them understand and respect self and others.

Estimated Time: Four sessions of 20-minutes.

Materials: Pen and paper, *Holmes-Rahe Social Readjustment Ratings Scale* (Holmes & Rahe, 1967).

Lesson 1

1. Introduction of yourself and activities. I am <name> and the activities we will be doing today may be used to address a stressful situation in your day such as before and/or after a test, or following difficult transitions in your lives. It is important to learn and practice these skills we learn today prior to the onset of a stressful event so that you may use them effectively.
2. Continue with: Stress is a natural part of every young person's life. Stress is any change, internal or external, positive or negative, to which a young person must adapt. Stress may cause students to become physically or mentally tired. Stress is usually related to everyday experiences, worries and challenges at school, home, in the community and within your peer groups. Identifying and acknowledging the causes of stress and expressing feelings about them are usually the

most effective tools to reduce stress, in addition to learning practical stress reduction skills. Therefore, the classroom activity we will be doing today is designed to teach you a variety of practical and fun stress reduction techniques.

3. Students will take The *Holmes-Rahe Social Readjustment Ratings Scale.* This rating scale is a two-part activity that provides you an opportunity to identify things in your lives that causes you stress, secondly we will talk about your reactions to seeing what stresses you and how to use some strategies to reduce or alleviate stress and/or tension. (30 to 45 minutes).

4. Discuss what the students think most teens feel anxious about. Counselor asks questions based on by responses students make on the *Holmes-Rahe Social Readjustment Ratings Scale.* Highlight stressful events with greatest impact on student.

5. Homework: Students are asked notice throughout the week when they feel stressed and to write down details (where, with who? how do they feel?). Encourage students to reflect on this activity on their own and practice basic strategies discussed to reduce stress until next session.

Lesson 2

1. Recap. Ask students if they reflected and/or used any strategies learned in the first session and how well they worked. (Counselor may utilize a Likert Scale.)

2. Ask some students share some log entries. When sharing, it is important to emphasize what the students identified as stressors, what reactions they may have had (physical, emotional, physiological, etc.) Were there similarities between the different situations? How did the students respond? Focus on the basic techniques used by students to calm down and how they helped, or did not help in relieving the stress.

3. Explain biological/psychological responses to stress and anxiety –The Counselor should address that each student responds to and resolves stress differently and the impact of ongoing or unresolved stress may lead to feelings of anxiety, depression, irritability, poor concentration, aggression, physical illness, fatigue, sleep disturbance and poor coping skills such as tobacco, drug and/or alcohol use.

4. Ask students to continue to keep a log, focusing more on biological/psychological responses based on what they learned in that group -when they are stressed, what caused them stress, and how did they feel (both physically and emotionally.

Lesson 3

1. Begin by asking students to reflect on when they recognized physical or mental fatigue.
2. Ask some students to share some of their entries. Examine the biological/psychological responses and have students come up with ways they think would best help diminish the anxiety. Counselor should emphasize students who develop stress reduction skills learn how to feel and cope better without hurting themselves or others. Identifying and acknowledging the causes of stress and being able to appropriately express feelings about them help us make better decisions in all areas of our lives.
3. Share and practice a few more techniques/exercises such as breathing exercises, meditations, etc.
4. Homework: ask students to continue to keep logs, focusing more on biological/psychological responses.

Lesson 4

1. It is important to reassess the student's progress by giving the *Holmes-Rahe Social Readjustment Ratings Scale* as a measure of growth and progress of handling stress and understanding the effects of stress on the body. It is a good post check for the student's understanding of the effects of stress on them to see that as time goes on there are different events that may change and cause stress, thus causing a physical response to that stress.
2. Ask students to complete the *Holmes-Rahe Social Readjustment Ratings Scale.*
3. Ask students:
   ✓ How their score has changed from the first test to the second.
   ✓ What life changes do the attribute to the change in score?
   This is important because everyone goes through different life events that will have physical effects on their body. It is important to identify

the changes that happen to them and how they can cope in a positive and helpful way. Focus on higher scoring, more dramatic changes and discuss the different coping strategies. For students who experience smaller changes, have them make adjustments to help lower their score, such as sleeping better, changing eating habits, etc.

4. Counselor highlights strengths/themes of what the students learned/shared and emphasize/encourage them to use the new tools/strategies they learned to handle stress and that this is a beginning for them to better deal with stressors in their lives.

Processing Questions:
- ✓ What have I learned about stress?
- ✓ What is it that I have learned stress does to my body?
- ✓ What events/situations make me feel anxious?
- ✓ How can I manage the biological/psychological changes that occur when I'm feeling stressed?
- ✓ What new strategies did I learn? When might I use them?

Cautions: It is important to observe if any students exhibit symptoms of anxiety throughout the classroom guidance lesson as they may be the precursor to a more serious issue. If a student exhibits an uncomfortable level of distress or anxiety, the child may be excused or referred for additional screening of anxiety.

References

Holmes, T. H., & Rahe, R. H. (1967). The Social Readjustment Rating Scale. *Journal of Psychosomatic Research, 11*, 213-218. doi:10.1016/0022-3999(67)90010-4

About the Counselors:

Stephanie Hammond is a School Counselor with Bio-Med Science Academy. shammond@biomedscienceacademy.org

Christopher P. Roseman, Ph.D., PC-CR, is an Assistant Professor in Counselor Education Program at the University of Toledo. Christopher.Roseman@utoledo.edu

What's on Your Plate?

Submitted by Dr. Ken Jackson

School Level: High.

Goals: Students will:
1. Understand the variety and effects of outside (ecological) forces that are acting in their lives.
2. Be able to apply this understanding to (a) resiliency, (b) career planning (interests and awareness), or (c) academic strategies/study skills— depending on the focus of the activity.

ASCA Standards:

A:B2.5 Use problem-solving and decision-making skills to assess progress toward educational goals

A:B2.7 Identify post-secondary options consistent with interests, achievement, aptitude and abilities

A:C1.1 Demonstrate the ability to balance school, studies, extracurricular activities, leisure time and family life

C:B1.7 Describe traditional and nontraditional career choices and how they relate to career choice

C:C1.3 Identify personal preferences and interests influencing career choice and success

C:C1.6 Understand the importance of equity and access in career choice

PS:B1.4 Develop effective coping skills for dealing with problems

PS:B1.12 Develop an action plan to set and achieve realistic goals

PS:C1.10 Learn techniques for managing stress and conflict

PS:C1.11 Learn coping skills for managing life events

Estimated Time: 25 to 55 minutes.

Materials: Paper plates (1 per student), colored markers or pens.

Special Directions: Drawing each step on the board or poster board may help students stay on track will help to guide students step by step with this activity. *(Italics refers to info shared with students.)*

Lesson

1. Introduction: Counselor begins with: "A variety of outside people and things affect our lives. Often times we forget the impact these may have. This activity will help us look at the big picture. The activity can help us identify things or people influencing how we feel about ourselves and others. We can also look at sources of stress that affect so many areas of our life including school work, taking care of ourselves and being in control of our academic lives. We can even use this exercise to understand why we have certain career interests and aspirations. This activity was first done in a large counseling group. As the students were processing it, one student called out, 'I get it. This is *what's on our plate.*' And the name was created."

2. Pass out the plates and markers to share. *Tell students they will be drawing a series of circles. Tell them to draw 4 circles on their plate (one inside another), making a dart board or bulls-eye.* Put a sample up for them (below). (2 minutes)

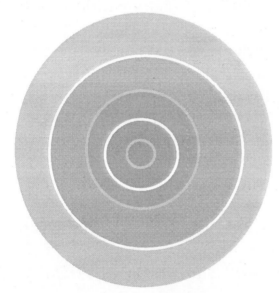

NOTE: The outside of the plate makes a 5th circle. They will be writing something in each circle.

3. *Skip the center circle (the bulls-eye).*

4. *In the second circle write in some of the people or things that directly affect your life. One example might be "family." Others could include "friends, school, sports team, church, extracurricular activities, jobs, etc."*

Demonstrate one example on the board. (This is the "micro level." More information in Brofenbrenner's levels can be found in the references). (5 minutes)

5. *In circle third space, draw lines showing how these groups might connect with each other. For example, how do friends feel about school; if good, they might use a smooth line; if bad, there might be a jagged line. If the family does not connect with the school, they might use a dotted line.* Students may start to see some confusion and complexity in their lives at this level. It gets "messy." This is a topic you can revisit in the later discussion section. (This is the "Meso level.") (5 minutes)

6. *In the fourth circle, write words about the groups you said affected your life ; where do they belong. A parent/guardians' jobsite could be listed, maybe with several work organizations. Other could be "school system, town/city, church denomination, sports associations, etc."* (This is the "Exo-level.") (5 minutes)

7. *In the fifth, outer circle, write the "big" things going on in the world that may affect everyone or the things they have already written down. This could include "economy, war, unemployment, civil rights, racism, homophobia, democracy, terrorism, etc."* (This would be the "Macro-level."). (5 minutes)

8. To help students reflect, ask them "what do you notice about their plates?" This may be done as a group or individually. For larger groups, a "think/pair/square/share" works well.

   a. Phase 1. A student picks a partner. (5 to 6 minutes)

   • *Share with your partner what is on your plate. Start with the first circle and work your way out. Then have your partner share.*

   • *What things/people on your plate seem to have the most effect on your life or how you feel?*

   b. Phase 2. After the pairs share, the pairs combine into groups of four. (5 to 6 minutes)

   • *Choose one or two people or topics to share with the rest of the group.*

   • *How do you feel about all of these influences?*

   • *How do these influences make you feel?*

   • *What title would you give your plate?*

   c. Phase 3. After they share, the entire group has a conversation. (18 to 20 minutes).

This process allows quieter members to share. NOTE: when members share what is in their circle, complete a demo plate on the board. Based on the focus of the lesson, students can discuss the following;

- *What are the stressors in your life? Do they explain how you may feel? Where do you get some support or strength?(personal/social)*
- *How do you think the things on your plate play a part in your career choices? (career)*
- *How do you think the things on your plate play a part in how you feel about school? –your ability to be successful in school? (academic)*

Based on the your theoretical orientation, you may concentrate on strengths or resiliency (Solution Focused), voicing one's oppressions (empowerment theory, narrative theory) or steps for creating changes in small areas (ecological theory reality theory).

Cautions: Focus on only one domain or topic on this lesson (personal/social, or career, or academic); otherwise students might be overloaded. The activity can be repeated another time with a different focus. (Usually the plates are not up for public display outside of the confines and confidentiality of the group.)

Adaptations: For an Intra-personal focus: The center circle may be used first. This is their internal life. They could put in how they feel (stressed, pressured), or career goals (specific occupations they are considering), or how they feel about their school work—depending on the focus of the lesson. Could be integrated into high school courses for co-curricular purposes: Literature classes (comparing personal and literary character identity and personal struggle) or History classes (social factors in historical figure's decisions).

Credit/References

Brofenbrenner, U. (1977). Toward an experimental ecology of human development. *American Psychologist, 32*, 513-531. 10.1037/0003-066X.32.7.513

About the School Counselor:

Ken Jackson, Ph.D. is the Head Counselor at Decatur High School, Decatur, GA. kjackson@csdecatur.net

Diversity is You: Exploring Differences and Similarities: Lessons 1 and 2

By Natoya Haskins, Ph.D., LPC and Anneliese Singh, Ph.D., LPC

School Level: High.

Goals: Students will:
1. Identify three characteristics that make them unique.
2. Identify three characteristics that make them similar to their peers.
3. Identify similarities and differences with others.
4. Identify three characteristics they learned about their partner.
5. Identify three characteristics they learned about themselves.
6. Identify three areas they would like to continue to explore in regards to diversity.

ASCA Standards:

PS:A1.1 Develop positive attitudes toward self as a unique and worthy person
PS:A1.2 Identify values, attitudes and beliefs
PS:A2.3 Recognize, accept, respect and appreciate individual differences
PS:A2.4 Recognize, accept and appreciate ethnic and cultural diversity

Estimated Time: One 40-minute and one 30-minute lesson.

Materials: Shrink a Village Information Sheet (Meadows, 1990), We are Unique and Similar Worksheet (Haskins, 2014), pens or pencils.

Lesson 1

1. Counselor says: Good morning, I'm Ms/Mr. _____ your school counselor. One of the main experiences we hope you have during your time here at (School Name) is to interact with individuals that are diverse. Self awareness is key to getting to know yourself and others. As such, today you will participate in a *Diversity is YOU* activity, where you will begin to discuss the difference and similarities you share with your classmates with the goal to help you understand and appreciate

your differences and the similarities you share with your classmates. (1 minute)

2. Pass out *Shrink a Village Information Sheet* (Meadows, 1991) and the counselor reads aloud. (2 minutes)

3. The counselor ask the following questions related to the information sheet (5 minutes)
   ✓ What did you already know from what I read?
   ✓ What surprised you about this information?

   Emphasize the differences and similarities students note in terms of cultural diversity in their answers.

4. The counselor shares: "We live in a world that is encompasses individuals that look like you and those that don't. We live in a world people look like you but have different values and beliefs. In our school we have a lot of diversity that often is overlooked or not discussed. Today we will engage in an activity which will allow you to develop an awareness of who you are and what makes you unique and similar to those in your class." (1 minute)

5. The counselor will pass out the *We are Unique and Similar Worksheet.* (1 minute)

6. Students complete the worksheet by themselves. Counselor says: "You will be asked to share only those things you feel comfortable sharing." (5 to10 minutes)

7. The students will pair with someone that they do not know well. Instruct them to share their answers with one another; and, then instruct the pairs to develop a list of similarities they share with one another. Counselor says: "For example in your pair you may determine that both of you are born in Florida, have a dog, play a musical instrument, and have an older brother." (10 minutes)

8. Process Questions to be asked after the students share in their pair (10 minutes):
   ✓ How did it feel to identify unique characteristics about yourself?
   ✓ How did it feel to identify similarities between you and your classmates?
   ✓ What surprised you about this activity?

9. Counselor says: "As a homework assignment you and your partner should engage in 1 in-school or after school activity together." (For example: eat lunch together, attend a football game, attend a club meeting, volunteer together). (1 minute)

Lesson 2: (2 to 3 weeks after initial classroom Guidance lesson)

1. Counselor begins with: "Good morning, I'm glad to be back with you. Remember, last time we met we explored the similarities and differences according to cultural diversity amongst your classmates. Over the last 2 or 3 weeks you had the opportunity to spend time with one of your classmates, today I would like to check in regarding your experience. During this time, share one insight you had about cultural diversity from your homework." (5 minutes)

2. Counselor says: "Take about 5 minutes to write down three things you learned about your partner and three things you learned about yourself" (5 minutes)

3. Students will then be asked to share 1 of the items they have listed (they can select either to talk about themselves or their partner). Emphasize that students should be mindful of both similarities and differences in cultural diversity as they discuss. (10 minutes)

4. Processing Questions: (depending on the comfort of the students and based on the counselor's discretion the students can either write down their answers or share verbally):
   ✓ How did the experience challenge your biases and assumptions?
   ✓ How will the experience inform how you interact with people that are different than you?
   ✓ What would you say to someone who has difficulty interacting with people different than themselves? Emphasize that students should be mindful of both similarities and differences in cultural diversity. (10 minutes)

5. At the end of this activity, the counselor should encourage the students to continue to seek opportunities to learn about differences and expand their understanding of diversity by volunteering and participating in activities that challenge you. In addition, the counselor should ask them to continuously reflect on these experiences and the impact they have on their understanding of differences. (3 minutes)

Cautions: The counselor should caution students against including information they feel uncomfortable sharing with the group, information that is insensitive or belittling to others (for example: highlighting differences in weight, personal hygiene, SES). If students are unsure they should raise their hand and ask the counselor for guidance while they are completing the *We are Unique and Similar Worksheet* (Haskins, 2014). If the counselor notes that individual students are having a difficult time or appear in distress regarding the activity a follow-up counseling session should be scheduled.

While some students may feel uncomfortable and give generic answers, the counselor should remember that this may be the first time these students have discussed this topic or participated in diversity activities. The activity should help the counselor facilitate an atmosphere where diversity will be embraced, whereas discomfort can slowly dissipate.

Adaptations: If students are unable to participate in an in-school or after school activity, students can complete a journal reflection regarding their interactions with classmates who are different than them and the impact this has had on their understanding of diversity.

References

Meadows, D. H. (1991). *The Global Citizen*. Washington, D.C.: Island Press.

About the Counselors:

Natoya Haskins, Ph.D., LPC is an Assistant Professor at the University of Georgia. nhaskins@uga.edu

Anneliese A. Singh, Ph.D., LPC is an Associate Professor at the University of Georgia. asignh@uga.edu

Shrink a Village Information Sheet

If we could shrink the earth's population to a village of precisely 100 people, with all the existing human ratios remaining the same, it would look something like the following (Please note the school counselor can edit the categories to represent the differences they would like to address).

59 would be Asian
14 would be American (North, Central and South)
14 would be African
12 would be European
1 would be from the South Pacific

50 would be women, 50 would be men
30 would be children, 70 would be adults.
70 would be nonwhite, 30 would be white
90 would be heterosexual, 10 would be homosexual

33 would be Christians
21 would be Moslems
15 would be Hindus
6 would be Buddhists
5 would be Animists
6 would believe in other religions
14 would be without any religion or atheist.

15 would speak Chinese, Mandarin
7 English
6 Hindi
6 Spanish
5 Russian
4 Arabic
3 Bengali
3 Portuguese
The other would speak Indonesian, Japanese,
German, French, or some other language

20 are undernourished
15 adults are illiterate
1 has an university degree
7 have computers

Adapted from Meadows, D (1991).
Meadows, D. H. (1991). *The Global Citizen*. Washington, D.C.: Island Press.

We Are Unique and Similar Worksheet (Haskins, 2014)

Directions: Please fill in the webs below with personal characteristics that make you unique and similar to your classmates.

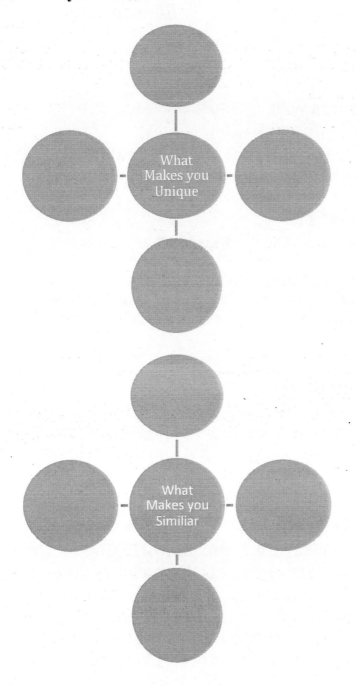

Developed by N. Haskins (2014)

School Counselors Share Their Favorite Classroom Guidance Activities

Don't Stand on Your Chair!
Lessons 1, 2, and 3

Submitted by Eric T. Beeson, LCPC, CRC

School Level: High.

Goals: Students will:
1. Identify various identity characteristics.
2. Differentiate between internal and external identity characteristics.
3. Build adaptive thoughts regarding personal identity.

ASCA Standards:

PS:A1.1—Develop positive attitudes toward self as a unique and worthy person
PS:A1.5—Identify and express feelings
PS:A1.10—Identify personal strengths and assets
PS:A1.11—identify and discuss changing person and social roles
PS:B1.7—Demonstrate a respect and appreciation for individual and cultural differences

Estimated Time: Three Lessons of 30-minutes each.

Materials: Two sturdy chairs and one chair broken or unsteady, Post-it notes of the same color (3 to 5 for each student); three folders labeled **Stable**, **Unstable**, and **Undecided**; Ceiling room; markers, tape.

Special Directions for Lessons 1, 2, and 3: All lessons begin with the school counselor bringing all the materials to the front of the room and arranging all three chairs side-by-side while placing the Post-It notes, folders, tape, and markers on a nearby desk. This activity requires the school counselor to stand on a chair at various points. It is likely that most teachers would not appreciate this behavior normally in their classroom; therefore, it is important to maintain the climate of the classroom while still engaging students with a high degree of energy and enthusiasm

Lesson 1

1. Counselor begins with: Ok, as we get started, I'd like you to raise your hand if you have ever stood on a chair. (Wait a few seconds while acknowledging students who raise their hands and then continue...) When I was younger, I liked to stand on chairs and imagine that I had just climbed a mountain or won an Olympic medal, but my mother didn't like it when I did this because she cared about me and didn't want me to get hurt. I am telling you this because at some point during the next three lessons, I am going to stand on my chair for a little bit to demonstrate our topic: identity development. With that said, I don't want any of us to climb or stand on chairs at any other time except this activity, okay? (Wait for students' acknowledgment before moving on.) (5 minutes)

2. The school counselor places a piece of paper on the sturdy chair in the middle of the three chairs that reads, "I am _____." The school counselor (or an eager student) then passes out 3 to 5 sticky notes (depending on class size) of the same color to each student. (Same color notes) helps protect students' anonymity.

3. The school counselor gives the following instructions:
"Each of you is going to get three sticky notes and I want you to write down words that you would use to fill in this blank. For example, if I were to fill in the blank, I might write, I am a school counselor or I am Eric. So, I'd like you to take a few minutes to fill out as many of the sticky notes as you can, but it's okay if you don't fill them all out. Whenever you are done, please raise your notes in the air and I will collect them. After I collect all of your notes, I will then read them aloud and place them on this sign." (4 minutes)

(In the spirit of empowering youth, it is very important to inform students regarding how these notes will be used. While students are writing, the school counselor observes students to identity any need for potential follow-up contact. For example, if the school counselor notices a student struggling to fill out the sticky notes, then the school counselor might make an effort to reach out to this student at some other time.

4. Student responses are then collected by the counselor and placed one at a time on the "I am" paper and then read aloud. It is important to arrange the sticky notes so that they can be easily removed. While reading the students' responses, the school counselor focuses on connecting similar ideas in order to promote universality amongst the

students. For example, if two or more notes read something like, "on the baseball team," then the school counselor would reflect these ideas by stating something like, "It seems like we have some athletes in the room." Similarly, if two or more notes read something like, "invisible," then the school counselor might reflect these ideas with something like, "It seems like it's important for us to know that we are noticed by others." (5 minutes)

(Care should be taken during this step to identify potential safety risks that should be addressed after the lesson. For instance, if a note read something like, "not going to be here tomorrow," then you would attempt to identify the student who wrote this note and follow-up with them after class, as well as encourage all students to visit you later during your office hours.)

5. After all responses are read, the school counselor processes the experience with the students. Potential processing questions are:
   ✓ What stood out (or surprised you) the most about this lesson?
   ✓ What was it like for you to hear those things read aloud?
   ✓ What was familiar to you about the notes we read?
   ✓ What did you hear that reminded you of yourself?
   ✓ Which notes did you most relate to?
   ✓ How have these characteristics changed throughout your life?
      o What caused the change?
      o What did you do to cope with the change?
      o How can you use this when other characteristics change in the future?
   ✓ What did it feel like when you heard that some of your peers shared the same ideas as you?
   ✓ Based upon what we've talked about today, what will be different for you?   (15 minutes)

6. The school counselor summarizes the processing while checking for any unfinished business with something like: "Thank you for taking the time to explore what can be a tough topic to talk about. From what I heard, we have a diverse group of students who have very different views of who they are and who they would like to be, and it seemed to me like trying to fill in this blank is still a work in progress. As we close up, I just want to ask if there is anything else you would like to get off your chest?" Depending upon the climate of the classroom, the school counselor might benefit from a closing round that asks students to compliment the student to their right/left in

order to identify and/or reinforce identity components that are uncovered (5 minutes).

7. After summarizing the lesson, the school counselor should build excitement and anticipation for Part II of this activity by saying something like:

"Now, earlier I told you I was going to stand on a chair at some point during the next three lessons, but that won't be today. Next time we meet, we will review these notes and talk about how we can use these things to build a more stable sense of identity. Also, remember what you said would be different because next time I will ask you how that's been going. Thanks and I'll see you next time."

Lesson 2

1. The school counselor begins by saying: "Thanks for having me back today. As we get started, I'd like to remind everyone of the dangers of standing on chair that we discussed last time. Even though I am going to stand on a chair to demonstrate an idea, please refrain from doing so at any other time."

2. Ask students to review the previous lesson. If students struggle to remember, the school counselor can help identify the key elements: the identification of identity characteristics and how these characteristics change over time. The school counselor can also ask students about what has been different since the last lesson. (5 minutes)

3. The school counselor tapes the folder reading "Unstable" to the broken/unsteady chair, the folder labeled "Undecided" on the sturdy chair with "I am _____" on it, and the "Stable" folder to the other sturdy chair (the chair without "I am _____" taped on it).

4. The school counselor continues by defining stable and unstable identity characteristics with something like: "Last time we heard some unique words that were used to describe you. It's interesting how the words we use often tell us a little bit about the way we think and the way we think typically tells us a lot about how we feel. Each of the words we wrote down, the descriptions, roles, qualities, etc., help to define unique aspects of who we are or as some people would call it, our identity. Some parts of our identity might be secret while others might be well known by everybody. Some parts of our identity might be defined internally, by you, while other parts might be defined externally, by others. Now, let's say that I am going to stand on one of these chairs, would you want me to stand on the stable, sturdy chair (point to chair) that's going to hold me up or would you want me to

School Counselors Share Their Favorite Classroom Guidance Activities

stand on the unstable chair (point to chair) that will probably collapse and send me falling to the ground? That's right it might be funny to see me fall to the ground, but I think we would all want to stand on the most stable, sturdy chair as possible. This is the way it is with our identity. Some parts of our identity might be unstable, meaning they are likely defined by others and are likely to change, while others might be stable, meaning they are innate qualities you have (e.g., like eye color, etc.), are normally defined by you, and are likely to remain the same. So, these chairs represent your identity. Since, you told me that it's probably best to stand on the stable chair, it's important for us to be able to identify parts of our identity that are stable and unstable. So, I am going to read each of your notes from last time aloud and I'd like you to help me identify which notes you would like me to put on the stable chair and which you would like me to put on the unstable chair. If we can't decide, then we can put them in the middle on the undecided chair." (1 to 2 minutes)

5. The school counselor then begins reading each note aloud. During this time, it is important to guide the students through this step by reflecting their statements and processing through any disagreements that might emerge regarding the stability of each characteristic. For instance, if one student would identify "athlete" as a stable, innate quality, but another student disagrees and says something like, "Being an athlete is something you have to work for and you probably won't be an athlete for the rest of your life," then the school counselor would validate each response while drawing out other students with something like, "It seems like we really aren't sure if this is stable or unstable, let's hear what some of the rest of you think." During this time, it is not as important to build consensus, as it is to validate the opinions of each student while managing the air time to ensure each student gets equal opportunity to share. If the students are not sure about the stability of a particular idea, then they can be left on the chair labeled "Undecided." (15 minutes)

6. After each note has been placed on a chair, the school counselor will assist students in processing the entire lesson and connecting it to future behavior change. Potential processing questions include: (15 minutes)

   ✓ What went through your mind as we had this discussion?
   ✓ Remind me, what is a stable identity characteristic?
   ✓ What is an unstable identity characteristic?
   ✓ Which ones (stable or unstable) do you have more of right now?

✓ Which ones (stable or unstable) would you like to have?

✓ What did you think about the idea of "secret" characteristics?

   o What might be an example of a "secret" identity characteristic?

   o How do "secret" identity characteristics affect the person?

   o What would you like someone with "secret" identity characteristics to do with them?

   o What can you do to help others share their identity traits with you?

✓ What was it like to disagree with your classmates?

✓ What was it like to agree with your classmates?

✓ Do you prefer to agree or disagree?

✓ What are the benefits of both agreeing and disagreeing with your peers?

✓ What did you learn about your classmates today?

✓ What did you learn about yourself today?

✓ What ideas did you have when you walked into class today that were challenged by this lesson?

✓ Taking in everything that we experienced here today, what will be different for you?

✓ What will you say, think, feel, and/or do differently?

7. The school counselor should summarize and validate the students' responses and focus on the importance of stable qualities and making sure students understand the concept of stable versus unstable identity characteristics. Also, it is important to ensure that students understand that having unstable identity characteristics doesn't make them unstable, it simply means that certain identity characteristics might be more stable than others. The school counselor should also affirm the students' ability to identify and defend various parts of their identity while respecting the views of others. (2 minutes)

8. Finally, the school counselor should build excitement and anticipation for Part III of this activity by saying: "I know that I said I was going to stand on a chair (stand on the sturdy chair labeled "Stable"), but you'll have to wait until our next lesson to figure out why I'm standing on this chair (step down from the chair and begin placing notes in the appropriate folders). Next time we meet, we will review these notes and talk about how we can use these things to build a more stable sense of identity. Also, remember what you said you would do differently because next time I will ask you how that's been going. Thanks and I'll see you next time."

9. Before leaving the room, the school counselor should place the students' notes in the respective folders to save for Part III.

Lesson 3

1. The school counselor begins by saying: "Thanks for having me back today. As we get started, I'd like to remind everyone of the dangers of standing on chair that we discussed last time. Even though I am going to stand on a chair to demonstrate an idea, please refrain from doing so at any other time."

2. The school counselor begins by placing all materials at the front of the room; however, in this part of the activity one sturdy chair should be labeled as stable, one sturdy chair should be labeled as unstable, and the broken chair can also be labeled as unstable. The school counselor then transitions by asking the students to review what was talked upon during the previous two lessons. If students struggle to remember, then the school counselor can briefly summarize focusing on the importance of identifying and building more stable identity characteristics.

3. Next, the school counselor should check-in with the students regarding what they have been doing differently since the last lesson with something like: "At the end of our last session, I told you that I would be asking you about what you have been doing differently since our last lesson, so what have you noticed since you started (insert a few students' responses from Part I and II)? Alright, well today I want to build upon this idea of constructing a more stable identity. Just to recap from last week, we identified (read notes from "Unstable" folder) as unstable, (read notes from "Stable" folder) as stable, and (read notes from "Undecided" folder) we weren't sure about whether they were stable or unstable identity characteristics." (5 minutes)

4. The school counselor reflects students' responses and transitions into the development of positive attitudes towards self as a unique and worthwhile person with something like: "Last week I told you that I would let you know why I was standing on the chair. Before we move on, I want to make sure we remember what these chairs symbolize. Who can remind me? (It is important for students to know that the chairs represent their identity or specific identity characteristics.) So, I want you to imagine that this chair represents some of the things you wrote down (stand on the chair labeled unstable) like (restate notes labeled as unstable). Now, while I'm standing on the chair, how do you think I am feeling?"

5. The school counselor reflects student responses and highlights the "good" feeling that one has when "on top" and "standing tall" with a variety of unique roles and pieces of identity. The school counselor then asks the students: "What would happen if this chair was pulled out from under me?"

6. After the students identify that the school counselor would fall down, the school counselor demonstrates a controlled fall to the ground. The school counselor then asks: "What do you think it felt like falling to the ground?

7. After some reflection of students' responses, the school counselor continues with: "So, sometimes the things we use to define ourselves are unstable, can be taken away from us, or change in some way, like when we (identify events from previous lessons that were known to cause changes in identity characteristics like divorce, injury, break-up, etc.). Sometimes we are responsible for the change and we can just step down from the chair, but a lot of the time we aren't and it feels like a chair has been ripped out from under us. Regardless of how it happened, when a piece of our identity goes away, it doesn't feel good, like falling to the ground. So now that I'm here on the ground, I want you to tell me what I should do next."

8. Students then discuss options for the school counselor and the school counselor reflects the students' responses before standing back on the chair and stating something like: "You are right I can get back on the chair (stand on the same chair again). This time, let's say that I am standing on the identity characteristic of "_____" (for the remainder of this example, the identity characteristic of "in love" will be used because it is typically one that is labeled as stable by students, but is likely more unstable; when completing this step, the school counselor should use a student's note that is likely mislabeled as stable). I believe I am in love, my partner is my whole life, and we will always be together. Things are going good right? But what happens if my partner breaks up with me or my parents move to another town? What would happen to my identity characteristic of "in love?" That's right, it would go away and what would happen to me? That's right, I would fall down again."

9. The school counselor completes another controlled fall to the ground and reflects the students' responses. From the ground, the school counselor identifies what it feels like to "fall from the chair" and connects this to what happens when pieces of the students' identity and/or roles change or go away completely. The school counselor

School Counselors Share Their Favorite Classroom Guidance Activities

should also be sure to identify that this was an identity characteristic that was labeled as stable before and ask something like, "So, we identified this characteristic as stable before, but we just saw it get ripped out from under me. What does that say about the stability of some of our characteristics?" The school counselor then continues with something like: "That's right. So sometimes we might think a certain aspect of our identity is stable when in reality it is not. Ok, so I've tried this twice and I'm stuck on the ground, what do you want me to do next?"

10. Inevitably, some students will say stay on the ground, others will say get back on the chair, and some might say nothing. The school counselor should repeat the controlled fall as many times as necessary to illustrate how trying the same thing over and over again will often result in the same consequences (e.g., defining your identity as being "in love" again and again will often lead to the same consequences). Special attention should be made to identify how each fall off the chair makes it harder and harder to get back up. This transitions nicely into the importance of building new strategies to prevent falls from the chair, prevent losing identity characteristics, and begin building truly stable identity characteristics. (10 minutes)

11. To build new strategies to uncover stable pieces of identify, potential processing questions include: (25 minutes)

✓ I'd like someone to start by telling me what you saw here today.
✓ What did this demonstration say to you?
✓ If you had to tell a friend what we did here today, what would you tell them?
✓ What does the chair represent? (Ensure comprehension that the chair represents pieces of their identity or their identity as a whole that is made up of the smaller pieces they have identified)
✓ Where do these pieces of your identity come from? (Be sure to distinguish between internal and external sources).
✓ What would it mean to you if you were in control of your identity?
✓ What would it mean to you if you were in control of the way you view yourself?
   o How would you like to view yourself?
   o How can we make that happen?
   o What are some things that could cause your "chair" to get pulled out from under you and/or change?
   o What can you do to make your "chair" more stable?
   o Tell me about a time when you felt like you "fell off a chair?"

o What happened?
o What did you do?
o What was the result?
o What did you learn from that experience given what you learned today?
✓ When I fell off my chair and lost track of who I really was, you told me what you wanted me to do, but now I want to ask you, what will you do in order to prevent falling off the chair?

12.   Ask students to list potential solutions that include creating a stable identity that is defined internally and avoiding the attribution of one's worth to any one piece of their identify. A key point to make is that if the "chair" goes away, they have a choice in how to respond. This discussion culminates with the following question to the students: "What is the easiest way to avoid falling off the chair?"

13.   After students respond, the school counselor closes with something like: "That's right. The easiest way to avoid falling off the chair is to not get on it in the first place! Don't stand on the chair! Imagine that I was walking around carrying this chair or carrying my (insert unstable identity characteristic), what would happen to me if the chair went away now? (Wait for some response from the students before continuing) That's right, the chair would still go away, but what would be different from before? Yes, I would still be standing because I was built on the most stable foundation, my own self. Sure, it might still stink a little when that piece of you goes away, but will it feel as bad as it did falling of the chair? Let's imagine that I filled in that blank from last week with "ME" or "Valuable Human Being," would that be stable or unstable? The reality is that our worth and our value never changes, we were born with, and there is nothing and no one that can change it or take it away; however, sometimes our view of our worth is what changes. Sometimes this isn't even our fault, we don't ask for it, but it still happens. So I'm here today to tell you that each of you has the ability to choose to view yourself as you truly are, valuable human beings with innate worth that no one and nothing can ever take away. It's about flipping our view of self. Instead of building on unstable characteristics that will likely lead to us falling, we can now choose to build upon a stable sense of identity. The choice is yours: Will you define yourself by what others say about you, what you look like, or who your friends are or will you define yourself by what you really are...a valuable human being...a unique YOU!

14.   The school counselor should close by asking students to share any final thoughts and allowing a few moments of therapeutic silence. After summarizing the students' comments throughout the lesson, the school counselor encourages the students to take out a piece of paper, complete the sentence "I am _____" again, and stop by the school counselor's office to talk about it.

Cautions: As with any lesson focused on processing of core issues related to identity development, it is likely that additional follow-up will be needed. Therefore, school counselors should leave their cards and explain their "open door" policy to the students. Teachers should also be informed of the nature of the activity to prevent any concerns they might have while you stand on a chair. Also, please use caution when standing on and falling off the chair in order to prevent injury.

Adaptations: Depending upon the students and the classroom climate, it may not be appropriate to stand on a chair. However, this activity is easily adapted with the use of puppets, figurines, pictures of celebrities, etc.

Credit/References

Jacobs, E.E. (1992). Creative counseling techniques: An illustrated guide. Odessa, FL: Psychological Assessment Resources, Inc.

About the Counselor: *Eric T. Beeson,* LCPC, CRC, is an Instructor of Mental Health Counseling at Emporia State University. ebeeson@emporia.edu

I AM

"A Village of 100" Lessons 1 and 2

Submitted by Jennifer Park, M.A., M.S. Ed.

School Level: High.

Goals: Students will learn:
1. About inequity and social justice issues.
2. To discuss sensitive issues respectfully and pose questions accordingly.
3. To work in small groups delegating work and communicating effectively.

ASCA Standards:

Standard A: Students will acquire the attitudes, knowledge and skills that contribute to effective learning in school and across the life span.
A:A3.2 Demonstrate the ability to work independently, as well as the ability to work cooperatively with other students*
Standard A: Students will acquire the attitudes, knowledge and skills that contribute to effective learning in school and across the life span.
PS:A1 Acquire Self-knowledge
PS:A1.2 Identify values, attitudes and beliefs
PS:A1.5 Identify and express feelings
PS:A2.1 Recognize that everyone has rights and responsibilities
PS:A2.2 Respect alternative points of view
PS:A2.3 Recognize, accept, respect and appreciate individual differences
PS:A2.6 Use effective communication skills
Standard B: Students will make decisions, set goals and take necessary action to achieve goals.
PS:B1 Self-knowledge Application
PS:B1.7 Demonstrate a respect and appreciation for individual and cultural differences.

Estimated Time: Two lessons of 40-minutes each.

Materials: Paper, pencil, computer access, Almanacs, library access (not mandatory), worksheet "*A Village of 100*" (Retrieved from *http://odtmaps.com/behind_the_maps/population_map/if-world-were-village.asp* or http://www.familycare.org/special-interest/if-the-world-were-a-village-of-100-people/)

School Counselors Share Their Favorite Classroom Guidance Activities

Lesson 1

1. ***Introduction:*** School counselor begins with "Inequities exist all around us. There are those who have plenty and those who do not. Our place in society has potential to change and is often in flux due to many factors. When we emphasize gratitude and compassion, we create an environment of understanding and hope. This activity opens the dialogue to examine some delicate, tough issues with a global perspective." (1 minute)

2. School counselor will review respectful dialogue with openness to questions and refraining from judgmental comments. Here is an example of guidelines: "People have different experiences and come from diverse backgrounds. What this means is that each student may have a unique perspective on what is important, what is valued, how he/she has grown up in a certain type of family situation, and how much exposure he/she has had to poverty, global news, lack of water and/or food, or lack of a home. For example, those who survive a hurricane or flood may have lost all their possessions and have to relocate to a new house. If you have not gone through something like that, you may think very differently about physical possessions and family compared to someone who has. We are going to discuss some challenging topics looking at real life. Before you speak, take time to listen to what your classmate is saying. Think about how others may perceive what you are stating. Do not interrupt. If you are not able to stay calm while sharing, do not speak, but collect your emotions. If a topic is close to your heart and bothers you, feel free to bring up a comment or question, but keep your voice composed and clear. Speak in an audible voice because we want to hear what you have to say. Allow others to respond to what you have to say without criticizing them. No talking while someone else is speaking. (5 minutes)

3. Pass out "*A Village of 100*," which condenses the world's population according to ethnicity, education, religion, literacy, poverty, etc. (1 minute)

4. School counselor will choose one ratio from the sheet and lead a class discussion covering what the ratio means, implications for individual students, community, and reflection on application to self. Example: "1 would have a college education. What percent is that? So, out of 100 people, only 1 would graduate from college. What does that mean? How does that affect your view of education? How many of you plan on attending college? If you are unable, what effect would that have on

your ability to obtain certain jobs?" Emphasize the privilege of education and encourage an attitude of gratitude. Also, how certain vocations "require" a college degree while others do not. What are the benefits of education? Of learning? (15 minutes)

5. Introduce the project with deadlines and procedure. Directions: In groups of 2 to 3 students, you will choose one or two ratios to explore. Convert the ratio into a percent and a decimal. Using the Internet and/or library almanacs and atlases, discover how valid the ratio(s) is and what implications there are on society. For homework tonight, ask an adult family member his/her thoughts about the ratio and for any potential solutions to address it if important to change. Write down an outline or rough draft with your thoughts as well: include initial reactions, if you think the ratio(s) ought to be changed, how you would address it and make changes in policy or advertise/campaign to bring awareness to the issue or need, and present ideas as solutions to rectify what you see as the potential problem. At the end of the next class, you will present your findings as a group and then, individually turn in a one-page typed (single-space) essay reviewing key points for homework. Before you leave today, someone from your group needs to tell me which two ratios you have chosen to explore in greater detail. I will address questions in your small groups. Break. (2 minutes)

6. Divide students into groups of 2 to 3 and have them discuss initial reactions to the ratios. Leading questions: Is this new information? How do you feel after finding out about the ratio? Would you like to change the ratio? Why? School counselor will walk around the room and monitor student productivity and interactions; also, answer questions accordingly. (15 minutes)

7. By the end of class, each group will tell the school counselor which two ratios they will present.

8. *Assign homework:* Students will:
   - Use computers, library, and/or almanac to research each chosen ratio.
   - Ask adult family member for thoughts about chosen ratios.

Lesson 2

1. **Introduction:** School counselor begins with, "Last class, I introduced various ratios from "Village of 100." We are handling some delicate topics that are real challenges today. Now that you have had some additional information, today, we will continue to examine your chosen ratios and see if there are some solutions to rectify the inequity." (1 minute)

2. Have students work in the same groups to discuss whether the ratio should be changed using information from the two homework assignments. Brainstorm solutions to the inequity. Each group should make a list of ideas. Students will organize a presentation reviewing which ratios were chosen and what each member thought about the ratio and what potential changes could be made. If there is access to the Internet in the class, allow students to use computers to research and/or type work (examples: http://www.childinfo.org/country_list.php; http://www.snopes.com/science/stats/populate.asp; http://www.census.gov/; http://en.wikipedia.org/wiki/World_religions; http://en.wikipedia.org/wiki/List_of_countries_by_percentage_of_population_living_in_poverty; http://www.miniature-earth.com/; (15 minutes)

3. Bring the class back together and assign an order for groups to present. Each group will stand in front of the class and share their thoughts and solutions for 1 to 2 ratios; each group will also answer three questions from the audience. (Divide the time equally for all groups to present: 5 to 10 minutes each.)

4. Large group discussion: School counselor will ask how the students' views of ratios have affected their thinking. Values? Concerns about society? The world? After gaining this knowledge, what difference does it make? If you had an audience with the President or United Nations, what would you share with him/them? Emphasize importance of awareness within self, community, and globally. Also, encourage students to know they have abilities and gifts to enact change towards a better future for the world. (10 minutes)

5. School counselor will conclude with remarks emphasizing the following points: The world is constantly changing. These inequities are not simple issues, and many disagree about whether to "fix" them and how to go about that process. This is a lesson to increase global awareness and talk respectfully about some difficult topics. Stress community, compassion, and understanding. (5 minutes)

Processing Questions:
- ✓ Which ratio stands out to you? What surprises you most? Why?
- ✓ How does this knowledge affect your life? Your perspective?
- ✓ Where you do you fall in the statistics? Where do you find yourself on this sheet?
- ✓ How would you feel differently if you were in the minority?
- ✓ If you are in the majority, how do you view the minority?
- ✓ If you had a meeting with the president, what changes/solutions would you propose? How can you help?

Cautions: This project was conducted in independent schools. Some statistics regarding malnourishment, illiterate population, or substandard housing may hit too close to home, so maturity of students must be assessed in planning stages before utilizing activity. Further, the topic of inequity often becomes heated, so guidelines (e.g., take turns in speaking, listen to your peers, if experiencing high emotion, refrain from talking until calmer, speak with trusted adult if upset) for discussion are strongly recommended. Clarify that statistics are changing, but the purpose of the activity is to shed light on demographics of the world and highlight a global perspective; also, to inspire change and the next generation to be those agents. The counselor may benefit from making a disclosure statement before the activity.

Credit/References

"A Village of 100" (many versions) (Retrieved from
http://odtmaps.com/behind_the_maps/population_map/if-world-were-village.asp or http://www.familycare.org/special-interest/if-the-world-were-a-village-of-100-people/) Original from Smith, D. J. (2002). *If the world were a village: A book about the world's people.* Tonawanda, NY: Kids Can Press.

About the Counselor:

Jennifer Park, M.A., M.S.Ed. is a Counseling Associate at Messiah College, a Counselor in private practice in PA, and a Ph.D. Student at Regent University. jenntep@mail.regent.edu

Conflict Resolution
Submitted by Tamika Collins

School Level: High.

Time Length: 40 minutes.

Goals: Students will:
1. Understand consequences of decisions and choices.
2. Identify alternative solutions to a problem.
3. Demonstrate when, where, and how to seek help for solving problems and making decisions.

ASCA Standards:

PS:A2.2 Respect alternative points of view.
PS:A2.3 Recognize, accept, and appreciate individual differences.
PS:A2.6 Use effective communication skills.
PS:A2.8 Learn how to make and keep friends.

Materials: **Conflict Resolution Scenarios** worksheet (Collins, 2012).

Lesson

1. Divide students into eight teams by having them count off 1 through 3 for groups of 15; 1 through 4 for groups of 20; 1 through 5 for groups of 25; 1 through 6 for groups of 30; and 1 through 7 for groups of 35. (1 minute)
2. Instruct each team to form a circle. (30 seconds)
3. Instruct students to stretch out both hands and grab the hands of two different students that are across from them in the circle. Say: "Grab one student's hand with one of your hands and a different student's hand with your other hand." (30 seconds)
4. Instruct students to untangle themselves without letting go of each other's hands. (5 minutes)
5. After each team attempts to untangle itself, lead the entire group in a discussion about the activity. (5 minutes) The discussion should include the following questions:
✓ *What was the explicit goal of this activity?*
✓ *Was your team successful at accomplishing this goal?*
✓ *What were some of the roadblocks to your team's success?*

✓ *What skills were important for each team member to exercise in order for your team to be successful?*

Skills to reinforce: **team work, good communication, listening to others, open-mindedness.**

6. Ask for volunteers to define the terms "conflict" and "conflict resolution". (3 minutes) Answers to reinforce: **Conflict is any issue or problem one has with another. A conflict may also be an issue or problem one has with intangible things, such as time or a schedule. Conflict resolution refers to the way in which one handles, or solves, his or her conflict.**

7. Inform the group that it is important to resolve conflicts in a manner that leads to a positive result for both parties involved. Ask for two volunteers to share a conflict in which they were involved that did not lead to a positive result, and, if they would like, share the negative result or consequence. (3 minutes)

8. Share the "Six Steps for Resolving Conflicts" (Drew, 2002). (5 minutes)

- **Step One: Cool Off**: Calm down before attempting to deal with the conflict. Breathe deeply, write in a journal, take a walk. Do not talk about the conflict with others as that may exacerbate the conflict.

- **Step Two: Use "I-messages"**: When you're ready to resolve the conflict, use statements that express how you feel about the conflict that do not place blame but instead allows you to take responsibility for the way you view the conflict. Avoid put-downs, sarcasm, accusations, and other negative language. An example is *I am annoyed that people are telling me that you are talking about me. Is this really happening?*

- **Step Three:** Each person restate what they heard the other person say: This is called reflective listening and ensures that both parties involved in the conflict are on the same page. This step helps to solve many conflicts because it clears up any confusion and misunderstandings that may have led to the conflict.

- **Step Four: Take responsibility**: In most conflicts, both parties have played a part in the creation of the conflict. Instead of recognizing this, however, each party places blame on the other. When each party takes some degree of responsibility in the conflict, resolution is possible.

- **Step Five: Brainstorm and agree on a solution:** There is not one single solution to a conflict. Each party should develop a solution and then compromise portions of each solution to develop a resolution that satisfies all.

School Counselors Share Their Favorite Classroom Guidance Activities

- **Step Six: Affirm, thank, or forgive:** Give some sort of closure to the conflict as a final signal that a resolution has taken place and both parties will move forward positively.

9. Give each team one of the typical high school conflict scenarios from the *Conflict Resolution Scenarios* worksheet. Team members are to discuss the scenario and then together develop and write down "What we WOULD do" and the consequences of those actions and "What we SHOULD do to appropriately and positively resolve this conflict" and the consequences of those actions. Inform the teams that each will role play its resolution for the entire group. (3 minutes)

10. Each team will discuss it's scenario by working through the "Six Steps of Resolving Conflicts" and plan its role play presentation. (7 minutes)

11. Each team (or as many as time will allow) will present its scenario by role playing the conflict and the appropriate resolution derived from using the "Six Steps of Resolving Conflicts." After each presentation, lead the entire group in a discussion about the appropriateness of each resolution and evidence of each of the six steps. (7 minutes)

Cautions: This is a rather long activity, thus it is extremely important to adhere to the time restraints listed. Using a timer that makes some sort of noise when time has expired will be helpful. If necessary, this activity may be divided into two separate activities or days: Day 1 Steps 1 through 8 and Day 2 (review) Steps 8 through 11.

References

Collins, Tamika. (2012). *Conflict Resolution Scenarios*.

Drew, Naomi. (2002). *Six Steps for Resolving Conflicts*. Retrieved from http://www.learningpeace.com/pages/LP_04.htm

About the School Counselor:

Tamika Collins, NCC, currently is a Professional School Counselor and Positive Behavior Interventions and Supports (PBIS) Coach and Character Education Chairperson at Jackson Road Elementary in Griffin, Georgia. Previously, she taught High School Social Studies.

Conflict Resolution Scenarios (Collins, 2012)

Scenario # 1: Tori and Krystal are seniors and have been best friends since 7th grade. They talk to each other about everything, know each other's secrets, and hang out with each other all the time. Tori began dating Marcus, a good friend of hers and Krystal's who they've known since 7th grade as well. Krystal doesn't have a serious boyfriend but all three still hang out together, sometimes just the three or the three of them with other people, too. This past weekend, Tori went out of town with her family but was in communication with Krystal and Marcus the entire time through text messages. However, during first period today, a classmate told Tori that she saw Krystal and Marcus at the movies together on Saturday. Tori had no clue they went to the movies together.

Scenario # 2: Kalynn Smith is a 2nd year member of the cheerleading squad and is excited that she is able to be more of a leader this year for the new girls. During practices, the cheer coach lets her and some of the old girls lead stretches, fix the new girls' motions, and teach cheers and dances. Kalynn loves cheering and wants the new girls to be perfect. Some of the other old girls tell her that she is too hard on the new girls sometimes. Kalynn believes that she got it tough last year as a new girl but it helped her be a great cheerleader and she's doing the same thing to the new girls this year to help them be great. Today during lunch, Kalynn's friend who isn't on the cheerleading squad told her that one of the new girls put up a post about her on Facebook *and* Tweeted: "K.S. is on some BS! Like…how did she even make the squad??? #CONFUSED"

Scenario # 3: Chasity and two of her four best friends are at the Homecoming dance together and are excited because this is the first of the last social events of their high school career. Chasity's other two best friends are not with the group because they have dates. Chasity is on the dance floor dancing and laughing with her friends when she glances to her left and sees her ex-boyfriend, Dwayne. Dwayne broke up with Chasity at the end of summer vacation before he went off to college but they still talk to each other and he comes to her parents' house to hang out when he comes in town to visit. Chasity immediately stops dancing to figure out why is he here because the only way he'd be able to attend is if he was a guest from someone at the high school. As Chasity walks towards him, she sees one of her best friend's who she didn't come with grab his arm and walk away but noticed that they had on matching colors.

Scenario # 4: Jessica and Taylor lived next door to each since they were preschool age until 6th grade when Jessica's family moved to a bigger house in a neighboring city. Jessica and Taylor were very close as young children but grew apart over middle and high school, but remained friendly when they did run into each other at parties or the mall or anywhere. Two weeks ago, Jessica attended her school's football game to support her boyfriend, D.J., who is on the team. While at the concession stand, Jessica runs into Taylor and sees that she is pregnant. She has small talk with Taylor about school and her family but is too surprised to ask Taylor whom she is pregnant by. That following Monday, Jessica is talking about the surprise of Taylor's pregnancy with one of her friends during Study Hall. One of the football players in Study Hall with Jessica over hears her conversation and interrupts saying "Oh he told you?!" Jessica and her friend ask him what he is talking about and he replies "D.J. told you he got that Taylor chick pregnant, huh?"

Scenario # 5: Riley and Abby are in the hallway talking during class change. Abby tells Riley that she just left chemistry with Mallori and overheard her talking to another student about being upset with Riley and wanting to fight her. Before she could even explain why or provide details about what Mallori said, Riley begins to walk very quickly down the hallway towards Mallori who is at her locker.

Scenario # 6: Danielle and Nicole have been friends since they were seven, and she and Simone have been friends since 9th grade; all three girls attend different high schools. Nicole and Simone met each other for the first time at Danielle's 17th birthday party earlier this spring, and over the summer all three girls went to the beach for a week with Danielle's family. Since then, Nicole and Simone became friendly, talking on the phone and texting each other from time to time. A month ago, Danielle shared with Nicole that she was getting annoyed with Simone because she was not being a good friend – not available to hang out and talk on the phone whenever Danielle wants. Nicole encouraged Danielle to talk to Simone about how she was feeling but Danielle never did. Two weeks ago, Nicole's dad gave her three free tickets he received to an NFL game. Nicole invited Danielle and Simone but Danielle said she couldn't come. Nicole and Simone went to the game and had a great time. Yesterday Danielle called Nicole and was still complaining about how she felt Simone wasn't being a good friend because she hasn't heard from her in "forever" and even said Simone must have a problem with her. Nicole replied that Simone didn't say anything bad about Danielle when they went to the NFL game. Danielle immediately began arguing with Nicole, accusing her of not being a good friend either because she did not know that Simone and Nicole were friends and could not understand why Nicole would talk to Simone or hang out with her after the way Simone has treated her.

Scenario # 7: Cherronda and Asia are in the 10th grade and have been best friends since the 3rd grade. Cherronda has been dating her boyfriend for five months and they always argue with each other. Cherronda comes to the lunch table everyday talking about her boyfriend and their issues and Asia listens to her best friend and sometimes even provides Cherronda with advice. Not too long ago, the two girls got into an argument because Asia hurt Cherronda's feelings when she told her that she didn't think Cherronda's boyfriend was good enough for her. The girls got over it, so Asia thought, until she recently found out from a friend of Cherronda's boyfriend that Cherronda has been talking about her. The friend said that Cherronda and her boyfriend are always accusing Asia of being a "hater" and jealous because she doesn't have a boyfriend.

School Counselors Share Their Favorite Classroom Guidance Activities

Scenario # :

What would you do?

Consequences:

What would you do?

Consequences:

Why would you act the way you said you would act?

EDITOR BIOS

Faith S. Colvin graduated with a Masters of Education in School Counseling from the University at Buffalo, the State University of New York; and is NYS certified as a School Counselor. Faith interned at PS 156 Fredrick Olmsted (5-12) in Buffalo, NY and Starpoint Intermediate School in suburban Buffalo. Faith also obtained her Bachelor of Arts at Bennett College for Women in Greensboro, North Carolina. Faith's interest includes closing the achievement gap and RTI. Group leadership experience includes a boys social skills group. Her group interests include social skills and divorce. Faith is also a Ronald E. McNair Scholar from North Carolina Agricultural and Technical State University.

Carla Giambrone, M.S. e-RYT, is a Ph.D. Student in School and Counseling Psychology at the University at Buffalo, the State University of New York. Carla is a vinyasa yoga teacher and has taught College Writing, Reading and High School English. She writes and develops life path programs, and created a 40-day mindfulness and yoga program that focuses on mind-body integration that she teaches to groups around the world. She incorporates writing and mindfulness into her teaching and research. Her research interests center around kinesthetic learning, and the efficacy of yoga to treat eating and mood disorders.

Sarah Catherine Korta graduated with a Masters of Education in School Counseling from the University at Buffalo, the State University of New York; and is NYS certified as a School Counselor. Currently, she is pursuing her Certificate of Advanced Study. Sarah interned at Cleveland Hill Middle School in Cheektowaga, New York and at South Park High School in Buffalo, New York. Sarah also obtained a Bachelor of Science at SUNY Buffalo State with a concentration in Marketing. Sarah created and implemented a girls self-esteem group, focused on activities designed to improve self-esteem, confidence, social skills, personal awareness, and empowerment for young girls. Sarah also has a passion for groups related to childhood nutrition and healthy lifestyle habits.

Katherine Maertin graduated with a Masters of Education in School Counseling from the University at Buffalo, the State University of New York in 2013 and is currently working on her Certificate of Advanced Study. Katherine has interned at Starpoint High School in Lockport, New York and at Global Concepts Charter School in Lackawanna, New York. Katherine also obtained a Bachelor of Arts in Health and Human Services in 2012 with a concentration in Early Childhood Education at the University at Buffalo. Her interests include working with study skills and organizational groups, the effects and prevention of bullying/cyberbullying and child/adolescent nutrition.

Eric Martin graduated with a Masters of Education in School Counseling from the University at Buffalo, the State University of New York, and is currently working on his Certificate of Advanced Study. Eric received a Bachelor of Science in Biology and Psychology from the University at Buffalo. His interests include college planning and preparation and study/organizational skills. Eric has interned at Kenmore East High School in Tonawanda, New York and West Seneca West Middle School in West Seneca, New York.

Meghan Mercurio graduated with a Masters of Education in School Counseling from the University at Buffalo, the State University of New York. She is currently a School Counselor in the Buffalo Public School District at Bennett High School. Meghan interned at Frontier Middle School outside of Buffalo. She also worked as a School Counselor at Pownal Elementary School in VT. Meghan also obtained a Bachelor of Science and a Master of Science degree at the University at Buffalo, SUNY majoring in accounting. Meghan enjoys working with groups and orchestrating various types of classroom guidance activities.

Lily Zawadski graduated with a Masters of Education in School Counseling from the University at Buffalo, the State University of New York. Lily has interned at Grand Island High School in suburban Buffalo..

Janice DeLucia-Waack is an Associate Professor in Counseling, School, and Educational Psychology at the University at Buffalo, SUNY and program director for the School Counseling Program. She is a Past President of **Association for Specialists in Group Work**, former editor of the *Journal for Specialists in Group Work*, and is a fellow in ACA, ASGW, and APA Division 49: Group Psychology and Group Psychotherapy. She is author of: *Leading Psychoeducational Groups for Children and Adolescents and Using Music in Children of Divorce Groups: A Session-By-Session Manual for Counselors*; and co-author of: *The Practice of Multicultural Group Work: Visions and Perspectives from the Field* (with Jeremiah Donigian), *Handbook of Group Counseling and Psychotherapy (2ⁿᵈ Ed.)* (with Cynthia Kalodner and Maria Riva), *School Counselors Share Their Favorite Activities: A Guide to Choosing, Planning, Conducting, and Processing* (with Louisa Foss, Judy Green, and Kelly Wolfe-Stiltner), and *Group Work Experts Share Their Activities: A Guide to Choosing, Planning, Conducting, and Processing Vol. 1* (with Karen Bridbord, Jenifer Kleiner, and Amy Nitza. She is currently on the advisory board for the Alberti Center for the Prevention of Bullying Abuse and School Violence at the University at Buffalo, SUNY.

CHAPTER AUTHOR BIOS

Laura Ache is currently a High School Counselor at a Title I school in Jacksonville, Florida. She earned her M.Ed. in Counselor Education from the S.O.A.R. Program at the University of North Florida. Her primary areas of interest are integrating pop culture into school counseling curriculum and innovative use of technology in school counseling as well as policy development for urban education. She has presented throughout the Southeast on topics ranging from small group work to classroom guidance, as well as technology-centered professional development seminars for practicing school counselors. She is current President-elect of the First Coast Counseling Association.

John Dagley serves as the Coordinator of the Counselor Education Program at the University of South Alabama. His professional experience has been shaped by central interests in career development and group work, particularly as practiced at all levels of schooling from elementary schools through higher education. Research and writing contributions have often focused on both the process and content of "career and transition groups." Among his scholarly contributions are co-authored books on *Intentionally Structured Groups*, and *Group Work in Schools*.

Dr. Carol Dahir is a Professor and Chair of the School Counseling Department at NYIT. She works extensively, nationally and internationally, with the design, implementation, and evaluation of comprehensive school counseling programs. Dr. Dahir served as the project director for the ASCA's *National Standards* development and *Planning for Life* initiative. She is a Past President of the New York State School Counselor Association and has served on the governing boards for the **American School Counselor Association** and the **National Career Development Association**. An established author of textbooks and articles, Carol Dahir continues to focus her writing, research, and presentations on comprehensive school counseling programs, college and career readiness, accountability, principal-counselor relationships, cultural competence, and continuous improvement for school counselors.

Ileana Gonzalez is an Assistant Clinical Professor at Johns Hopkins University who recently earned her doctorate degree from the University of Maryland. Her research interests include examining the commitment of urban school counselors to social justice and advocacy efforts. Dr. Gonzalez is the coordinator for the School Counseling Fellows Program, an accelerated social justice based graduate program for students who intend to practice in urban environments and are committed to education reform. Prior to her doctoral work, Dr. Gonzalez was an urban School Counselor in South Florida primarily serving Caribbean immigrant populations. Dr. Gonzalez is a strong believer in equity and access to a quality education for all students, and believes school counselors are the key to achieving these outcomes.

Dr. Caroline J. Lopez is an Assistant Professor in the School Counseling and School Psychology program at Chapman University. She teaches group counseling for masters students. Prior to this, Dr. Lopez was a at both an Elementary and Middle School Counselor.

Rebecca A. Schumacher worked in public education as an Elementary Teacher in Indiana, and Professional School Counselor and District Level Administrator in Connecticut before earning her Ed.D. in Counselor Education (specializing in School Counseling) at the University of Maine. Much of her public education experiences have been devoted to working with poor and underserved populations in urban schools. She currently is Program Director and Assistant Professor for the School Counseling Program, at the University of North Florida in Jacksonville. Her primary areas of interest in research and teaching include group work in schools, preparation and professional development of school counselors, and supervision for school counselors. She has presented and trained extensively throughout the country, primarily on group work for school counselors. Her recent publications include topics on supervision issues for school counselors, group work for classroom guidance, small group work for school counselors, implementation of school counseling models, and service learning for urban school counselor preparation. She is Past President and a Fellow of the **Association for Specialists in Group Work**.

Carolyn Stone is a Professor of Counselor Educator at the University of North Florida where she teaches and researches in the area of legal and ethical issues for school counselors and school counselors impacting the opportunity, information and achievement gaps. Prior to becoming a Counselor Educator in 1995, Carolyn spent 22 years with the Duval County Public Schools in Jacksonville, Florida where she served as a Middle School Teacher, Elementary and High School Counselor and Supervisor of Guidance for 225 counselors. Carolyn was the 2006 President of the **American School Counselor Association** and is in her tenth year as their Ethics Chair. Dr. Stone was awarded the *Mary Gerke Lifetime Achievement Award* by ASCA in 2010 and the *Bob Myrick Lifetime Achievement Award* by the Florida School Counselor Association in 2012. Carolyn is a Past President of the **Florida Counseling Association** and the **Florida Association of Counselor Educators and Supervisors**. Carolyn has delivered over 500 workshops in 49 states and 22 countries. She has authored six books, dozens of journal articles and serves the courts as an expert witness in cases involving school counselors. Her professional path in elementary and high school counseling, middle school teaching, supervisor of guidance for the nation's seventeenth largest school district, and counselor educator has prepared her with first-hand experience and understanding of the professional world of school counselors.

Dr. Christine Suniti Bhat is an Associate Professor in the Department of Counseling and Higher Education at Ohio University. She teaches group counseling at the master's and doctoral level. Dr. Bhat has extensive international experience as a Counselor and Psychologist in Australia and the USA in diverse work environments such as the Australian military, non-profit agencies, schools, and universities. She is Past President of the **Ohio Counseling Association** and served as Process Observer on the Executive Board of the **Association for Specialists in Group Work** for two consecutive terms. Dr. Bhat is a licensed Professional Counselor in Ohio.

Luis Antonio Tosado II, Ph.D. is a Clinical Assistant Professor at the University at Buffalo, University at Buffalo. He is a National Certified Counselor and a National Certified School Counselor. His Professional School Counseling experiences have been in urban middle schools and high schools, in Texas and Maryland. Dr. Tosado's research interests are related to the college aspirations, preparation, and attainment of Latino youth and English Language Learners. He is also interested in the leadership role of school counselors in urban school districts and working with military families. Before beginning his Professional School Counseling career, Dr. Tosado served as an Elementary Teacher in a suburban school district.

Dr. Amy Upton is currently an Assistant Professor and Director of the School Counseling Program at the University of South Alabama. Amy earned her doctorate in Counselor Education from Old Dominion University in 2012. Her professional work experience includes sixteen years of service as a School Counselor at both the middle and high school levels. Her primary research interests include school counselor development and professional identity, school counseling program development, and school counselors' leadership practices, responsibilities and opportunities.

Kelly Wolfe-Stiltner is a licensed School Counselor at an elementary school in Fort Wayne, Indiana. Ms. Wolfe-Stiltner received her Bachelor's degree in secondary education from Ball State University and Master's degree in School Counseling from Indiana University Purdue University Fort Wayne. Ms. Wolfe-Stiltner also has five years of teaching experience at a residential treatment facility. She also has taught a Professional Orientation and Ethics Class to school counselors. Ms. Wolfe-Stiltner's areas of interest include group work, grief work, ethical and legal issues in school counseling and the role of the school counselor. She has served as a Media Committee Co-Chair and committee member for the **Association for Specialists in Group Work.**

Author Index

Author Index (cont.)

WHAT IS ASGW?

The Association for Specialists in Group Work, founded in 1973, is a division of the American Counseling Association. As counselors who are interested in and specialize in group work, we value the creation of community; service to our members, their clients, and the professions; and leadership as a process to facilitate the growth and development of individuals and groups. The purposes of the Association are to establish standards for professional and ethical practice; to support research and the dissemination of knowledge; and to provide professional leadership in the field of group work. In addition, the Association shall seek to extend counseling through the use of group process; to provide a forum for examining innovative and developing concepts in group work; to foster diversity and dignity in our groups; and to be models of effective group practice.

As a member of ASGW, you receive:

The *Journal for Specialists in Group Work*, current issues in print

Access to all past issues of the *Journal for Specialists in Group Work* online

The Group Worker, the ASGW Newsletter, print version three times per year

Access to past issues of *The Group Worker* online

Reduced registration rates for ASGW bi-annual conferences, group training events, and CEUs

Reduced prices on ASGW products: books, DVDs, and group products

Access to Member Only part of website, www.asgw.org

Joining the Association for Specialists in Group Work (ASGW)

Membership type	ASGW		ACA		total
Professional	$40.00	+	$165.00	=	$205.00
New Professional	$27.00	+	$94.00	=	$121.00
Student	$27.00	+	$94..00	=	$121.00
Regular	$40.00	+	$165..00	=	$205.00

Joining ASGW only

Regular	$40.00 +	$10.00 =	$50.00

Join on-line at www.counseling.org or www.asgw.org
Or join by phone with VISA or MasterCard...
call: 1-800/347-6647